Unlocking Kabbalah

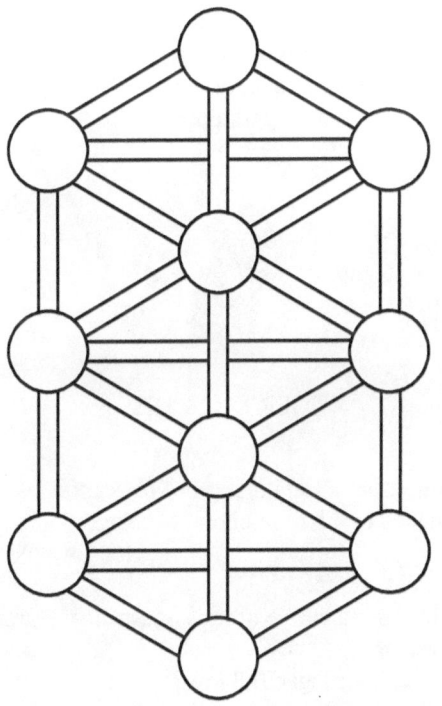

A New Synthesis of Astrology, Tarot, and the Tree of Life

Thomas Weems

TIGER TAIL PRESS

Copyright © 2024 by Thomas Weems

All rights reserved. No part of this book may be reproduced in any form without written permission from the author.

Library of Congress Control Number: 2023922179

Tiger Tail Press
Richmond, VA
www.tigertailpress.com

TIGER TAIL PRESS

Publisher's Cataloging-in-Publication Data
provided by Five Rainbows Cataloging Services

Names: Weems, Thomas, author.
Title: Unlocking kabbalah : a new synthesis of astrology, tarot, and the tree of life / Thomas Weems.
Description: Richmond, VA : Tiger Tail Press, 2024.
Identifiers: LCCN 2023922179 (print) | ISBN 978-1-7372798-1-5 (paperback) | ISBN 978-1-7372798-2-2 (hardcover) | ISBN 978-1-7372798-3-9 (ebook)
Subjects: LCSH: Cabala. | Tree of life. | Astrology. | Tarot. | Success--Psychic aspects. | Spiritual life--Judaism. | BISAC: RELIGION / Judaism / Kabbalah & Mysticism. | BODY, MIND & SPIRIT / Divination / Tarot. | BODY, MIND & SPIRIT / Astrology / General.
Classification: LCC BM723 .W44 2024 (print) | LCC BM723 (ebook) | DDC 296.7/2--dc23.

Contents

Part I
A New Model of the Kabbalistic Tree of Life 3
Part II
The Diamond Sphere 25
The White Sphere 37
The Black Sphere 43
The Indigo Sphere 50
The Blue Sphere 56
The Red Sphere 63
The Yellow Sphere 71
The Green Sphere 81
The Orange Sphere 89
The Purple Sphere 94
Part III
The Psychological Study of the Tree 107
Magic and Manifestation 123
Part IV
Judgment 137
The High Priestess 142
The Hanged Man 146
The Fool 153
The Wheel of Fortune 157
The Sun 163
The World 166
The Tower 169
The Magician 175
The Empress 180

The Emperor: Aries 184
The Hierophant: Taurus 188
The Lovers: Gemini 192
The Chariot: Cancer 196
Strength: Leo 200
The Hermit: Virgo 204
Justice: Libra 209
Death: Scorpio 213
Temperance: Sagittarius 218
The Devil: Capricorn 223
The Star: Aquarius 228
The Moon: Pisces 233

Conclusion 238

Part I
Introduction

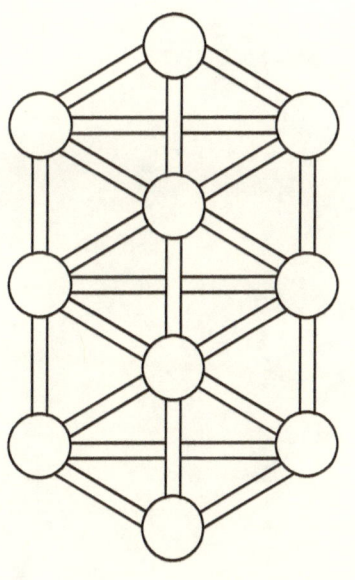

A New Model of the Kabbalistic Tree of Life

This book presents a rather novel way of looking at an ancient tradition. The premise is that the central motif of the Jewish mystery teaching known as Kabbalah, which we call the "Tree of Life", is in fact *not* the original design as it was first imagined, but rather a modification thereof. This idea is not as outlandish as it may sound. One has only to make a cursory glance at the diagram itself to see that it raises certain questions. And yet, these questions have remained entirely unanswered. In fact, they are seemingly not even asked. The primary source materials of the Kabbalah - the *Sepher Yetzirah*, the *Bahir*, and even the vast and sprawling *Zohar* - give no apparent account for the origin or rationale behind this mysterious symbol. Given that the Kabbalah as a whole was primarily an oral rather than a written tradition, it is probably safe to say that the doctrines of Kabbalah, including the Tree of Life itself, evolved in secrecy over an untold number of generations before coming down to us in the form that we know them today.

That being the case, the aim of this book is not to attempt an analysis of the Kabbalah based on historical material. The actual origins of the Kabbalah are shrouded in deep mystery, and the existing literature that we know of is written in such an obscure and opaque style as to be virtually impenetrable to anyone who doesn't have access to the unwritten backstory. The intent of this book is instead to offer an *interpretation* of the Kabbalah which attempts to get to the heart of what the Tree of Life actually represents. To this end, the course of inquiry has been to assume that the Kabbalah evolved within a wider context of occult philosophy, and to use a combination of synthetic and intuitive reasoning to piece together a coherent narrative.

This is of course a very subjective approach, and so it would be helpful to elaborate on the method of the journey. There are two principal ways of understanding a matter. One is purely through the intellect, in the manner of formulating abstract concepts and weaving together the relationships between them. The other way of understanding is more grounded in the senses and in physical experience. Some might call it "practical" understanding, as it is the kind of understanding that often comes from the practical experience of a thing. Knowing how to ride a bicycle is an example of this. It is not something that can be learned by simply reading a book or by hearing it explained. One has to actually immerse oneself *physically* into the experience in order to internalize it.

This is no less the case when it comes to plumbing the depths of metaphysical ideas. We can spin up any number of intellectual theories with very abstract concepts about God, truth, beauty, spirit, and so forth. And certainly, it is not wrong to say that a solid grasp of logical and abstract reasoning is necessary to arrive at a coherent philosophy about anything. But without some kind of *visceral* and living sense of what these words actually mean, they remain empty concepts, without impact and without weight. To go forth into the realm of metaphysics, therefore, requires the application of both reason and intuition, the solar mind and the lunar mind. It requires that we engage in a process that some would refer to loosely as *channeling*, or what Carl Jung described as *active imagination*.

Understand that this term "channeling", although it may have outlandish connotations, doesn't necessarily imply the presentation of strange or otherworldly personalities. More broadly, the word *channeling* signifies a process of opening up to the intuition in a way that allows ideas and inspirations to flow into our awareness from other sources. This is not by any means a rare faculty that is limited to a few extraordinary individuals, but rather a capability possessed by everyone. Artistic and creative types often describe this experience when they speak of inspiration as having come to them seemingly from somewhere outside of themselves. And this description is more than just a metaphor. There is a very palpable feeling of engaging with some *other* power that comes with this mode of tapping the intuition.

It is in this sense that we say that delving into the realm of metaphysics requires more than just an intellectual grasp of the subject matter. One must *feel into* the underlying energies of existence in order to assimilate them and actually live them. This business of opening to the intuition demands that we start with a certain approach and a certain attitude. The British occultist Dion Fortune once said that the subconscious comes from a stage of evolution prior to language. That is why it speaks to us in terms of symbolism and imagery rather than verbal thought. And so diving down into the metaphysical matrix of existence means getting below the level of verbal thought, below the plane of logic. It is a journey that is experiential rather than mental. It means dipping into the watery realm of force and power, the realm of feeling rather than thinking. And so the process of this expedition is to first feel into the universal truth that one is pursuing, and then to allow the mind to find the words and thoughts in which to frame it. This, as opposed to starting from a set of mental constructs which have no actual *weight* behind them, is the deeper and more penetrating mode of understanding. Logic or *Logos* is simply the structuring of thought, the ordering and organization of ideas. But logic must start from direct perception and felt experience. It cannot create order out of nothing.

This requires a willingness to assume a receptive and somewhat passive role in the process. The lunar mind is fluid and non-linear, and so you have to be willing to allow the thought process to meander a bit in the course of exploration, because the intuition can take unexpected turns and get you to the destination in ways that you didn't expect. This, however, is not the same thing as the mind simply wandering about because it is distracted and lazy. It is a meandering with a sense of purpose always in mind, a kind of free orbit about a center of gravity. And generally speaking, it is not so much a mental concept that you are following but rather a sensation or a feeling. The development of this idea can be hindered by the rational mind putting the brakes on a movement because it doesn't immediately seem to make any logical sense. But if you resist the urge to hit the brakes, then the idea can continue to unfold and expand in the subconscious. Worry is the chief obstacle to following the intuition. Worry that you are going to get it wrong, or that there even *is* a right or wrong, is an instinct that must be let go of in order to be fruitful in this endeavor. In the realm of the intuition and the subconscious, you must get over the impulse to judge whether something is "true" or "false", because that is entirely beside the point. The point is that the intuition will attempt to follow the watercourse way to get you to the understanding that you seek, and so a train of thought that seems irrelevant may in fact lead you indirectly to another train of thought which becomes the key to understanding.

With all of that in mind, we come back to the main premise. My assumption is that most readers will already be familiar with the basic concepts of Kabbalah, but for those who are not I will give a brief outline. The Kabbalah is best understood as a mystical and esoteric interpretation of Judaism. In keeping with every other mystical philosophy across all ages and cultures, the starting point of Kabbalah is the concept of God as "*Ayin Soph*", which in Hebrew means literally "Without Limit". Some sources further elaborate this concept of God as the "Three Veils of Negative Existence" - beginning with "Ayin" (which means "Nothing" but can also serve as the qualifier "not" or "without"), from which proceeds "Ayin Soph" ("The Limitless") and finally "Ayin Soph Aur" ("Limitless Light"). What is particularly striking here is the association of God with the concept of *nothingness*. This is actually a common thread in all strains of mystical thought. It is a foundational idea in Eastern religion (such as *The Tao* as the source of all things, or the concept of *Brahman* as the ultimate reality in Hinduism). But the idea is also found among the ancient Greek philosophers, who in contrast to the anthropomorphic gods of Mount Olympus insisted that there was an even higher power above these gods, a *Unity*, from which all things were created. The crucial thing to understand here is that the idea of God that is put forth is not a *mere* nothingness, but rather a formless, shapeless energy in which all things *potentially* exist. Every created thing is defined by its boundaries and its limitations. Without the limitation of form, the created thing cannot be said to have any *tangible* existence whatsoever. But limitation is not an attribute that we can ascribe to the highest creative power, and so God must be understood as a creative energy without limit and therefore without any form or shape. In that respect, God must appear like a "nothingness" in relation to the physical senses, or even to the rational mind which deals in formal concepts. But this nothingness is by the same token an infinite possibility and an infinite power. It is a nothing that is also *everything* at the same time.

The Tree of Life is the core *structural* concept of Kabbalah. It represents a series of archetypal ideas that emanate out of Ayin Soph to form the framework of the created universe. These ten emanations are known individually by the term *Sephirah* and collectively by the plural form *Sephiroth*. The Hebrew root word *Saphar* signifies "to enumerate" or "to count", though it can also mean "to recount" or "take account of" something, from whence we have the word *Sepher* ("book"). In the context of Kabbalah, the Sephiroth can be interpreted as ten enumerations that proceed forth from Ayin Soph as the fundamental cosmic principles underlying existence. These principles are known as:

1. Kether - Crown
2. Chokmah - Wisdom
3. Binah - Understanding
4. Gedulah or Chesed - Greatness or Mercy
5. Geburah or Din - Strength or Judgment
6. Tiphareth - Beauty
7. Netzach - Victory
8. Hod - Splendor
9. Yesod - Foundation
10. Malkuth - Kingdom

The fourth and fifth Sephiroth have alternative designations of Gedulah and Geburah (Greatness and Strength) or Chesed and Din (Mercy and Judgment). Most sources refer to them as Chesed and Geburah, and so that will be the convention used herein.

These ten Sephiroth are arranged in a specific formation, as shown in Figure 1. At the top of the diagram is a triangle formed by Kether, Chokmah, and Binah, with Kether forming the apex and Chokmah and Binah being the right and left points of the base respectively. Beneath this triangle is an inverse triangle with Chesed on the right, Geburah on the left, and Tiphareth beneath them. Below this triad is another downward triangle formed by Netzach on the right, Hod on the left, and Yesod beneath them. Malkuth lies at the bottom of the Tree directly beneath Yesod. This arrangement places the Sephiroth into three columns. The Pillar of Mercy is on the right consisting of Chokmah, Chesed, and Netzach. The Pillar of Severity on the left consists of Binah, Geburah, and Hod. Between them sits the Middle Pillar which is Kether, Tiphareth, Yesod, and Malkuth.

In addition to the ten Sephiroth, the Kabbalah postulates a set of twenty-two paths which are depicted in the Tree of Life diagram as connecting lines between the various Sephiroth. While there are theoretically fifty-five possible connections between all of the Sephiroth, only twenty-two are considered to be of primary significance. These would seem to be the paths between Sephiroth which are directly proximate to each other either laterally, vertically, or diagonally. If the Sephiroth are the primary building-blocks of existence, then the twenty-two connecting paths can be thought of as secondary building-blocks, each of which synthesizes in some way the energy of the two Sephiroth which it joins. In this respect, the relationship between the Sephiroth and the paths can be thought of as analogous to the relationship between atoms and molecules.

The number twenty-two is also significant for two other reasons: there are twenty-two letters in the Hebrew alphabet, and twenty-two Major Arcana in the Tarot. The correlation between the Major Arcana and the paths of the Tree is a more recent idea, popularized by the French occultist Eliphas Levi in the 19th century. The correlation between the paths and the Hebrew letters goes back much further, however, and is much more integral to the Kabbalistic tradition. As to which letters and which Tarot trumps map to each path, there is no singular agreed-upon convention. There are of course multiple interpretations given

A New Model of the Kabbalistic Tree of Life

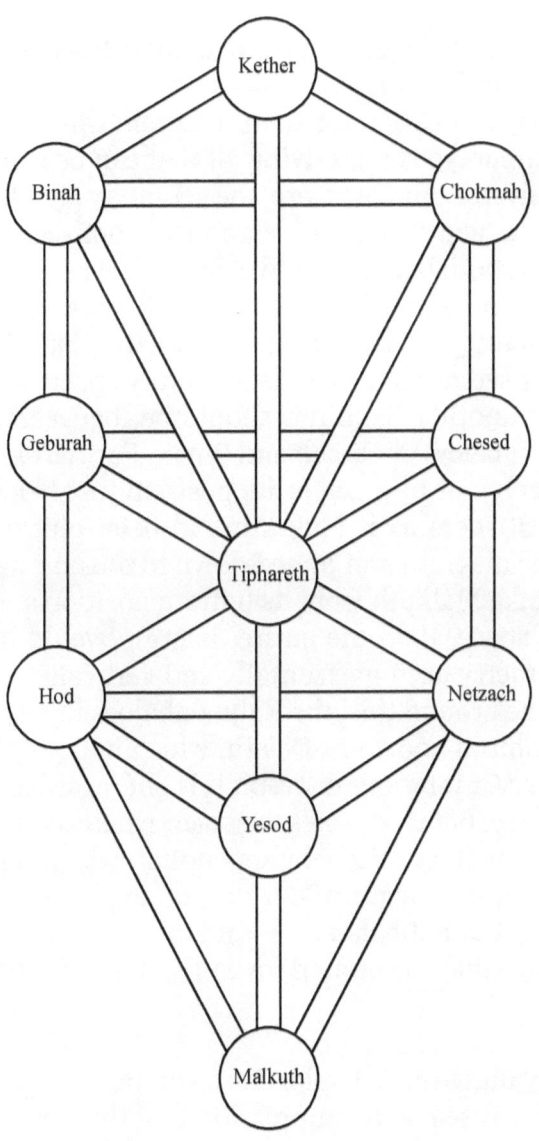

Figure 1
Traditional Tree of Life

by different sources, but no one system has been settled upon as authoritative.

The Tree of Life has been a source of endless fascination to occult philosophers for centuries, and it is not difficult to understand why. There is an abstractness to the diagram which suggests a set of Platonic archetypes underlying all that can be comprehended about the universe. Furthermore, the geometry and the symmetry of the Tree hint at a structured relationship between these archetypes which is both balanced and elegant. But as we contemplate this diagram more thoroughly, eventually one has to notice a certain peculiarity to it. There is a symmetry, but also a broken symmetry. It seems as if there is an empty space on the Middle Pillar where another Sephirah should be, between Kether and Tiphareth just below Chokmah and Binah. Furthermore, Malkuth looks strangely out of place in its position just below Yesod. It would almost seem as if Malkuth had been plucked from the middle of the diagram and pulled down to the bottom. Indeed, if we were to take Malkuth from its bottom position and put it into this central space, then the entire diagram would have a more perfect symmetry both horizontally and vertically. To add to all of the intrigue around this, the Kabbalah does in fact posit a sort of *quasi*-Sephirah known as Da'ath, which means "Knowledge". Da'ath is a very mysterious concept. It is not regarded as an actual Sephirah *per se*, but it occupies the space where a Sephirah ought to be. It is a shadowy and nebulous notion which highlights the obvious gap in the diagram, but doesn't explicitly fill it. Da'ath stands within the Kabbalah as a kind of vague hint that there is something not fully accounted for in the Tree of Life as we have received it.

This is really quite remarkable. Once you put it all together, it is very difficult to escape the impression that the Tree of Life as we have it today represents a conscientious alteration of a simpler and more intuitive diagram. The question is... *why?* Who might have made such a modification, and to what purpose? The honest answer is that the Kabbalah does not seem to speak to this question anywhere. In fact, it does not even acknowledge the question.

A New Model of the Kabbalistic Tree of Life

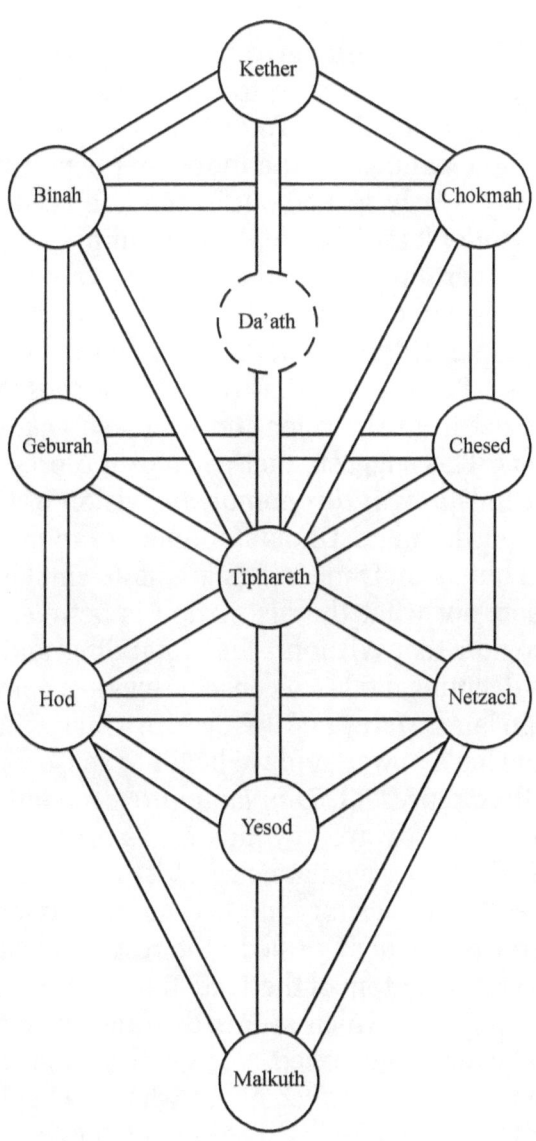

Figure 2
Tree of Life with Da'ath

The Tree of Life is simply taken as axiomatic, but the precise origin and explanation of it seems impossible to trace.

If the Tree of Life is indeed derived from a more primitive concept, how can we then attempt to reconstruct and understand this hypothetical *proto*-Tree? To do this, we would have to first understand the meanings of the individual Sephiroth. But this too is in no way clearly spelled out by the Kabbalistic literature. If we try to understand the Sephiroth simply by their literal names, we will certainly not end up getting very far. The name of the first Sephirah, Crown, is clearly symbolic in some sense, but rather opaque. It implies perhaps an aspect of God as ruler of the universe. But the fact that the symbol chosen is an item which is distinct from the ruler and which sits *above* the ruler is very curious. This suggests that perhaps it represents an idea which transcends any *anthropomorphic* vision of God that we might have. Wisdom and Understanding are more philosophical concepts, but as their meanings are quite similar it is rather difficult to sort out what the distinction is between them. It is interesting to note that Wisdom, Understanding, and Knowledge are all words denoting modes of consciousness - a point which will come up again later. Mercy and Justice are a bit easier to grasp as operations of God's power, and we begin to sense a relationship forming as they represent *complementary* modalities. Beauty and Splendor suggest ways in which God's presence appears to us, but the distinction is again unclear. Victory is also a bit vague. Over whom or what is victory implied here? Foundation would appear to serve a supporting role to the rest of the Sephiroth, as it is placed near the bottom of the Tree. But the very bottom-most Sephirah is Kingdom, which seems to stand in relation to the Crown as that which is governed over. On the whole, these names don't seem to tell us very much about what the Sephiroth actually represent. So how might we begin to understand them more clearly? To get to the bottom of this, we will have to attempt to piece together a conceptual framework based on clues from the Kabbalistic tradition.

Let's look first of all at Kether. As the first emanation from Ayin Soph, it is said to be the most primal, abstract, and radical expression of God's energy, and therefore is largely incomprehensible to the rational intellect. It is often visualized as the infinite energy of Ayin Soph condensed into a single point. This single point represents the primal Unity that transcends the multiplicity of manifest existence. Another way to think of Kether is that it depicts the transition from the Zero of Ayin Soph to the One of primitive existence. The Zero and the One are conceptually not that far apart. They both represent a state of *undividedness*, and so the difference between them is more qualitative than anything else. This is a very mysterious doctrine to be sure, but we can encapsulate the meaning of Kether by saying that it stands at the blurred boundary between Existence and Non-Existence.

An important clue to the meaning of Chokmah and Binah is that they are also referred to in the Zohar by the Aramaic terms Abba and Aima, which mean *Father* and *Mother*. This points to Chokmah and Binah as representing the fundamental masculine and feminine, active and passive energies of existence, or Yin and Yang if you will. It also offers us a slightly different shade of meaning between Wisdom and Understanding. "Understanding" implies to us a more feminine, empathic, and passive mode of awareness, whereas "Wisdom" suggests a capacity to actively apply one's understanding in a beneficial and productive way.

Another clue to understanding the Tree is the relationship between Chesed, Geburah, and Tiphareth. This relationship seems to receive special attention in the Zohar, in which Tiphareth is seen as the balancing influence between Judgment and Mercy. Judgment without Mercy would be unnecessarily harsh and cruel. But Mercy without Judgment would allow evil to run unchecked. Tiphareth therefore establishes the necessary equilibrium between the two. This relationship, as simple as it is, tells us a great deal about the essence of the Tree as a whole. Tiphareth is regarded as the central Sephirah of the Tree, and its role in this central position is the balancing of opposites. The Zohar elaborates on this further by equating Chesed to water, Geburah to fire, and Tiphareth to air. This elemental symbolism sums up the cosmic order quite powerfully as the balance between Fire and Water. This three-fold relationship is extended to the overall structure of the Tree in the form of two left and right pillars balanced by a middle pillar. The Tree of Life can therefore be seen to depict the cosmic order of things as *polarity in equilibrium*. The fact that this equilibrium is described as "Beauty" is especially poignant. It evokes a particularly Hellenistic and classical notion of Divine Harmony as being everything in just the right measure and proportion - an idea encapsulated by the Greek word *Logos*.

The last key to understanding the Tree of Life, and perhaps the most important, is the astrological mapping. This system correlates each Sephirah to one of the concentric spheres of the heavens as envisioned by classical astrology. These attributions are as follows:

Kether - The Primum Mobile or "prime mover"
Chokmah - The sphere of the zodiac
Binah - The sphere of Saturn
Chesed - The sphere of Jupiter
Geburah - The sphere of Mars
Tiphareth - The sphere of the Sun
Netzach - The sphere of Venus
Hod - The sphere of Mercury
Yesod - The sphere of the Moon
Malkuth - The sublunary sphere or realm of the four elements

This is potentially the most valuable clue to understanding the Tree, as it gives us an entire range of astrological attributions to apply to most of the Sephiroth. To fully penetrate the meaning of each of these Sephiroth then, we would have to meditate upon the qualities and characteristics assigned to the corresponding planet, and then try to distill from those qualities an abstract, archetypal principle which summarizes the energy represented by that planet. At the same time, we must figure out how these principles fit into the framework of polarity and equilibrium that the Tree of Life describes.

A New Model of the Kabbalistic Tree of Life

With this in mind, our first order of business in constructing our *proto*-Tree is to move Malkuth up to the place of Da'ath. Now of course, as soon as we do this we have to begin interrogating the implications of such a move. This begins with the question, what does Malkuth actually represent in the first place? According to the astrological model, it represents the "sublunary sphere". In classical astrology, this means the realm below the sphere of the Moon. That is to say, the realm composed of the four elements of Fire, Air, Water, and Earth. So for all practical purposes, Malkuth represents the physical world in which we live. But given that the Sephiroth signify archetypal principles, we need to refine our definition of Malkuth somewhat and say that in some sense it stands for the *essence* of physicality. In religious or esoteric terms, the experience of physical existence has always been characterized as the experience of *limitation*. Our journey in this world is framed as a journey of travail and suffering, a constant struggle of overcoming resistance in order to get anywhere that we want to be in life. But interestingly enough, this also resembles the traditional astrological description of the influence of Saturn. So if we take Malkuth to be the essence of Saturn and move it up to the place of Da'ath, then the diagram begins to fall into place in a way that seems much more orderly and symmetrical. We have three Sephiroth at the top representing a Divine Trinity in some sense, and the seven lower Sephiroth represent the seven astrological bodies that were known to the ancients.

This figure becomes even more interesting when we consider the geometry of the seven lower Sephiroth. Collectively, they form a wheel with the Sun at the center. This wheel consists of six paths around the circumference, and six paths forming spokes as it were from the Sun to the other planets. This makes twelve paths altogether, which equals the number of signs in the zodiac. If we equate the spokes to the so-called *positive* or active signs and the perimeter to the *negative* or passive signs, then the logic of this diagram becomes quite compelling. As I will attempt to show in the remainder of this book, the astrological attributions to both the planets and the signs come together quite neatly if we assign the zodiac signs as follows:

Mars to Sun: Aries
Saturn to Mars: Taurus
Saturn to Sun: Gemini
Saturn to Jupiter: Cancer
Jupiter to Sun: Leo
Jupiter to Venus: Virgo
Sun to Venus: Libra
Venus to Moon: Scorpio
Sun to Moon: Sagittarius
Mercury to Moon: Capricorn
Sun to Mercury: Aquarius
Mars to Mercury: Pisces

This brings us to the question of what astrological correspondences, if any, apply to the three upper Sephiroth? Modern astrology recognizes three major planets which were unknown to the ancients - Uranus, Neptune, and Pluto. The ancient astrologers conceived of the astrological bodies as inhabiting nested concentric spheres around the earth. The order of those spheres from innermost to outermost tracks to the order of the Sephiroth going up the Tree from Malkuth. Following this pattern, one might logically conclude that Uranus would subsequently fall in the place of Binah, and Neptune in the place of Chokmah. Despite the reasonableness of this expectation, my reflections on the symbolism of both the planets and the Sephiroth lead me to the conclusion that Neptune tracks more neatly to Binah, Uranus to Chokmah, and Pluto to Kether. The reason for this apparent reversal of order of Uranus and Neptune is not at all clear. The best that we can say perhaps is that the outer planets have all been described as *transpersonal*, and the three upper Sephiroth are similarly thought of as transcendental, and so in some sense these three principles are seen as standing outside the normal structures and relationships of physical reality.

The final form of the re-imagined Tree of Life, with Tarot attributions to the twenty-two paths, is shown in Figure 3. Given that this is an altogether novel representation of the diagram, I have chosen to forego the traditional names, and instead depict them simply as ten spheres of diverse colors based loosely upon the Golden Dawn color scheme. The rationale for this is twofold. First of all, the traditional designations are, in my opinion, more obfuscating than helpful. Second, I find the picturing of these archetypes in the likeness of colorful jewels to be more evocative of the primitive simplicity and *pure energy* that they ultimately express. While the verbal labels may seem to offer more in the way of definition to the intellect, the color scheme appeals more to the subconscious, which reads their energies intuitively.

The ten spheres, with their astrological correspondences and key concepts, are defined as follows:

The Diamond Sphere: Pluto - Consciousness
The White Sphere: Uranus - Change
The Black Sphere: Neptune - Space
The Indigo Sphere: Saturn - Consistency
The Blue Sphere: Jupiter - Power
The Red Sphere: Mars - Will
The Yellow Sphere: Sun - Coherence or Integrity
The Green Sphere: Venus - Essence
The Orange Sphere: Mercury - Form or Appearance
The Purple Sphere: Moon - Force

The keywords given above are naturally oversimplifications that will require deeper elaboration, but they are chosen carefully to give an intuitive sense of the logical structure of this diagram and the story that it tells.

At the top of the Tree is Consciousness. Just as there is no story without a listener, and no play without an audience, there is likewise no existence without a *subject* who experiences it. Consciousness is therefore the first and foremost principle, because without it there is no reason for anything else to exist. The nine remaining spheres can be divided into three triangles. The White, Black, and Indigo Spheres - in the aspects of Time, Space, and Eternity - form the Existential Triangle. Together these

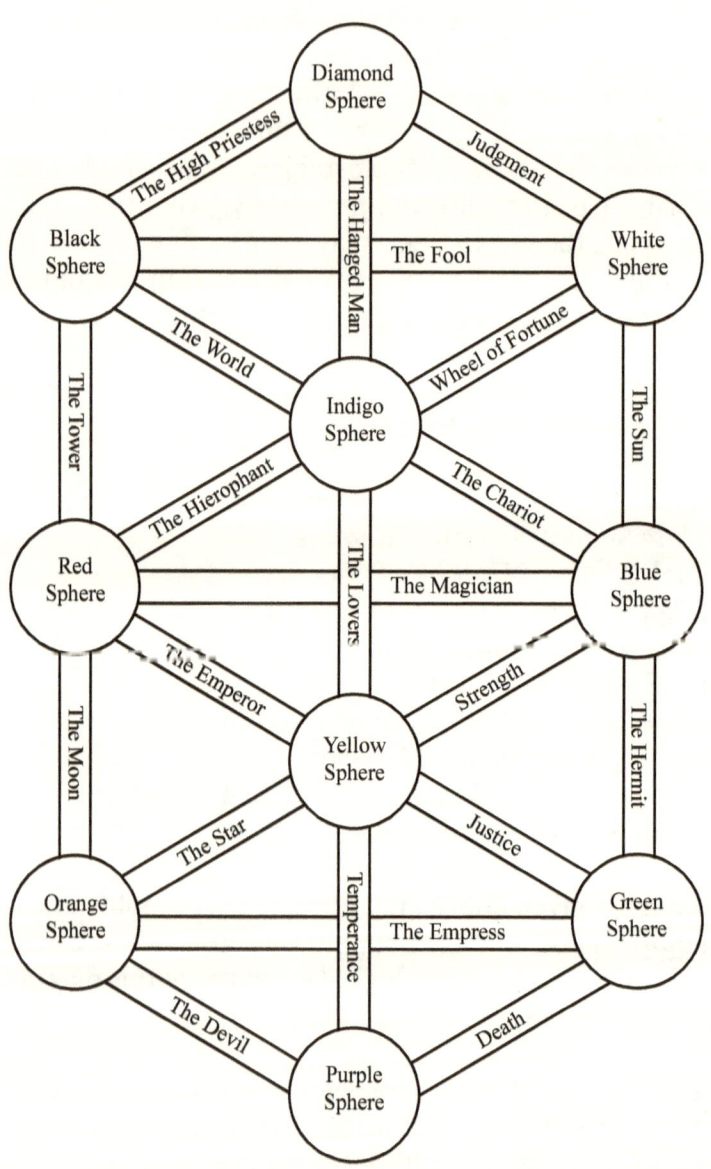

Figure 3
Tree of Life Revised

A New Model of the Kabbalistic Tree of Life

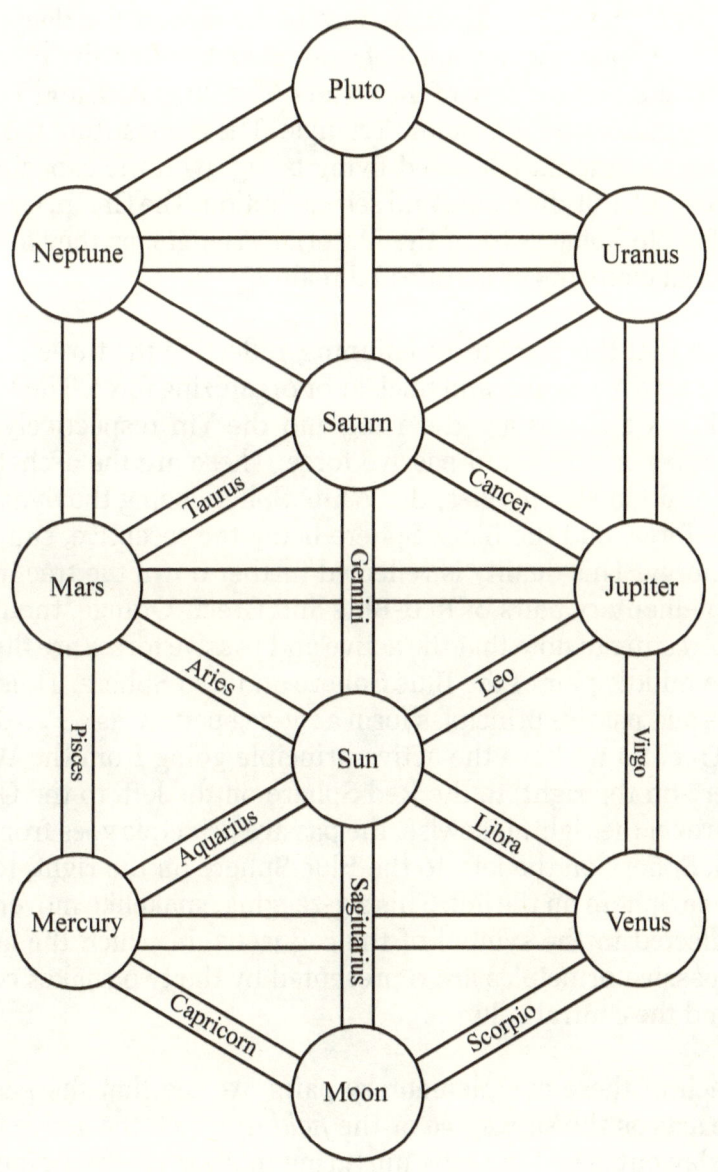

Figure 4
Revised Tree with Astrological Correspondences

constitute the primeval backdrop of existence, in which all of experience plays out with Consciousness at their center. In the Book of Genesis, the Black Sphere is the face of the deep, and the White Sphere is the Spirit of God (*Ruach* – literally "breath") that hovers over the face of the waters. The Blue, Red, and Yellow Spheres make up the Organic Triangle. These constitute the core elements of the individuated living being, with the capacity for self-control, self-direction, and self-definition. The Green, Orange, and Purple Spheres form the Material Triangle, as they are the principal elements of manifested reality.

We see that there are three columns, reflecting the three principles of active, passive, and nuclear or organizing force. The White and Black Spheres are the Yang and the Yin respectively, the principles of active and passive force. These are the archetypal male and female energies, the White Sphere being the dynamic, active force, and the Black Sphere being the receptive, supportive energy. This duality is reflected further down the tree in the complementary pairs of Red-Blue and Green-Orange, though it is interesting to note that the active and passive forces are flipped in the middle pair of the Blue Sphere and Red Sphere. Thus, the active and passive principles form a zig-zag pattern as we go down the Tree. So we have the active principle going from the White Sphere on the right, to the Red Sphere on the left, to the Green Sphere on the right. Likewise, the passive principle goes from the Black Sphere on the left, to the Blue Sphere on the right, to the Orange Sphere on the left. This zig-zagging, snakelike movement is reflected in the symbol of the caduceus, in which the active and passive principles are represented by the two snakes coiled around the central column.

In each of these complementary pairs, we see that the passive force acts as the *substance* or the *field* in which the active force can play out. The Yin is the nurturing mother-energy because it provides the Yang with the material that it needs to work with. With the White and Black Spheres, for instance, space is the field in which movement is possible. Likewise, the Blue Sphere is the domain of control in which the Red Sphere is able to exert its influence. And finally, with the Green and Orange Spheres, the form is that through which essence is expressed.

The central pillar represents those principles which are the nuclear, organizing force of existence. Saturn and the Sun in particular form a double-center of the Tree, because the universe is held together jointly by the principles of *consistency* and *coherence*. Consciousness, in a higher sense, is the center of all experience. Because from the philosophical standpoint known as *subjective idealism*, the interplay of manifested existence is empty and void without the perceiving subject to experience it. The Purple Sphere, finally, is a special case. It is the *raw force* of nature on which the material world rests. It is the engine that drives manifestation.

Also represented on the Tree are the four elements of Fire, Water, Air, and Earth. The active spheres represent Fire, as they are all warm, dynamic, and energetic in nature. The passive spheres are the element of Water, as they embody the idea of fluid substance in some sense. The Black Sphere, as space, represents undifferentiated universal substance. It is the mother-substance out of which all material forms crystallize. The Blue Sphere, Jupiter, represents the idea of a *pool* of resources with which one can operate. And the Orange Sphere, Mercury, embodies the concept of a plastic, malleable substance that can be readily shaped into whatever form is desired. The Diamond and Yellow Spheres are the element of Air. They embody the principles of both *clarity* and *levity*. Finally, Earth is represented by the Indigo and Purple Spheres, as these express both the *stability* and the *impactfulness* of material reality.

It should be obvious from the relationships described above that these spheres can never be understood in isolation from each other. They are all intimately interrelated, and that is how they come alive in our own experience. Taken separately, they are groundless. But together, they form an organic whole.

The rest of this book will explore each of the ten spheres in detail, as well as the paths between them, to which I have attributed the twenty-two Major Arcana of the Tarot. But first, there is one final point that needs to be made abundantly clear, and that is that the manner in which these energies manifest through the lens of any given human experience will be greatly shaped by the evolution of the individual concerned. This is a crucial point to understand, because in traditional astrology certain planets were regarded as *malefics* (Mars and Saturn) whereas others were deemed *benefics* (Jupiter and Venus). In truth, none of the energies of this Tree are malignant or negative. They all serve a positive and beneficial role in the framework of creation. It is rather the *filter* of the personality through which they pass that determines the positive or negative representation thereof. This applies to zodiacal as well as planetary energies. Furthermore, these rays can be filtered through cultural influences which may impart a certain spin that is not truly essential to the core energy, but is rather a *side effect* of the cultural or personal influence. But while the transmission may be distorted through the lens of human personality, the underlying energy is, in all cases, an expression of the Divine Harmony.

Part II
The Ten Spheres

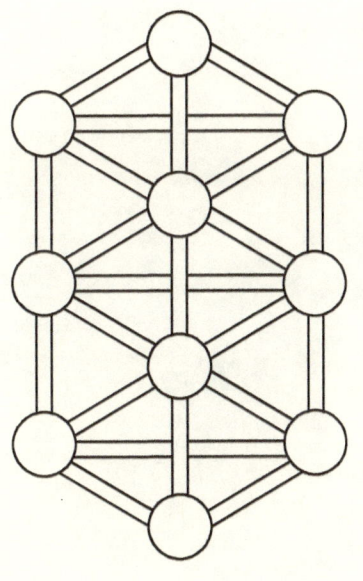

The Diamond Sphere

The apex of our Tree is the crystal-clear diamond of consciousness. By this we mean not everyday, mundane consciousness, but rather *pure consciousness*. Why would we liken pure consciousness to a diamond? Because it is *clear* and it is *sharp*. It *cuts through* the illusions that weave together the fabric of human society. In the heightened state of pure consciousness, we see the world with the utmost clarity. And most importantly, we see with the understanding that our consciousness is itself a *point of power* from which change and creation and manifestation radiate forth into the world.

Being the first and uppermost sphere of the Tree of Life, consciousness represents the beginning of existence. In direct contrast to the materialist philosophy, which claims that consciousness is a mere *side effect* of matter, the esoteric philosophy has always asserted that the material world is an extension of consciousness. This notion was articulated by the English thinker George Berkeley as the philosophy of *subjective idealism*. The crux of this philosophy is that there is no meaningful way to speak of existence apart from that which is experienced by a perceiving consciousness. That is why consciousness is the very root of this Tree. All experience occurs within the space of consciousness.

The opposing and consensus view of reality is that the objects of experience have an independent existence apart from consciousness, and that their sensible qualities are simply surface phenomena which are distinct from the underlying thing-in-itself. Berkeley's counter-argument to this idea is that if you strip away all of the sensible properties from a thing, there is nothing left over but an empty and meaningless abstraction. The very *reality* of the thing lies in its perceptibility, which is meaningless without the one who perceives. Thus, there is no real substance to anything apart from the perception of it by consciousness.

The typical objection to this argument is that things obviously persist when we are not observing them. If I see a tree, and then walk away from it and come back to it later, the tree is still there, which means that it must have an independent existence apart from my seeing it. This is a compelling case to be sure, but the counter-argument of esoteric philosophy is that *consciousness is everywhere*, and everything is conscious at some fundamental level. As Berkeley framed it, the consciousness of God *pervades* all of existence, and thereby *sustains* all of existence. This idea is expressed very eloquently in the Zohar itself, which states that if the all-seeing eye of God were to close for even a fraction of an instant, the entire universe would cease to exist.

So does this mean then that Kether represents the consciousness of God? Or does it represent human consciousness? This is where things start to get complicated. Kether is both God-consciousness *and* human consciousness, because it is the *universal* principle of consciousness, which is the same in God and humanity and all that has consciousness. And if God-consciousness is everywhere then everything in fact, down to the tiniest atom, has consciousness. The pattern of the universe is fractal in nature, and so each sphere on the Tree represents a principle that is reflected both above and below, in the macrocosm and in the microcosm.

In the Hebrew Old Testament, there are multiple designations for God. The name of God which corresponds to Kether is *Ahaiah*, which literally means "I am". And this is precisely what the Diamond Sphere is - the pure, abstract state of self-awareness. It is the "I am" in Descartes' famous formula "Cogito ergo sum". I think, therefore *I am*. Understand that in this statement Descartes was starting from a state of absolute philosophical skepticism. He begins with the question: how can one know with certainty that anything in the world is true? And the one thing that he realized to be undeniable is that *consciousness is*, because without the "I" there could be no question. This is the beginning of all truth, that *I am*. And this is the one truth that remains constant. While the world that we observe through our senses is perpetually shifting and changing, our *consciousness* of this world is the one thing that is always present in the experience. It is the foundation of all experience, the one central point around which the entire theatre of life unfolds. And what is most mysterious about this central point of consciousness is that there is seemingly *nothing to it*. This is the truly remarkable thing about consciousness, that it has no sensible qualities of its own. You cannot measure it or handle it or describe it in terms of any tangible attributes. It can only be understood as a kind of *field* in which sensible experiences take place. This is why we refer to consciousness as the Diamond Sphere. It is a clear, pure, and transparent brilliance.

Consciousness can therefore be described as an irreducible substance. A singularity. There are no *parts* to it that can be picked apart from one another. It has neither length nor weight nor color nor odor. It is simply a transparent clarity. In a certain sense, it is *nothing*, insofar as it has no tangible parts or attributes. And yet consciousness is more than just nothing. It is a nothing that is also a something. And not *just* a something but *everything* - because just as consciousness is capable of reflecting all that can be experienced, it is also capable of conceiving all that is conceivable. Thus, it contains every possibility within itself. This is indeed the most significant truth to understand about the Diamond Sphere, that it is the root of *all possibility*. Consciousness is not just a static reflection of perceptions and experiences. It is also a *point of power*. It is the doorway through which the Limitless Light projects all possibilities. Consciousness is a *subject*, meaning that which creates the experience. It is the experiencer who drives the experience.

That which is a singularity is indestructible. What has no parts, cannot be broken apart. Nor can it be rationalized as an accidental side-effect or by-product of parts. Consciousness is an eternal, fundamental principle of existence.

Each of the spheres on the Tree of Life brings a certain power or capability to the one who meditates upon it and absorbs its truth. The principal power to be gained from meditation upon the Diamond Sphere is the discovery of one's *Core Self*. This Core Self is the source of all creative power, and it can only be truly grasped through the invisible, transparent, and formless nature of consciousness. In the language of the Kabbalah, it is called the *Yechidah*, which derives from the root word *Yachad* meaning unity. The Core Self is a oneness, and we can only understand oneness as that which is indivisible. And only that which has no parts which are capable of being separated from one another can be indivisible. This is the essence of consciousness - formless, indivisible, indestructible... the eternal central point from which *all possibility* emanates. The Yechidah is the No-Thing, the One-Thing, and the All-Thing.

There is a leap of understanding here that is far too big for words, because it asks you to recognize that your true identity is not the physical form or even the personality that bears your name. What other people call "you" is simply a mask of the True Self. It is a convenient fiction. Consciousness itself is above the mind and above the body. The mind is simply a *technology,* just as the body is a technology. When you step into a car and drive it, the vehicle becomes a powerful extension of your will. But you don't suddenly imagine that you *are* the vehicle. There is always a clear distinction between the vehicle and your *self*. This is the shift in perspective that comes from grasping the nature of the Diamond Sphere. When you shift the *locus of identity* from the mind-body complex to the Yechidah, then the Yechidah rises above the mind-body machine and governs over it, using it as a technology. This is a position of tremendous power. When the identity is no longer bound to the thoughts and emotions and impulses of the personality, then it is no longer subject to being thrown about by the automatic gyrations of the machine. It is instead in a position to intelligently re-direct the energies of the machine. Quite simply, the personality becomes as a puppet, and the Yechidah is the puppet-master.

When you experience this level of pure self-awareness, it is perceived to be so far above ordinary human consciousness as to seem distinctly *super-human*. The All-Thing sees through the eyes of the personality as one standing in the uppermost chamber of a high tower, looking out across a vast horizon. And as for all of the storm and stress and turmoil that the personality acts out on the landscape below, it all looks so very *small* from up here. In this cool, calm detachment from the theatre of existence, the drama of life is simply a thought in the mind of the One. This,

The Diamond Sphere

in essence, is the very ideal of Eastern philosophy as expressed in Yoga and Buddhism: to be above it all, and thereby to be *free* from it all. Which is not to say that one can ever be, in this lifetime, completely free from the limitations of time and space. But one can attain a *psychological* freedom of self-determination, a freedom that comes from the *clarity* which sees everything in its proper perspective. Unlike the human consciousness, which is enmeshed in its web of limiting beliefs about what everything means and how it all ought to be, the diamond clarity of pure consciousness *cuts through* all of these illusions and *transcends* the fabric of false awareness that defines human existence.

This diamond consciousness is therefore beyond human. It is like a whirling vortex from which all of the universe emanates. Kether is called the Crown because it is not anthropomorphic, but rather a primitive and transcendent existence that sits *above* the human form. It is not the king himself (which is Tiphareth - that which holds together the thing that we call a personality), but rather the sovereign Spirit that assumes the aspect of the king. The king is a man who is born and grows and lives and dies. But "The Crown" is forever. It passes on from one ruler to the next. And it is by no means coincidence that the symbol of the Crown is in the shape of a circle - the most perfect geometric expression of simplicity, unity, and eternity.

Astrologically, we correlate the Diamond Sphere to Pluto, and as we study the astrological interpretations of Pluto, we seem to find a striking contradiction. Up to this point, we have described the Diamond Sphere as a pure and transcendent consciousness of the utmost clarity. And yet of all the astrological symbols, Pluto is generally treated as the most troubling, disturbing, and dangerous. In spite of this rather bad reputation, I stand by the conviction that none of the astrological signs or planets are in any sense *inherently* negative. It is rather the clarity and insight of the human personality through which these energies pass that determines whether the expression will be productive or counter-productive. Pluto is no exception to this rule. Being the astrological representation of the highest and most *radical* principle of existence, Pluto carries in a sense the most powerful energy. And with the most powerful energy comes the greatest potential for things to go sideways. It is a responsibility that not everyone can handle successfully.

The key thing to understand about Pluto is that it is, in a very real sense, "beyond good and evil" as Nietzsche would say. Pure consciousness is *amoral* insofar as it recognizes that what we commonly call "good" and "bad" are not absolute truths written upon the fabric of reality, but rather *projections* of what the limited human ego finds pleasing or threatening. Now to be clear, this does not in any way mean that someone who experiences transcendent awareness immediately becomes a cold-blooded psychopath. Far from it. The *clear-seeing* that characterizes pure consciousness does not typically lead to amoral and antisocial behavior, because most people possess an innate instinct for *balance* which guides their interactions with other people. This is the influence of the Yellow Sphere, which lends a kind of moral compass that is much more substantive than the rules and norms of society, which can often be quite arbitrary and superficial.

Human morality typically expresses itself in the way of judging things as either "good" or "bad", depending on whether they are helpful or harmful to oneself or others. The rules of judgment are in theory supposed to be applied consistently and equally, but in practice they can prove to be highly relative and malleable according to the context. Which is another way of saying that human beings tend to finesse their own rules of judgment to suit their own needs. Transcendent awareness, on the other hand, is completely *above judgment*. It does not see a thing as "good" or "bad" or "right" or "wrong". Everything simply *is what it is*. And it has to see things this way because that is the clearest and truest perception of reality. Judgment is essentially *negation*. To judge something as wrong or bad is to assert that it does not have a right to exist, that it *should not* exist. And yet, the thing *does exist*. And so, in a very real sense, judgment is a false consciousness, a false perception of reality. Transcendent awareness must necessarily rise above judgment in order to see the world as it truly is.

This is a perspective which naturally makes a lot of people uncomfortable. The typical objection to this way of thinking is that if we don't judge certain things as good and bad, then everything is permitted, and injustice becomes the norm. Certainly, there is a distinct danger of this if some other regulating influence is not present. The crucial thing to realize is that the instinct which impresses a *natural* harmony and order onto things is quite different from the impulse that labels things as right and wrong. In particular, the impulse to affix the labels "wrong" or "bad" onto something is a distinct attempt to *shut down* whatever we don't like. It is a peculiar kind of flawed logic that aims to invalidate and thereby negate the existence of whatever we refuse to accept. But it is *not successful* in actually doing this. And so this energy of shutting-down that we attempt to impose on other things and other people simply reflects back upon ourselves and shuts down our own energy. This is an unavoidable side-effect of standing in judgment. The harder we judge, the more we shut down our own energy. Judgment is a bit like banging one's head against a brick wall. It is only when we stop banging our heads and take a step back, that we can begin to move the energy in constructive ways. This is the key understanding of the philosophy of non-judgment as it is expressed in Buddhism or Taoism. To let go of judgment is to both *see* the pure energy and *liberate* the pure energy that exists within ourselves and within the world around us. Whereas judgment is about negation, transcendent awareness is all about *possibility*. Seen through the lens of non-judgment, everything shines with the radiance and power of its limitless possibility.

Pluto is therefore, in one aspect, a liberator of primal energy. This can be a very dangerous thing, however, if there is not a proper understanding of how to balance and harmonize that primal energy. Like the energy of nuclear fission, it can run disastrously amok if it is not channeled constructively. The clarity of Pluto rips the veil off of reality and reveals the God-like power of *all possibility* that is at the heart of everything, and most importantly at the heart of oneself. To those who are unprepared, there is a very real danger of becoming drunk on the experience of this power.

In its negative projections, therefore, Pluto often manifests as *abuse of power*. It is almost like a light that is so bright that it overwhelms the ability of the human personality to process it and contain it. Manipulation, rule-breaking, and overstepping of boundaries are the hallmarks of an unregulated feeling of internalized God-power. There is also a very distinct element of *nihilism* where Pluto is involved. Kether is the point that emanates out of Ain Soph Aur, and so it is the border between existence and nothingness. With the perspective of non-judgment, there also comes a perception that there is no intrinsic *meaning* to anything. This could be interpreted on the one hand as a very negative realization - that all of existence is essentially empty. On the other hand, as Nietzsche pointed out, the stripping away of all layers of meaning could be seen as revealing the limitless possibility that underlies all things, a kind of *positive nihilism*. In any case, the interesting thing about nihilism is that even after you have stripped away all of the meaning from everything and reduced it all to nothing, there is still one thing left over - which is the inescapable reality of one's own existence. And in this *blank slate* of meaningless existence that stands before us, we are faced with the responsibility of *owning* our own free choice to shape the future that lies ahead. This is indeed the very essence of *existentialism*, which is a decidedly Plutonian way of being in the world.

As we unpack the full meaning of Pluto, a central theme that emerges is the relationship between clarity, truth, and power. To see clearly into a matter is to understand the truth of the matter, and to know the truth is to possess power within the domain of that truth. Jupiter is also associated with power in a certain sense, but it is of a different nature. The power of Jupiter comes from direct ownership of a space or a resource, whereas the power of Pluto is that which comes from a strategic vantage point. Pluto embodies the dictum that *knowledge is power*, insofar as it possesses insight into how things work. Pluto is very cunning in this respect. It penetrates into the root causes of things. It finds the vulnerabilities and weaknesses. Power is knowing how to manipulate the levers and the fulcrums and the soft points. Pluto above all represents a *penetrating awareness*. You could say that the superpower of Pluto is to penetrate into the heart of things. The

Plutonian impulse can express itself as an intense desire to pick locks, figuratively (or literally) speaking. This represents an archetypal drive to get to the bottom of all secrets, which is a desire to *know* what has not been known. And so it is fundamentally a drive of consciousness. The *cogito ergo sum* must penetrate into the truth of its experience, in order to be the master of its experience.

Pluto seems to be associated with manipulation, and in a peculiar way this could be seen as an aspect of its transcendent nature. That is to say, the transcendent awareness is able to occupy a vantage point *outside* of the system. And from this vantage point, which is both outside the system and above it, the transcendent awareness is able to exert a vector of influence *obliquely* to the plane of manifestation, from a direction that cannot be met head-on. Pluto is therefore associated with forces that are secret, hidden, and inscrutable. This is a very esoteric concept to grasp hold of, as it raises a metaphor of operating from a higher dimension than the plane upon which you wish to act. And yet this is a very succinct image of the Diamond Sphere. It is the Core Self that lies behind the manifest form of the personality. Insofar as most of us are fully identified with the personality, we are enmeshed within the personality and enmeshed within the web of mental and emotional influences to which it belongs. But the Core Self, if we can shift our focus of awareness into it, is above the personality and above time and space. It therefore occupies a transcendent viewpoint from which it can manipulate the personality and manipulate reality.

Pluto has a reputation for acting sharply, incisively, and sometimes drastically. One way of describing this is to say that Pluto expresses an uncompromising *will to truth*, and in certain circumstances it may bring about what we call a "moment of truth". *Illumination* is the key concept of the Diamond Sphere, and illumination sometimes requires the sacrifice of that which is not grounded in truth. The Plutonian aspect of the Diamond Sphere is best understood as the impulse to *revelation*, to tear away the false facade that encumbers the clear seeing of reality. And because this sphere also represents a non-identification with the personality, there is a decidedly *impersonal* way in which Pluto goes about tearing down what is not real.

This can become quite uncomfortable when we resist the facts. Pluto has precious little tolerance for intellectual dishonesty, or superficiality, or softening of the truth in any way. One could say that the principal action of Pluto is *cutting through the crap*. It cuts through the lies and cuts through the illusions, and it doesn't care in the least about your emotional attachment to those illusions. Pluto has no mercy for that which is inauthentic. And so its influence is often experienced as a force which shatters that which has outlasted its usefulness. When we hold on to something which is no longer serving our authentic nature, Pluto will clear it away. Perhaps the most useful way of understanding Pluto is to say that it represents the clearing away of stuck or blocked energy. It strips away that which is not essential to our Core Self. This can be easy, or it can be decidedly difficult, depending on how invested one is in a false self-image. If the resistance is strong, then Pluto can manifest as a sudden crisis which forces us to go through a profound transformation of awareness - a symbolic death and rebirth if you will.

This clarifying action can be looked at as a process of *purification*. To see things clearly is the key power of the Diamond Sphere. But to *see oneself clearly*, without any illusion, is by far the most important power. And the willingness to ruthlessly jettison the dead weight of whatever is not truly part of oneself - this is the most Plutonian exercise of all. The Greek word *apocalypsis* literally means "revelation". And indeed, the Book of Revelation can be seen as a metaphor for the revelation of the True Self through the Plutonian process of self-purification, a process of separating the wheat from the chaff in one's own constitution. It is an undeniable fact that whatever is pure is more powerful than that which is impure. And a pure, authentic self is much more powerful than a false and inauthentic self. And so what is most valuable about the clarity of the Diamond Sphere is that it allows us to see through to the truth of our underlying drives and feelings, without the distorting filters and rationalizations of thought. Where there is clarity, there is no dilution of self. Clarity sees the raw, unfiltered facts of existence. It does not apply any layer of moralizing over the bare truth of what is. Nor does it interpret the world through a filter of how we want it to be, or how we think it ought to be. Clarity breaks everything down into its raw, elemental, primitive, and primal energies. It strips things down to their purest form, and that which is pure is stronger than that which is diluted.

This raw and unfiltered aspect of Pluto is part of what makes it seem so frightening and so difficult to come to terms with. Pluto has a way of ripping away the layers of illusion that society takes comfort in. If we think of society as a complex construct of lies, then Pluto is what tears the lid off of this whole facade. It is oftentimes associated with the "dark side" of human nature, but this is not exactly accurate. Pluto simply *reveals* the unintegrated aspects of human nature. It blows the lid off of the attempt to cover over the untamed instincts. With the clarity of the Diamond Sphere comes a brutal ripping away of all pretenses of moral posturing, and subsequently all of the emotional impulses that have been suppressed rise to the surface. So despite its rather maligned reputation, Pluto is actually that which *shines a light* on the unresolved conflicts. It is like turning over a rock and finding all manner of vermin underneath. Pluto is not itself responsible for the vermin that we find there. Pluto is simply the turning over of the rock.

This honest exposure of what lies beneath can be overwhelming or even catastrophic, but there is always an opportunity to arrive at a higher level of awareness. The important thing to understand is that the energies that are brought to light and purified are much less dangerous than those which continue to operate unconsciously through distorted filters. There is often a fear that if we take off the rose-colored glasses and see ourselves as we really are, then the truth will be too much to bear. But when we see all phenomena, both internal and external, as simply pure energy, then this fear begins to dissolve. Pure energy does not naturally tend toward ugliness and disharmony. It is the distortion and the blockage of energy that causes disharmony. And so ultimately the influence of Pluto presents to us as something dark and terrible because we have not yet figured out how to engage with it and process it. If we meet it from a place of denial and unconscious resistance, then it will tend to act with explosive decisiveness. But if we approach it with a willingness to let go of our illusions, then Pluto can bring the flash of illumination that sorts everything out.

Pluto is sometimes associated with survival or the will to survive, but this really has more to do with the way in which Pluto forces a certain *clarity of intent* in times of crisis. In those moments of imminent danger where the very fabric of our world is about to fall apart, it is Pluto which strips away all of the layers of self-doubt, uncertainty, guilt, shame, and whatever else we normally carry around which would stand in the way of realizing our goal. In a time of crisis, Pluto has a way of stripping us down to our most fundamental, primitive, undiluted self. Everything that is fake goes out the window, and that is exactly where we need to be in order to navigate the moments of greatest decision.

In rounding out this discussion of the Diamond Sphere, it is worth noting that we have focused a great deal on some of the more difficult astrological interpretations of Pluto. The reason for this is that astrology on the whole has tended to take a negative bias toward the outer planets - Pluto in particular - focusing mainly on the disruptive influences that they manifest in human affairs. This is rather unfortunate, because the difficult or challenging manifestation of an archetypal energy is not its primary expression. It is rather a *secondary* aspect that results from the passage of that energy through the distorting filters of human personality. The primary expression of each one of these spheres is *positive* in nature, and the only way to truly get to the heart of these energies is to grasp each one of them by their positive and beneficial essence. The expression of Pluto can be difficult or it can be easy. In its easy expression, it is quite simply the sparkling tranquility of Buddha-mind, the crystalline radiance of illumination in which all the world appears pure and clear and innocent again. This is the key concept of the Diamond Sphere that we must move forward with.

The White Sphere

The White Sphere represents *movement*. Or to be more accurate, it is *movementness*. That is to say, it represents the impulse toward movement: dynamism, verve, and the spirit of *pure energy*. The key formula of this sphere is that *energy* equals *change* equals *flux* equals *time*. These are all one and the same principle. Time is nothing other than flux, and there is no time apart from flux. Dynamism equals life, which is the capacity to move and to make things move.

The White Sphere is the universal creative father-energy, driving things forward. Space is the empathic mother-energy that embraces all beings. The White Sphere is the essence of *becoming*. It is renewal, and everything that is new. It is the creative urge, which is manifested in spontaneous play and untamed excitement. Imagine it as a whirling, writhing white vapor, a chaos in never-ceasing flux. The White Sphere embodies the pure joy in the flux of life.

In the symbolism of Hinduism, this is the Dance of Shiva in which nothing is permanent, and the White Sphere delights in impermanence. Creation and destruction are two sides of the same process, which is out with the old and in with the new. Such is the flow of life itself. Life is constant change and constant movement forward. The White Sphere stands for metamorphosis, progress, and the driving force of evolution. Its symbol is the dragon which breathes magical fire, and the fire is the life of all things.

Levity is the essence of this sphere. It is light-hearted, joyous, exuberant, and ebullient. Depression is always experienced as a *stagnation* of the vital energy. Motion and circulation of energy is what defines a bright and healthy temperament. To have levity, one must embrace the acceptance of change and impermanence. It is the nature of levity to not be overly attached to outcomes or to worldly concerns. The spirit of *not taking life too seriously* is the very tonic of life. This energy is inherently anti-depressant and stimulant in nature. It is the essence of caffeine, sugar, and all forms of excitement. It is speed for the sake of speed and motion for the sake of motion. Carnival rides exemplify the essence of the White Sphere, as do races, and dance. This is an energy that cannot stand still. It is revolutionary for the sake of revolution.

The White Sphere can be described as the root of the creative impulse, because it is the primal drive to both experience something new and to manifest something new. It is always on the path of reaching out to new things. In this mode of activity, it is also the power of *renewal*. The White Sphere has been called by such names as *spirit*, or *pneuma* in Greek, and *ruach* in Hebrew, all of which describe it as something like a breath or a wind. This points to a function of the White Sphere as stimulating the *circulation* of life-force. We can imagine the influence of the White Sphere to be like a cool, cleansing breeze that blows through and clears away all of the stuck and stagnant energies. This purifying breeze sweeps away all of the dust and cobwebs of the mind and soul, leaving a clear and free channel for the flow of creative energy. And so by opening up to this free flow of energy, we experience a special kind of life-giving and youth-restoring rejuvenation.

In its creative capacity, the White Sphere is associated with brilliance and genius, because it engenders an entirely new way of looking at the world. Fundamentally, it is the primal creative urge of the Divine. It is the impulse to bring creation itself into being, and to make worlds happen. This impulse is of an altogether different order from any goal-oriented or specified will, because it is much more abstract than that. The creative impulse is all about expressing *something* new, *anything* new. It is about creating something that has not been seen before, novelty for its own sake. With this impulse there comes a boundless curiosity, and an endless desire to explore. And so the desire to go forth into unknown territory with no particular end-point in mind is a perfect expression of the White Sphere's energy.

To fully understand the White Sphere, as with any of these principles, you must recognize the *reason* why it is what it is, that there is in fact a purpose behind it. For instance, you could think of the White Sphere simply as energy in the purely physical sense. But this would not capture the underlying essence of it. This would be a materialistic and mechanistic understanding. You must also understand the *motivation* that is behind it. It is the motivation to experience new modes of being and new modes of creation which propels the physical energy that drives the universe.

Likewise, the Black Sphere is more than just empty space. It is also the *reason* why space exists, which is to serve as the place in which these new modes of being can play out. That is the *impulse* which lies behind the existence of space. And that purpose and impulse is inseparable from the space itself, just as the impulse to explore new modes of existing is inseparable from the physical energy that pulsates in every wave and particle. And standing above both of these spheres is the impulse toward experience itself, pure consciousness, which is the impulse to envision a universe.

So the White Sphere is not just an objective phenomenon in the form of physical energy. It is also, and more importantly, a subjective principle. That is to say, it is the feeling of *excitement* that propels the movement of the universe. None of these spheres can therefore be properly thought of as a static principle. Each one is a *dynamic* principle with a driving motivation behind it.

It is worthwhile to reiterate here the overarching pattern in which the spheres on the left and right columns form complementary pairs of active and passive principles. The passive principle serves as a vehicle, field, or substrate in which the active principle manifests. Change operates in the field of space. Will operates in the field of what we can control. And essence manifests in the substrate of form. Space and flux taken together constitute the field of all possibility, the field of creation. Consistency, in the form of the Indigo Sphere, is the axis around which that field revolves.

Astrologically, the White Sphere is represented by the planet Uranus. Uranus is often said to have a very intellectual or detached quality to it. This is actually an expression of the desire for *mobility* which Uranus embodies, which can only be maintained by a spirit of levity and detachment from anything that would weigh it down emotionally. The *freedom to move* that Uranus values above all else demands that it not be burdened with any form of sentimentality or attachment. It is based in the idea of impermanence as the way of things and as the way of life, indeed as the very essence of life itself. And so this desire for freedom cannot be attached to any one form of manifestation. Uranus embodies the perspective of the Greek philosopher Heraclitus, who famously said that you can never step into the same river twice.

Like Mars and Venus, Uranus represents the active side of the fundamental Yin-Yang polarity. But Uranus is a much purer, more refined type of energy than either Mars or Venus. It does not have the emotional or sexual overtones of Venus. Nor does it have the aggressive and linear determination of Mars. Uranus is a much more abstract kind of energy. And because it is so abstract, the action of Uranus can often seem directionless or even wanton, with a proclivity for flipping everything upside-down just because it can. The key to understanding Uranus is that fundamentally it is change for the sake of change. Because movement is the essence of life, and without movement and circulation of the vital energies, there is simply death. It is not moving toward an end-state because there is no end-state. There is simply life everlasting. This directionless outpouring of energy is represented by the spirit of *play* - that state of taking nothing seriously, in which the ebullient movement toward no concrete goal in particular is embraced with full delight and excitement. It is the energy of the White Sphere that erupts in the form of *laughter*.

This is not to say that Uranus cannot serve a useful purpose. It is first and foremost the stimulator of innovation *par excellence*. The ability of Uranus to think outside of the box and to explore new territory is the source of every revolutionary idea that advances humanity a step forward. But there is an almost *accidental* quality to the way in which Uranus stumbles into innovations of actual utility. Uranus is at its best when it doesn't take the outcome all that seriously, but simply allows the free flow of imagination to land on the occasional idea of practical value.

This brings us to the association of Uranus with the idea of *genius*. A genius in any field of endeavor is someone who takes the subject to a whole new level, through a willingness to think outside of the lines and to see things in an entirely new way. One thing that has often been said about genius is that it is akin to madness, and this trope of the "mad genius" is a very apt illustration of how the White Sphere fundamentally operates. There is a distinct *wildness* to the White Sphere. It is untamed, unchained energy with an overwhelming urge to be free. The decidedly non-linear, unstructured, and *non-deterministic* mode in which the White Sphere acts can best be described as *Primal Chaos*. This free-ranging indeterminacy of the White Sphere is what truly defines it. It could be anything, anywhere, at any moment. In the White Sphere, we have the feeling that anything is possible, and it is in the Primal Chaos that we see new possibilities taking shape. This chaos permeates all of space. It permeates every atom and every cell. It is the field of *all possibility* surrounding and penetrating material existence. And it is essential to recognize here that the White Sphere *has to be* the source of the unpredictable element, because movement that is predictable cannot create anything truly *new*, and so the White Sphere must therefore embody this chaotic undertone.

The chaotic nature of Uranus can lend it toward some negative interpretations, but we must understand that the Primal Chaos is not an inherently destructive force. It is in fact the core creative energy of the Divine. It is primarily when that energy is blocked, repressed, or otherwise maladapted that it can act out in ways that are destructive or irrational. The urge for freedom is a very powerful force, and if this urge is frustrated then it will find its outlet rather explosively. So we could accurately say that destructive chaos is a misfire of creative chaos. Now to be clear, there is definitely some truth to the adage that creation always involves the destruction or passing away of an old order. And Uranus is certainly not afraid to break a few eggs to make an omelette. But the important distinction to understand here is that genuine creation always leaves you in a higher state than before. And so Uranus in its purest manifestation will always be seen to have an *uplifting* influence.

The last thing to understand about the White Sphere is the stark contrast that it makes with the Indigo Sphere. The latter embodies consistency, constancy, and predictability, and so on one level it represents the very *mechanistic* laws of physics that turn the wheels of the physical universe. The White Sphere, by comparison, is the realm of pure *magic*. It is the antithesis of predictability, and therefore it represents the creative power that defies all of the rules. Whereas the Indigo Sphere sets limitations and lays down the law, the White Sphere is the power that tells us that *anything is possible.* If we imagine the Indigo Sphere to be *cosmic ice,* then the White Sphere is a *cosmic fire,* whirling and writhing chaotically with no distinct shape or form. The White Sphere is however not experienced as a fire that scorches or burns, but rather as a fire that *dances.*

The Black Sphere

With the Black Sphere, we have the idea of *space* - the Mother Ocean - which includes both the *meaning* of space as well as the experience of *being in space*. This is one of the spheres of the Existential Triangle, which consists of Space, Time, and Eternity. The Black Sphere is the most existential of all the spheres, however, because it represents the splitting of the original Oneness into the world of duality. The idea of space is implicit in the idea of separation, as there can be no separation without a space between two entities. Only in space can there be an I and a thou, a self and an other. This concept is illustrated quite plainly in the root of the Hebrew word Binah - *Bin*. On the one hand, the word means to discern, to separate, to draw distinctions. At the same time, it carries the meaning of *between*, or an interval between two things. It is this betweenness that defines the matrix in which existence can manifest. The One suffers separation in order that it may create a world, and that it may experience itself therein through the reflection of duality.

To be a distinct being is to be *immersed* into this duality. We are all in a certain sense "thrown" into space. Every living soul, separated from the primal Oneness and separated from its kindred spirits, must undergo this experience of profound *aloneness* in order to exist as an independent, sovereign being. But the fruit of this separation is the magnificence of creation, and so the Black Sphere of Mother Ocean is truly the most bittersweet of all the spheres on the tree. It embodies more than anything else a deep, fundamental sorrow mixed with profound beauty. Separation is the price that we pay for our existence.

And yet, at the same time the Black Sphere embraces a key paradox, which is that this separation *is not real*. To grasp this, we must recognize that every finite thing that exists occupies a certain portion of space. It can be measured by the space that it takes up. But in order to be measurable in terms of space, a thing must in some sense *consist* of space. It is made of space, and yet it presents itself differently from so-called "empty" space. That is to say, it is a portion of space expressing itself through certain qualities and modifications. Another way of putting it is to say that matter is nothing more than a *precipitation* of space, like an iceberg congealing upon the surface of the black polar sea. And like those icebergs that crystallize out of the ocean, and dissolve back into it, all of the various manifestations of finite existence are simply cinematic fluctuations on the surface of the *one space*.

And so the paradox of the Black Sphere is that it represents both duality as well as the interconnectedness of all things which belies that duality. For this reason, it is the realm of both *psychic* and *mystical* experience. It represents that ability to blend into the underlying matrix of reality, to become one with that matrix, and to thereby feel into the ripples and emanations of all other beings which are a part of it. This state of profound connectedness with one's surroundings can only be arrived at through a transcendence of that intellectual function of the mind which draws boundaries and distinctions, and which creates definitions around all of the multifarious elements of existence. It is a distinctly *Zen* state of mind beyond logic and reason, and so it tends to become an experience of pure *feeling*. When the intellect is stripped away, then feeling is the only real *substance* of existing. In this grasping of interconnectedness, one experiences the feeling of subtly melting back into the fabric of space. It is as if your boundary dissolves, and yet there is not a complete loss of self, because you are still a distinct center of force and awareness. One becomes like a wave moving across the ocean. To be a finite being is to be an *articulation* of space, which is at the same time *seamless* with space. It is not a complete dissolution, but rather a blurry and ambiguous boundary between oneself and The All, an open border through which information passes freely. The mystery of Binah is the ability to merge with everything - to see deep into the heart of existence, and read the secrets of all things.

This experience of non-separation is what makes the Black Sphere the root of compassion and empathy, for it is here that we come to realize that we are all expressions of the One Substance. In this awareness, all conflict is seen as an illusion, and one truly begins to understand the injunction to "love thine enemy". Because even the enemy is a facet of the same universal fabric as oneself.

Astrologically, the Black Sphere corresponds to Neptune. Neptune has a very complex set of interpretations, many of them with a somewhat negative flavor. Some of the keywords used to describe Neptune are *illusion, deception, fantasy, dissolution, addiction, martyrdom, idealization, romanticism, mysticism*. All of these descriptors in some sense come back to the idea of the dissolving of boundaries, in particular the boundary between the self and The All. The negative shades of interpretation all tend to point toward a sense of detachment from reality. It would be more fair, however, to say that Neptune operates at a *deeper level* of reality than the mundane reality. Like Uranus, Neptune operates beyond the range of Saturn, which represents the circumscribing and limiting aspects of existence. Saturn therefore represents our consensus "reality" in the sense of that which we are forced to struggle against because it offers resistance to us. Uranus and Neptune represent a more fluid level of existence which is nevertheless just as real, but real in a different fashion. Neptune points to the watery indeterminacy of space in which all forms are latent. It is like the blank sheet of paper on which any conceivable form can be circumscribed within the outlines of the pencil. And so it is true to say that any and every possible form, an *infinity* of forms, is dormant within the blank space of the paper.

And so with Neptune, there is this underlying sense that reality is fluid, and could be literally anything, if only the limiting influences of one's existence could be transcended. Fundamentally, this perception is not wrong. And yet the limiting influences do have to be addressed and negotiated. And so the challenge of Neptune is whether or not one can balance its dreamy visionary boundlessness with a practical capacity to operate within life's limitations. Where the influence of Neptune is very strong, the frustration with limitation can be equally strong. And this can easily lead to a life of magical thinking and escapism, especially in the form of alcohol and drugs, which already have a tendency to loosen the structure and the boundaries of the self. For the

Neptune influence to really operate effectively in the world, it requires some assistance from a more focusing and disciplining influence such as that of Saturn or the Sun. Where this assistance is present, Neptune is capable of manifesting tremendous insight and creative vision. Without it, Neptune simply dissipates.

The quality of romanticism with which Neptune paints the world is important to understand. Neptune is a planet of *big feelings*. This follows as a matter of course from the dissolution of personal boundaries. When the line between one's self and the rest of existence becomes permeable, then the energy of *everything* comes rushing in. This is not unlike the feeling that one experiences when gazing up into a starry sky, or looking out across a broad landscape from the top of a mountain. The immersion into vast open space is the experience of being *merged* with the vastness of space. This feeling can be so profoundly moving that in some cases it equates to an ego inflation that borders on megalomania. In this respect, the influence of Neptune is in some ways not unlike the influence of Jupiter. In point of fact, Neptune, Jupiter and Mercury are all related to the idea of boundaries.

Mercury = defining one's boundaries
Jupiter = expanding one's boundaries
Neptune = dissolving one's boundaries

The difference between Jupiter and Neptune is that whereas Jupiter may give one a feeling of being somewhat larger than life, it still retains a grounded sense of being a distinct individual. Neptune, on the other hand, gives the sense of becoming merged into something far bigger than any one person. And this is precisely where the romantic and idealistic flavor of Neptune comes into play. Neptune transforms one into a visionary. It brings the feeling of being part of something grand and overwhelming in either a spiritual or world-historical sense.

It is not surprising that these feelings tend to surface more intensely when material circumstances are most unstable. In times of insecurity, when personal undoing or even death is seen as a real possibility, we may start to reach out for some way to make meaning out of one's suffering. And what better way to find this meaning than through a narrative of personal sacrifice? This may manifest as a martyr complex or even as a messiah complex. In any case, there is a paradoxical *inflation of self* that comes from the boundary-dissolving experience of Neptune. This is indeed the peculiarity of Neptune, that the dissolution is experienced not as annihilation but as *boundlessness*.

On the upside, this Neptunian sense of selflessness - which is at the same time a profound expansion of self - may be expressed as tremendous heroism. The person who feels that they have given up all attachment to their own small existence, and has nothing left to lose, is capable of complete fearlessness. In fact, one of the more striking aspects of Neptune is that it creates a capacity for emotional resilience. There is an ability to absorb difficulties more easily, because the loosened boundaries between the self and everything else causes the emotional impact to be distributed into the ether. The vastness of space into which one merges seamlessly acts like a heat sink for all of the excess psychic turmoil which would otherwise fracture a personality that was more rigidly self-contained. And so the upshot is that someone with much Neptune can absorb much sorrow. "Beautiful sadness" is one way of experiencing Neptune, either through poetry, music, narrative, or even through an addiction to creating drama in one's own life.

We could say that the emotion of deep sorrow is itself an experience in which one feels the dissolving of boundaries. Sorrow is most commonly experienced as a feeling of separation from what we love. And the psychological and emotional reaction to this separation is a feeling of dissolution of boundaries, which at some level represents an attempt to overcome the separation and get back to the unity with All. There is a distinctly watery aspect to the feeling of sorrow, as if everything about oneself has become fluid and loosely held together. One may even feel as if the world itself has become watery and nebulous. The best way to manage this emotion is to let go of fighting it and simply give it the space that is needed to recalibrate the psychic structure. The acceptance of sorrow, and the willingness to embrace it, can then be a window into a higher vision of our union with everything.

Needless to say, it is necessary to put limits around this and commit to moving past sorrow once it has worked its alchemy. Otherwise, there is a danger of becoming addicted to one's sorrow and glorifying it beyond all reason as a way of life. At that point, it becomes a full-blown neurosis and martyr complex. Sorrow is by no means the only way of experiencing the Neptunian vision. Nor is it the highest expression of Neptune. To be sure, for many people sorrow may be the only way in which they have ever fully tapped into the transcendent experience of the Black Sphere, and that is all well and good. But this may lead to a mistaken notion that sadness is in some sense equivalent to transcendence, when in actuality it is best seen as a bridge that points the way, rather than a formula that one relies upon to reproduce the experience.

The Neptune influence is often felt as a profound dissatisfaction with the limitations of self, of society, or of life in general. The nagging feeling that Neptune provokes - that there is something far grander and far bigger beyond the surface level of reality - can be immensely tantalizing. That intuition of some hidden mystery, or hidden treasure beyond the veil, may lead us to feel as if we are chasing after a romantic ideal that is always just out of reach. More pointedly, it leads to a feeling that the human personality is itself obscuring some tremendous inner truth that we *ought* to be expressing, and yet the personality is too dense or too confused or too stupid to allow this light to shine through. This can very easily drive one to a feeling of despair, which manifests as an impulse toward self-denial, self-undoing, or self-destruction. The martyr complex is a very natural expression of this impulse. If one's own self is not a worthy expression of the ideal, then the next best thing is to sacrifice that self to something which *is* worthy. It then becomes natural to project that desire for worthiness onto someone or something else that can become the symbolic representation of the ideal. The reality, however, is that the object of this projection is likely no more and no less flawed than oneself, and so disillusionment is commonly the outcome. It would be easy to say that Neptune leans toward an overly romanticized and unrealistic view of other people, and of the world in general. But the truth is much more complex than this. The intuitive conviction that Neptune feels - that despite our human flaws we are all sparks of divine light - is fundamentally correct. It is simply necessary to adapt this understanding and adapt one's expectations to the practical limitations of human existence. Once we have come to terms with the acceptance of these limitations, then Neptune can learn how to work its creative magic within the parameters of earth-bound life.

As a final word touching upon the topic of magic, we will point out that the influence of Neptune shows us the fluid nature of reality. The matrix of the Black Sphere contains literally every possibility as a potential within itself. Science itself has caught up to this idea in the last century, and physics no longer speaks of particulate matter as discrete billiard balls, but rather as clouds of probability. From this perspective, the line between fantasy and reality becomes hazy and ambiguous. Like Schroedinger's cat, the Black Sphere is able to contain multiple possibilities, multiple realities, and even contradictions within itself. Neptune is therefore the realm of fiction, story-telling, and myth. But the peculiar and startling thing about a myth is that despite its "unreality", it has a remarkable ability to move the masses. How is a fantasy able to do this, if it does not possess some inherent power of influence from the heart of the matrix itself? Esoteric literature has a word for a fantasy that acquires a kind of *quasi*-reality if it is believed in by enough people. The term is *egregore*, and it denotes a myth or a symbolic fiction which, by virtue of receiving the attention and psychic energy of a large enough group of people, enters into what Jung called the "collective unconscious", where it exerts an independent psychic influence upon humanity as a whole. Thus the fictional world of a myth, even though it seemingly has no point of contact with our tangible reality, can nevertheless have a profound influence on the vector of culture and society, thereby shaping our tangible reality in the final outcome. The seemingly miraculous power of suggestion, as recounted in the annals of hypnosis as well as medicine, bears witness to the fact that the boundary between reality and fantasy is not as clear as we are accustomed to believe. And so if any given possibility is a latent potential within the matrix, then magic becomes a matter of gliding into that potential, filling it with one's energy, and drawing it out into manifestation.

The Indigo Sphere

The Indigo Sphere represents the principle of *consistency*. In physics, we know this as the law of inertia. An object at rest tends to stay at rest, and an object in motion tends to stay in motion. This is really nothing more than a principle of *self-sameness*. That which is, continuing to be what it is.

In traditional astrology, Saturn was regarded as a malefic and unfortunate planet, but this simply represents a failure to see Saturn from the proper angle. Consistency is the very foundation of our existence. It is the solid ground on which we stand. Indeed, it is impossible to imagine the universe as we know it without the principle of inertia to hold things together into a stable structure. Without consistency, the universe would be nothing more than a perpetually shapeless chaos, unable to crystallize into anything enduring. From this perspective, the beneficence of the Indigo Sphere is impossible to overstate, because it literally makes our world possible. Without that rock of stability that Saturn provides, we would have nothing to hold on to. It is Saturn which establishes the eternal kingdom of God.

In Greek mythology, Kronos castrates his father Uranus, who was born of Chaos. This is clearly symbolic of the peculiar relationship between the White Sphere and the Indigo Sphere. Uranus represents the never-ceasing pure motion of the White Sphere, which is indeed a swirling chaos in which nothing stable can last for long. The chaos of Uranus is necessary to drive the creative power of existence. But in order for what we call a world to even exist, Saturn must check and contain that great whirlwind of chaos with the principle of inertia and stability. Astrologically, Saturn is said to correspond to the skeleton, and it is fair to say that the Indigo Sphere is the skeleton of the universe.

At the same time, there is undeniably a double-edged quality to Saturn, because the resistance to change that it sets before us also presents an obstacle to our desires. Saturn gives us structure and foundation and defense, but it also frustrates our attempts to shape our environment to our liking, and so it introduces the necessity for hard work and patience. It is for this reason that Saturn is often perceived as an oppressive force that limits our freedom. But what is missing here is an appreciation of how Saturn provides a stable environment in which freedom can even be possible. Without the stabilizing influence of Saturn, all of one's efforts would be pointless and void, because they would simply dissipate into nothingness. The same could be said of our social structures and law and order. While they may be seen as limiting in certain respects, they actually create an environment that is much easier to move through than the pure friction of anarchy, in which the resources provided by a structured society no longer exist, and in which all of one's "freedom" must be expended on simply surviving.

Nevertheless, the tension between Uranus and Saturn brings forward a persistent and prominent feature of human experience. It is the problem of frustration and impatience. The desire to bring about significant changes in one's experience runs headlong against the inertia and resistance of the world around us. This frustration is universal. It is the reason why Saturn has traditionally been regarded as a malignant influence in astrology. The reality is that none of the astrological influences are inherently bad, but our relationship with them may be difficult due to our lack of understanding. In today's culture especially, which values speed and freedom, the influence of Saturn is generally one to which we are not well adapted. It is therefore of utmost importance to grasp the correct attitude toward Saturn's influence. The proper mindset of the Indigo Sphere is to learn how to appreciate the process and not just the outcome. By way of illustration - if I am at point A and my destination is point B, then naturally I want to be at point B sooner rather than later. This means that I may hurry to get to point B as quickly as possible. But then what have I actually done here? I have *devalued* the entire distance between A and B. I have made point B the only thing that matters, and everything in between is merely a nuisance that I am struggling against.

This devaluation and struggle against the world at large is an inherently unhealthy way to exist. It creates a *friction* that only serves to grind you down over time. It also represents an impulse to detach from the world altogether, as if you could simply jump to point B instantaneously without traversing the continuity of space in between. This inability to be grounded and situated within the world is also unhealthy. This is why the urge to hurry which is so typical of modern life should be replaced with an intention to move at the proper pace. This is often expressed as an admonition that you should slow down in order to do anything successfully, but it would be more accurate to say that you should *match the pace of the medium through which you are moving*. Any environment that you are working through has its own consistency and continuity. And there will be a natural pace at which one can move through that consistency without generating friction. To match the pace of the medium, and to respect the road that leads to the destination, means that we are in alignment with the whole of existence rather than fighting our way through it. This is the true meaning of patience.

Another benefit of pacing ourselves is that we absorb experience more deeply. Whenever you give attention to something, you put your energy into it. This is why it is better not to hurry through something important. When you hurry through something, you do not put full consciousness into it. Not only do you not give it energy, you also do not assimilate it. We assimilate new things by paying attention, by *being aware*. This is why it is so essential to move at the proper pace. If your digestive tract were in a hurry to get food in and out, it would absorb very little of the nutriment that the food contains. When you make a conscious effort to pace yourself, then your awareness sinks in deeply rather than superficially, and it is far better to absorb one thing completely than a hundred things superficially.

This ability to absorb a thing deeply is the difference between practical understanding and intellectual understanding. Practical understanding is an aspect of the Purple Sphere, which we will explore later. Suffice it to say that the influence of the Indigo Sphere teaches us the values of patience, endurance, perseverance, steadfastness, and discipline. These are all attributes that serve to ground us in the physical world and provide practical understanding, which leads to success at worldly things. Just as the soil nourishes a plant, we get nourishment from the Indigo Sphere when we are grounded and respecting the pace and consistency of our medium. When we appreciate the consistency of the world around us, then we become attuned to it, and it will serve us well by keeping us rooted and sustained.

On a more psychological level, the Indigo Sphere gives us a stable sense of identity. The person who lacks the consistency that Saturn provides is one who tends to be purely reactive, someone with no fixed center of gravity, who is agitated and swayed by the circumstances of the moment. He is like a bobbing cork that floats downstream, buffeted this way and that by the random currents. Such an individual does not have a firm nucleus that he can call himself. Saturn is what makes the personality, and thereby the will, immovable and impervious to outside forces. It is an ability to not react emotionally to whatever happens to be going on around you. This ability to maintain a *firm stillness* is what gives one a stable center and a fulcrum of power. Saturn is the fixed point of self which is not thrown off balance by external circumstances.

Philosophically, this is embodied as the ideal of stoicism, as well as the Buddhist ideal of non-attachment. On the negative side, this can sometimes present as an emotional coldness. This is a common complaint where the Saturnian influence is badly represented in the personality, in which case it manifests as a general freezing over of the emotional affects. The challenge of Saturn is therefore to learn how to be capable of both passion and equanimity at the same time. This can be a tricky balance to wrap one's head around, but the key concept to keep in mind is that the *center* must be stable while the *perimeter* is mobile. Picture it figuratively as the fixed nucleus of an atom surrounded by the swirling chaos of the electron cloud. With this metaphor, you can begin to understand how to express the full range of emotional lability, as long as it remains tethered within the orbit of a stable center of being. This represents a capacity to be emotionally *active* rather than *reactive*. It is the power to constructively harness one's emotional energy, which is a far different thing than being emotionally rigid or shallow.

The relationship between the White Sphere and the Indigo Sphere is worthy of special attention. We have said earlier that the White Sphere is time, the Black Sphere is space, and the Indigo Sphere is eternity. The White Sphere corresponds to time because the very idea of time is meaningless without change and flux. If there were no movement, then there would simply be no way to measure time. And yet the Greek name for Saturn, *Kronos*, was generally equated with *Chronos,* which means time. How do we square this? Well, the curious thing about time is that we do not experience it as *merely* change and flux. We experience time as having a certain *continuity* and linear progression. And the only way that we can experience the movement of time in this manner is if it takes place against the backdrop of something *enduring*. That is what we call eternity. Eternity is that which stays ever the same behind the swirling flux of time, and the only place that you can ever find eternity is in the *now*. Eternity can never be found by sending the mind far back into the past or far ahead into the future. It can only be found in the *stillness* of the present moment, because eternity *is* stillness. That stillness is the *context* in which we interpret the changes that take place around us. It is the underlying stillness that provides a sense of continuity to our experience. Eternity is the backdrop on which those changes and experiences are assimilated. The occult philosophers assigned each day of the week to one of the seven planets of ancient astrology. In this system, Saturn corresponds to Saturday, which is the Hebrew Sabbath, the day of rest. Rest is a space of reflection and processing. It is that holy sanctuary of inner silence from which the bustle and impermanence of the outside world can be observed, measured, interpreted, and made *meaning* out of.

There is one last key concept to touch upon vis-a-vis the Indigo Sphere, and that is *knowledge*. In the traditional Tree of Life, the Indigo Sphere occupies the place of the hypothetical sphere known as Da'ath, which literally means "knowledge". The reason why this name is so appropriate is because only that which is

The Indigo Sphere

consistent is knowable. Whatever is unpredictable and perpetually fluctuating cannot be known with any degree of reliability. Knowledge requires predictability. The Indigo Sphere is therefore the basis of *science*, because the goal of all science is to grasp those rules of existence which are consistent, predictable, and thereby controllable.

The Blue Sphere

As we come down from the existential realm of the Indigo Sphere and above, we step into the realm of *individuation*, which is defined by the Blue, Red, and Yellow Spheres. The Blue Sphere is where the individual being stakes its territory and establishes itself as a center of influence. The Blue Sphere represents *power*, which means the ability to make things happen. Power is circumscribed by the sphere of that which we can directly manipulate, and so a keyword of the Blue Sphere is *ownership*. At the most fundamental and concrete level, this means ownership of our body and mind. These are the things that we have direct, immediate control over. On a more abstract level, ownership encompasses one's extended assets. This can be personal property, such as a house, a car, or a bank account. It could also be intangible assets, such as skills or knowledge. In the broadest sense, the Blue Sphere can be thought of as *resources* and *abundance*. The most abstract and universally understood form of abundance is of course money, but there is far more to the concept than just this. To truly understand abundance we must think beyond money. Abundance is the ability to manifest what you need, when you need it, and there are limitless ways to co-create with the universe to make this happen.

The word that most succinctly describes the Blue Sphere is *having*, and the key phrase is *I have*. Along with this having comes the feeling of *I can*. Of the Red Sphere, the key phrase is *I will*. The Blue Sphere and the Red Sphere together form a Yin-Yang, Fire-Water polarity. The Blue Sphere is the watery element insofar as it represents the *pool* of resources at your disposal, and thus the *potential* of what you can do with those resources. The Red Sphere is the fiery element insofar as it represents how you choose to actively direct that potential. So on the one hand, I can say that *I have* my body and all of its functions - my eyes, hands, feet, and so forth. And there is a vast range of things that I can potentially do with this body. That is the Blue Sphere. On the other hand, I can say that *I will* go into the back yard and use my hands to plant a garden. That is the Red Sphere, the executive force of the will that directs the application of one's potential.

The Blue Sphere is a capacity to manifest, and so in this sense, it is not just your potential but also your *potency*. This is an important distinction to keep in mind, as the Blue Sphere is not just a *static* having but rather a *dynamic* having. It is not a possessing of resources just to possess them. Rather, it is a possessing of resources with the express purpose of doing something constructive with them. The urge to put resources to creative use is baked into the energy of the Blue Sphere. And so we could say that it is inherently *expansive*. It is not a mere holding-on to something but an overflowing fullness of potential, a *pregnant* potential with an inherent desire to create and make something of itself.

In astrology, the Blue Sphere is embodied by the planet Jupiter, of which the keywords include *expansion, growth, optimism, confidence, generosity, magnanimity*. It is not difficult to tie these all together with the concept of power and potency. Let us first look at the idea of *growth*. To grow is to expand one's range of creative capacity. As a child, one grows in physical strength, but there is also the growth of one's mental capacities which can continue well into adulthood. We experience growth in our knowledge and our talents and our skills, and through the application of those skills in the form of work we grow our financial resources. Those financial resources can in turn be used to grow in even more ways, through travel and hobbies and furtherance of one's education. Through the expanding of our horizons, we acquire a wider range of human experience to draw upon for the expression of our creative capabilities. The influence of Jupiter can be summarized by the word *wealth*. But again, we have to understand this word in a dynamic sense. The wealth of Jupiter is not a limited resource that eventually gets used up and runs out. Jupiter represents the kind of wealth that keeps providing because its creative capacity is endless. And so we speak of a wealth of talent, wealth of experience, wealth of knowledge, and wealth of creativity. Jupiterian wealth is that domain of personal resources that can always be converted into something of value.

With this understanding of Jupiterian wealth, it is easy to see why confidence and optimism are naturally Jupiterian attributes. When we have the resources and the capabilities to succeed, then it is natural to believe that we *will* succeed. Jupiterian optimism comes from a natural proclivity to see the *potential* in every situation. Whereas Saturn sees the limitations and restrictions, Jupiter sees the possibilities. With Jupiter, we have a willingness to take risks because we feel that we are bigger than anything that life has to throw at us. It is the fullness of having what we need to succeed, and that fullness flows naturally outward, not just in bold and decisive action but also in an intangible energy that mysteriously moves forces in our favor. Jupiter is often associated with *luck*, but it is important to understand where luck comes from. Luck is not something that is arbitrarily handed down from above. Luck is a force that emanates from the energy of confidence and optimism. It is the Law of Attraction in motion.

This intangible yet substantial power of confidence is also spoken of as the power of *faith*. Faith is an understanding that confidence does not necessarily need to be based on any objective measure of capability. It can actually unlock and unfold latent potentials just by acting as if they were already a reality. Even science recognizes this power of faith, and calls it the placebo effect. Jupiter says "I can do anything", and believes it, because it feels instinctively that the power of God is within. This is where the influence of Jupiter intersects with the religious instinct. The creative drive of Jupiter is expansive, and with that expansion comes a sensation of being larger than oneself, as if overflowing with the creative power of the Infinite. This intoxicating sensation of creative potential instills the feeling that "with God all things are possible". It is well to remember here that each of the spheres on the Tree operates on both a macrocosmic as well as a microcosmic level. The Kabbalistic names of the Blue Sphere are Chesed and Gedulah, Mercy and Greatness. Mercy is the principle of Divine Providence, that potential to manifest anything which saturates the very fabric of reality. Greatness is the feeling of expansion that Jupiter arouses. It is experienced quite literally as an expansion of the energy body, and for those with a philosophical leaning, it will be seen as tapping into a power larger than oneself.

The Blue Sphere

The religious associations of Jupiter must in some sense be tied in with the fact that Jupiter inspires the more *ennobling* qualities of humanity. Virtues such as generosity, magnanimity, and graciousness are all Jupiterian attributes. The reason for this comes down to a very simple dynamic, but once it is fully understood it explains a great deal. Jupiter reflects noble character because one who has a fullness of potential and resources can *afford* to be noble and gracious in dealing with other people. The expansion and abundance that Jupiter provides inspires a feeling of confidence that we can give freely and still have more than enough left over. This extends to more than simply giving money or gifts, or even giving of one's time. It includes the ability to give our thoughts and feelings without fear of criticism or judgment. It is the ability to express openly. It is also a capacity to handle conflicts with grace and fairness and understanding, because we have confidence in our ability to maintain control of the situation. One who has genuine inner security and confidence will naturally act in a noble fashion. The inverse is equally true. That is to say, someone who operates from a perception of lack finds it much harder to deal in a noble manner. The least admirable of human attributes are motivated by a sense of powerlessness. Pettiness, vindictiveness, greed, the urge to lash out - all of these are driven by a fear of losing control. With the expansive energy of Jupiter, this is never a concern. The Blue Sphere is like the blue of the sky, limitless and free. And what is free and abundant has no reason to behave in a manner that is in any way *small*.

The flip side of generosity is gratitude, which is the *feeling* of being provided for. Gratitude for what you have is a naturally expansive energy. The more you feel this energy, the more it works on your behalf, magnetically attracting even more resources and more abundance. Lack of gratitude is the *feeling of lack*, which can only attract more lack. It is understood that a person who has no gratitude cannot behave nobly. Such an individual constantly feels as if he has very little, and therefore he must inevitably behave in a *small* manner. The thing that most undermines the power of Jupiter is the belief in scarcity. If you act as if your time is limited, or your energy is limited, or your skills are limited, then you inhibit your ability to take the risks that are necessary to expand. If you treat yourself as a limited resource, then you will hold back your own growth. What are the mindsets and attitudes that most sharply limit our ability to expand? Fear of failure, fear of appearing foolish, feelings of not being worthy, petty ego... all of these are attitudes that make us feel small and act small. Worst of all is the belief that life is a zero-sum game, and that one can only benefit at the expense of someone else. This conviction is a mindset of despair from which no admirable human qualities can emerge. This is why it is often said that generosity attracts more abundance. The natural current of Jupiter is to bring forth value. And like any other muscle, the more it is exercised the stronger that current becomes.

Now we have said that the Black Sphere is space, and in a certain sense the Blue Sphere is a reflection of the Black Sphere, insofar as it represents the space that you occupy, or the space that you take up in the world. Jupiter is the very act of taking up space, and so in this respect, it is associated with *grandiosity*. Grandiosity is often seen as a negative quality, and for this reason, many people are instinctively afraid to take up space. And yet, it is impossible to *not* take up space. Taking up space is a completely natural thing, and so Jupiter teaches us that it is incumbent on each individual to find the space that they rightfully occupy, and then fill it. This does not have to be in a manner that is pompous or overbearing or over-the-top, but one should have no qualms about taking up a *comfortable* amount of space. This is most readily attended to in terms of the physical space that we occupy, and the ways to enhance our physical space include an upright but relaxed posture, open body language, and expansive and expressive gestures. Some people operate on a conscious or subconscious assumption that it is more considerate to others to occupy a small space. But the reality is that most people are more comfortable around someone who knows how to comfortably take up space. In taking up our natural space, we *exude* an energy that is naturally beneficial to those around us. And so it is quite fair to say that Jupiter expresses its natural *generosity* by taking up the space that is appropriate to it. One thing that is important to keep in mind is that we do not need a *reason* to take up space. What most people fail to understand about the nature of Jupiter is that they think that some proof of *worth* is required in order to project the power of Jupiter. Nothing could be further from the truth. The essence of Jupiter projects itself. In fact, the more determined you are to prove your worth to other people, the more you are sitting in an energy of powerlessness. The mere *willingness* to take up space is itself a generator of Jupiterian power.

Jupiter is associated with travel and learning and expanding one's horizons, which is simply another way of widening the orbit that one occupies. The physical body is in fact only the narrowest sense in which we take up space. In order to fully comprehend the scope of the Blue Sphere, you must embrace the understanding that boundaries are fuzzy. If you ask a quantum physicist to describe an electron, he would say that it does not occupy a specific point in space. Rather, the electron is likened to a "cloud" of probabilities, which is the sum of all possible places that it could be at any given moment. Likewise, the Blue Sphere is far more than just the immediate physical space that we occupy. It is the space of all potential influence that we can exert, by way of not just the physical body but the energy body as well. An expansive energy body is what makes some people seem "larger than life". We can come to a better understanding of this by focusing our attention on the energy body, and observing how it exudes beyond the physical. This is a very simple exercise that should not be underestimated. The ability to sense one's own presence beyond the boundaries of the flesh is a powerful stimulator of Jupiterian current. To expand the personal energy outside of the body even by a few inches is to instantly *feel* larger than oneself, and in a certain sense to liberate the personal energy from the limitations of the physical. The impact on one's personal vitality and charisma is immediate and substantial.

In closing, the last attribute that exemplifies the Blue Sphere is *mastery*. To fully understand the essence of the Blue Sphere you must experience the *feeling* of being in control, and this begins first and foremost with self-control, self-command, and self-mastery. This expresses itself most clearly in a certain *gracefulness* of bearing and carriage. To deliver one's words and gestures in a manner that is smooth and concise, such that every expression is no more and no less than what it needs to be... this is what projects an aura of personal strength and robust character. To exhibit a certain *purity* and deliberation in one's actions telegraphs a level of self-possession that commands respect. In addition to the impression that it makes upon others, this habit of graceful bearing eliminates energy leaks and accumulates the body's magnetic power. An essential element of self-mastery is the power of *stillness*. This is the very essence of control. Pure action is just as much stillness as it is movement. It is the "no more" half of the formula "no more and no less". To simply *sit still* is a highly effective exercise in self-control. An added benefit of this practice is that the concentration required tends to still the mind. Therefore, it is an effective form of meditation. And by stilling the mind, we come closer to *pure will*, which is a concept that we will explore with the Red Sphere.

The Red Sphere

With the Blue and Red Spheres, we are entering the realm of the *Organic Triangle*. The Blue Sphere represents individuated life, or the sphere of influence governed by a single conscious being. The Red Sphere is the *will* of that individual being. It is the force that aligns the resources of the Blue Sphere into a specific purpose and direction. It is the executive, decision-making function of the organism. Insofar as it seeks to alter the existing order of things, the Red Sphere can be thought of as a reflection of the White Sphere. But whereas the White Sphere is pure energy in an abstract sense, the will is a focused application of energy toward a specific goal. The White Sphere is diffuse whereas the Red Sphere is directional.

Given that the will is of such primary importance to the existence of every individual, a deep study of the Red Sphere will necessarily focus on the cultivation of *strength* of will. This begins by recognizing the difference between *true will* and false will, or inauthentic will. False will is a feature of the false personality, which is the mask of inauthenticity that we wear. False will is what we *think* that we are supposed to want based on outside influences, which hypnotize us into believing that this thing or that thing is what we need to be successful, or happy, or worthy. True will is what we *know* within our inner being to be our genuine destiny in life.

Authenticity is the key power of the Red Sphere. To be authentic is to be real, and to be whole. False personality and false will create a force of drag that dissipates away the vital energy. It is like trying to drive a car with the parking brake on. Authenticity is the self-awareness with which to see through the false narratives that your own mind has placed upon you. And we should have no doubt that the mind is extraordinarily adept at spinning webs of illusion which conceal our own authentic nature from ourselves. This is why we need to understand that in the hierarchy of forces that make up the individual, the will stands *above* the mind. The mind will naturally try to persuade us otherwise, because it is very cunning in that way. It will argue that reason must dictate that this-or-that course of action is the "correct" or "reasonable" decision. But this is in fact an inversion of the chain of responsibility. Reason is a *technology* in the service of the will, not the other way around. Reasoning is a *means*, of which the will is the *end*. To embrace your authentic will, you must therefore cast aside the pedantic tyranny of a reasoning that demands a *"why?"* for everything. There can be no accounting or explanation for one's *true will*. True will has no justification or reason why. If you have to offer a rationalization for it, then it is not will. It is simply derivative, a means to something else. Now of course, this is not to say that we should *never* have to account for our actions. Most of what we do in the day-to-day has to make some sense in the overall context of things. But when it comes to decisions about your individual *purpose* in life, your true will cannot be expected to answer to a *why*. Because any answer to *why* can be countered with another *why*, and so every chain of reasoning eventually comes back to a *"just because"*.

This point, while it may seem a bit odd, is quite essential to truly understanding the essence of will. Will is a spontaneous *motivating drive* whereas mind is an adaptive mechanism. That which is done for "reasons" is very different from that which is done with motivation and excitement. The one has an energetic abundance that the other does not. And to live within that energetic abundance, it is essential to be tapped into an authentic will which stands upon its own initiative and its own sovereignty.

Now here is a point that will be even more challenging for some people to understand - true will *is not attached* to the outcome. That is to say, it does not calculate the odds before deciding to act. True will simply acts based on the conviction that the goal is worth pursuing. The worst thing that one can do is to deny your own will because you don't think that it is attainable. The will does not have to be realized in order to be valid *as will*. If you set out to do a thing, but do not succeed at it, never think to yourself that you would have been better off if you had not made the attempt at all. This is how you undermine the will and cripple its vitality. This way of thinking atrophies the will and completely devalues its worth. We should never measure the validity of our will by success or failure. True will does not take heed of the probabilities.

Most of us are familiar with the story of the fox and the grapes. A fox sees a very succulent-looking cluster of grapes hanging from a vine, but after several attempts is unable to reach them. Rather than admit defeat, he says to himself "Ah, who cares... those grapes are not worth it. They are probably sour anyhow." This story succinctly illustrates the principle of *cognitive dissonance*. But we might ask... is the fox actually wrong to tell himself this false narrative? Is he not better off convincing himself that he doesn't want what he can't have? The answer is *no*... because he has then *denied his own will*, which is a form of self-disempowerment. He has allowed the machinations of his mind to shut down the *vital energy* that a clear, authentic will instills within us.

This is a point which will be difficult to grasp for many, but it is key to everything just the same. A will that is not attained or even attainable is no less potent than a will that is actualized. The motivating energy is still there. It can still be tapped into and channeled in constructive directions. You must simply acknowledge it and allow it to be what it is, rather than shut it down through the false narrative of denial. To allow the contradiction of desiring something that you don't have is to allow the will to speak its truth and hold its power. Most people have not yet learned the skill of embracing contradiction. The mind does not like contradictions, and so it will try to resolve the contradiction through cognitive dissonance and denial. Either that, or one will sink into self-pity, which is worse than useless. True will does not experience self-pity, and it should never be confused with any form of longing or yearning which *suffers* on account of not obtaining what is desired. Pure will never suffers in this manner, because it is an active and not a passive energy. If it is frustrated in reaching its goal, then it will either seek an alternate route or else attempt to smash its way through. And if it can do neither of these things, then it will forthrightly embrace the contradiction. But pure will never stops to languish in self-pity, and it will not deny its own truth. The difference between *willing* and *wanting* is that wanting is a feeling that you lack something, and therefore you are incomplete in some way. Authentic will never feels incomplete. It is already endowed with a sense of completeness and wholeness. Will is positive and active, whereas wanting is negative and passive. Will is a going-forth, while want is a sucking-in. We should always be striving to will rather than to want. It is incumbent then, to cultivate an attitude that you are complete and whole as you are. You do not need anything outside of yourself to make you whole. Wholeness comes from the limitless power of *pure being*. When you possess this wholeness, then you are able to embrace contradiction.

In the field of electronics, it is understood that oppositely charged particles have a natural attraction toward one another. A battery is a device in which the positive and negative charges are held apart from each other in a state of suspension. The unresolved pressure of the attraction between these charges is what constitutes the *voltage* or driving force of the battery. It is this voltage that powers the flow of electricity when the battery is placed into a circuit. A will that is not realized but still acknowledged just the same becomes a *voltage* which has considerable power that can be channeled to constructive ends. But will that is denied and repressed becomes a poison that will eventually work itself out in some form of neurosis or dysfunction.

In traditional astrology, Mars was regarded as a "malefic" planet and was typically associated with conflict and aggression. This is not, however, an accurate reflection of the genuine energy of the Red Sphere, which would be better described as a strong and healthy *assertiveness*. In fact, in its clearest expression, The Red Sphere carries the same sense of levity and humor as the White Sphere. There is a radiance to it much like the radiance of fire, and in this respect, it is not unlike the radiance of the Green Sphere. The White, Red, and Green Spheres are all of a similar Yang energy, and so fundamentally they all express a bright and optimistic quality. Mars is best described as the energy of *taking action*, and doing so without fear. It has a lightness and a bounce to its step that does not shy away from taking risks. The more difficult qualities that have been associated with Mars - such as anger, hardness, and belligerence - are all products of the *friction* that the will encounters in its environment. This friction is experienced outwardly as hindering or limiting factors, but is translated inwardly as a frustration that lashes out in the form of aggression. These are manifestations of a will that is not operating at its highest potential. When the will flows with natural ease, it has an aspect that is direct and assertive but also cheerful and bright. To put it most succinctly, the genuine essence of the Red Sphere is not in fighting but in *speaking one's truth*. To speak one's truth means not just in words, but also in actions. And not just in actions, but in thoughts as well. That is to say... being truthful with oneself. An overly-aggressive person is someone who has not actually learned how to be *comfortable* speaking his own truth. And so a key characteristic that we can attribute to the Red Sphere is that it *shines like truth*.

Now to be sure, speaking one's truth will sometimes entail fighting for one's truth, especially when that truth is unwelcome. The energy of the Red Sphere is not by its nature prone to seek a fight, but it does indicate a *willingness* to stand up for oneself and a willingness to hold one's ground. This, however, does not have to be prosecuted in a way that is mean-spirited or abrasive. Someone who is not clearly tapped into their Mars energy might think that they have to adopt a hard posture in order to cultivate the skill of assertiveness. This is a false understanding that comes from mixing the Mars energy with the energy of friction, which invariably makes it feel coarse and dull and heavy. The refined essence of Mars is actually *light* and *swift,* with the sparkling brilliance of a flame. And so standing up for oneself in a natural and healthy manner will be expressed with dignity, grace, and charisma. It is fair to say, however, that human beings have generally had a difficult time coming to terms with their authenticity, and integrating it into their personality. It is not customary to speak one's truth. Society militates against it. And so it is not surprising that the Mars influence has so typically been bottled up and manifested in maladaptive ways. The purification of the Mars energy is therefore one of the most important goals that we can undertake.

This requires us to separate the wheat from the chaff, so to speak. We must get a clear insight into what the Red Sphere *is* versus what it is not. First and foremost, the Red Sphere is an *affirmative* energy. It is the energy of *yes*. Antagonism, on the other hand, is the energy of *no*. It is an energy of shutting-down, and of shutting other people down. To be argumentative or critical or judgmental is to implicitly attempt to shut down the creative expression - and to a certain extent the life-energy - of somebody else. Its underlying motivation is to *suppress*. But the curious thing about this energy of *no* is that you cannot engage in the shutting-down of someone else without shutting down yourself at the same time. This becomes quite obvious when you start to actually *observe* and pay attention. When you engage in negative thoughts or words against somebody else, it will feel as if a dense and heavy energy is embracing you. And this density will feel constrictive, as if it is sapping and giving resistance to the natural flow of your life-force. This is the energy of shutting-down. Whenever you attempt to project it upon someone else, it invariably reflects back upon yourself. The energy of *no* exerts a shutting-down on all who engage in it. On the other hand, when you direct positive thoughts or words at someone else, the effect upon you is a lighter and freer sensation. That is the energy of *yes*, an energy which invigorates and encourages the taking of action.

Now to be clear, this mustn't be taken to imply that one should never express disagreement or set boundaries. You can always say "no" to arguments or demands or behaviors that you disagree with, as long as it is done respectfully and without ill will. That is not at all the same thing as what we are calling the *energy of no*. The energy of *no* is when you attempt to deny or tear down someone else's basic humanity or self-worth. It is essentially *devaluation* in any form. To say that someone or something is wrong, stupid, bad, or worthless - this is to stamp a gigantic *no* upon it, as if it had no business to exist. This is really the core motivation of negative judgment. It expresses a frustration at the fact that something that one does not like is allowed to exist, and so the denunciation of it is an attempt to negate it by declaring that it *has no right* to exist. This is of course completely ineffective. In fact, it is comically ineffective. The offending reality continues to exist, and so that energy of negation has no place to go except to bounce right back upon the one who sent it. Whether you feel that your judgment is "justified" or not is irrelevant. The energy of shutting-down will reflect back upon you regardless, as it behaves very much like a law of physics. You are much better off to have a *sense of humor* about what you can't change, than to stew in the devitalizing vapors of impotent criticism.

It goes without saying that many will reject this point of view, and will cling to an emotional investment in the energy of shutting-down, believing that there is some moral high ground to be had in denouncing very loudly whatever they believe to be wrong or stupid. Whether this is actually a moral virtue is debatable, and whether it leads to better outcomes is equally up for question. One thing that must be apparent to anyone, however, is that the *habit* of being judgmental and fault-finding will naturally make one extraordinarily sensitive to the threat of criticism from others. A person with such a tendency can't help but develop over time a morbid fear of making mistakes, or of doing anything that could be perceived as "incorrect" in any way. This habitual energy of casting *no* upon everything will therefore invariably place a heavy weight upon the feeling of personal initiative, and the willingness to take risks. On the other hand, someone who does not take the position that everything must be subjected to evaluation and judgment will have far less concern about appearing "wrong" or "foolish", as he will simply take it for granted that everyone is wrong and foolish at some point in life, and that this is just as it should be. This attitude of not taking life so damn seriously is precisely the energy of *yes* that encourages boldness, action, and a willingness to push the envelope. In that respect, it is quite fair to say that *vanity* is an affliction of the weak-willed. The person who has to appear better than others, or at least *right* at all costs, puts himself into a very narrow box. It is the individual who is not afraid to look stupid, or to fail epically, that is capable of achieving anything.

There is one last point to make about the power of will, and it is perhaps the most important of all. To have will, you must *take ownership* of your decisions and their consequences. Without this, you have nothing. There are those who will always find someone else to blame for every disappointment and failure in their life. To do this is to simply create a narrative that one *has no agency*. And as long as you stick to this narrative, you will have no capacity to steer your own destiny. Even if there is justifiable blame to be laid somewhere else, there is no value in clinging to it. The road ahead depends upon the choices that one makes in the now. This is why people who suffer from an insecure vanity are so lacking in real willpower. They are unwilling to take ownership of their disappointments, and so they must constantly deflect responsibility onto someone else. The strong-willed individual knows that it is better to own a mistake or a failure than to own victimhood, because the latter implies a lack of personal agency. To take responsibility is the deepest essence of the will, and it applies not just to one's actions, but also to one's beliefs, values, and ethics. In the final analysis, the energy of Mars is about owning who you are, and how you exist in the world. It is above all the understanding that no matter what life throws upon you or what it takes away from you, the one thing that cannot be taken away is your truth. To stand up for that truth and defend it with your honor is the true code of the Red Sphere.

The Yellow Sphere

The Yellow Sphere stands for *integrity*, which means wholeness. When your actions are consistent with your beliefs, this is wholeness. When your beliefs are consistent with each other, this is also wholeness. When your goals are consistent with the overall well-being of the world in which you live, then this is the next level of wholeness. Integrity is the force that binds the parts together into a whole. It is harmony, coordination, and peace. This is coherence, as well as cohesion.

When you feel as if your conscience is troubled, or if you are experiencing remorse or regret, then this is an indication that there is division from within. The parts disagree and war against one another. The individual with a bad conscience is not whole. It is truly an unhappy state to be divided from within, because your strength is then severed in two. Half goes one way, and half goes the other way. Together, they cancel each other out and amount to zero. To possess integrity is to be like a disciplined and united army, the force of which is irresistible. He who has integrity within himself is a power to be reckoned with. But he who stands in integrity with the world around him is unstoppable, because he has the force of the whole world behind him.

Integrity in the social realm is law and order. We are speaking, of course, about natural and just law, not arbitrary or tyrannical law. It is the law of basic respect for one's fellow citizen. Integrity is that synergy in which the cooperation of the parts allows them to both be more and accomplish more than they could on their own. It is organization, and also the definition of what is *organic*.

The Yellow Sphere defines what we would commonly think of as the "moral order", for lack of a better term. But we have to clarify exactly what this means, lest we confuse the matter with ideas that are not at all in tune with what we are aiming at. By "moral order" we do not mean to imply a kind of abstract set of rules, a litany of "shalls" and "shall nots", for which one is either rewarded or punished. This is a much too rigid and static concept of morality which lacks the organic and fluid qualities that the Yellow Sphere denotes. It is not to say that a well-established rule system does not have its place in human relations. Rules of conduct represent an attempt by human beings to codify in some sense the moral order that they perceive instinctively at a basic level. But the lens of human intellect and understanding is imperfect, and so the rule systems devised by society will always have some degree of imperfection. Some rules will be frankly unjust. Some will be well-meaning but short-sighted. Others will be ambiguous and questionable depending on the context. It is not enough then to say that the essence of morality consists of simply following a set of rules. We must distinguish between the *letter* of the law and the *spirit* of the law, and the Yellow Sphere is most definitely on the side of the spirit of the law. Thus, the moral order embodied by the Yellow Sphere cannot be expressed as a rule set but rather as this general principle: if your action is in harmony with the good of the whole, then the whole will move in your favor. If your action is against the good of the whole, then the whole will move against you. This is the universal law of equilibrium. It is nothing more than the *integrity of the whole*, keeping all things in balance.

It is vitally important to understand that there is no element of judgment or *punishment* in this idea of cosmic justice. The urge to punish, humiliate, or shame is an entirely human impulse. It is an impulse stemming from a sense of insecurity and fear, which overcompensates for its feeling of powerlessness by lashing out with an unbalanced vindictiveness. The higher power that we call God is far beyond this level of insecurity, and therefore has no reason to respond to human shortcomings with anything resembling wrath or revenge. The law of equilibrium simply aims at the *correction* of imbalances. The application of equilibrium in one's personal life therefore demands that we disavow any attitude of *self-righteousness,* which will invariably exceed its boundaries and perpetuate a cycle of imbalance. The notion that one is entitled or even obligated to inflict vindictive punishment or humiliation on another is not only bound to result in atrocities, it is also poisonous to whomever is possessed by such a mindset.

The Yellow Sphere

It is simply *unhealthy* on all levels - moral, mental, emotional, and physical. Whether you think that someone else *"deserves"* to be punished is irrelevant. The damage done to one's own inner harmony is suffered just the same. For this reason, the urge to pile *shame* on another, or even upon oneself, should be recognized as counter-productive. There is nothing in this to imply that one cannot be firm and decisive in the application of balance. Balance will sometimes mean establishing boundaries in a very strong way. And it will often mean taking ownership of one's own mistakes. But balance must never be executed with malice or animosity. Otherwise, it would not be in balance. Any morbid attachment to self-loathing or devaluation of others must be seen as simply unhealthy and neurotic. The energy of the Yellow Sphere is above all harmonious, brilliant, joyous and beautiful. It is an energy of *hygiene* at all levels of one's being. Anything that is morbid or unclean is disinfected in the clear light of the Yellow Sphere.

This brings us then to the very important question of *anger*. Is anger ever justified, and is it possible to express anger in a way that is healthy and wholesome? The best answer to this question is to say that the basis of what we experience as anger is an intense and instinctive focus of energy, directed at the elimination of an imbalance. It is experienced as a rush of adrenaline that provides an additional boost of willpower in moments of decision. This is a valuable and necessary energy, but it must be distilled into its pure form in order to function in the right way. This means that the negative elements of self-righteousness, insecurity, and vindictiveness must be taken out of it. Furthermore, the will must be direct, clear, and one-pointed in intent. That is to say, it must aim for the correction of imbalance with swift, decisive efficiency and nothing more.

What we are talking about here is really the application of the Red Sphere at the behest of the Yellow Sphere. And the Red Sphere, fundamentally, is not anger. It is *pure will*. When it becomes bogged down in mental churning and rumination, then it deteriorates into a festering and destructive anger. But when it does not go into the weeds of overthinking itself, then pure will moves naturally and swiftly to the correct and just resolution of a problem. Most people do not know how to express this kind of pure will in a healthy way, because they cannot express it honestly. Instead, it is filtered through layers of fear, dissembling, self-doubt, and so forth. When people lack confidence in their own instinct for asserting balance and boundaries, then they begin to rationalize their feelings and frame the situation in terms of "I am right, and they are wrong". This has a way of simply derailing the energy of the will and sidetracking it into intellectual arguments and counter-arguments. This is where the energy gets stuck and deteriorates into anger. It is no longer a pure and focused intent to set things in order, but has instead become a frustrated indignation that is not altogether sure of itself, and must therefore exceed all reasonable measures to prove that it is right. The urge to beat a dead horse is a hallmark of morbid and unhealthy frustration. This is where the understanding of *balance* becomes so essential. To recognize just the right amount of force needed to restore balance, and to *not exceed it,* is the correct application of the will to justice.

Now to be clear, the idea of integrity has a much broader range of meaning than just the moral concept. It is a universal principle of binding-together that operates on many different levels. Integrity of the body is what we call health. Integrity of the mind is reason. Integrity of emotion is poise, calm, and equanimity. Integrity of action is uprightness. And integrity of form is beauty. All of these things represent the idea of balance and wholeness, and they must all be understood as facets of the same principle. That is to say, if you try to think of the Yellow Sphere as simply dumping these separate qualities into one bucket, you will miss the point. They are all different manifestations of the same core concept. Taken together, they give a much clearer picture of what integrity looks like, as opposed to more reductionist notions of "right" or "wrong". Integrity is an energy of coherence in which both individually and collectively, we have the capacity to grow and thrive.

As with all of these spheres, it is necessary to understand what the Yellow Sphere *feels like*, as opposed to simply understanding it on an intellectual level. The energy of the Yellow Sphere is golden

The Yellow Sphere

and warm, soothing and beautiful. Being a *centripetal* force, it instills a certain tone and tautness to the nerves and muscles, which renders one dynamically ready and alert, but also calm and relaxed at the same time. It is the *magical equilibrium* of all of one's internal forces. It is also the balance between Fire and Water, Yin and Yang. What this means in practice is striking a balance between being active and being passive, knowing when to push forward and when to yield. This is the key to success in all things. It is also the formula of *peace*. This word "peace" is a difficult one for some to embrace, because they believe that it is an entirely passive energy. This is incorrect. Peace is the equilibrium of active and passive. It has all the dynamic vitality of active forward energy, but tempered in just the right amount to produce a harmonious and beautiful result.

The Yellow Sphere is principally a *binding force* of unification, and the power of self-balance comes from being securely bound together within. It is the state in which all of our components are well put together into a coherent unity. This is not a restrictive binding in any sense of the word, but rather the wholesome feeling of being held together quite soundly - to be of *sound* mind and body. The Yellow Sphere is the glue that holds the universe together. It is not a rigid glue however, but rather a malleable glue which gives the constituent parts the freedom to move in their own way, yet still keeps them together as an organic whole. It is the power of *focus*. More specifically, focus of *self*. It is efficiency and precision. It is every part doing exactly what it needs to do - no more and no less. The power of the Yellow Sphere is the bringing to bear of all of one's forces into a single, focused direction. This is the essence of *virtue*. What we call "vice" is simply an element of the psyche that has cut loose from the overarching design and has run amok with its own agenda. It has rebelled against the master plan, and expends its energy in a direction that does not serve that plan. Vice is a state of being pulled apart from within. The Yellow Sphere is the binding force that aligns all elements with the true will. The Yellow Sphere operates as a *medicine* on all levels, because it is the knitting-together of all the parts into wholeness and perfection.

Most people tend to think that being virtuous is something difficult, and that it is some kind of uphill struggle. To be virtuous is actually not that hard. One simply has to *let go* of the false beliefs that pull you in directions against your true nature. It is a matter of jettisoning the dead weight. The temptation to succumb to vice is usually driven by the absence of a clear sense of purpose. Where purpose is lacking, there is a void that needs to be filled with whatever stimulus or distraction is available. This emptiness often comes with a desperate imperative to prop up and maintain a *false* sense of self. This projected image of a self will typically be curated to appear as powerful or as capable or as talented as possible. But without an underlying sense of purpose, the false self tends to become something of a parasitic empty shell, feeding on everything and everyone around it. The definition of *virtue* - which ultimately derives from the Latin word for courage or potency - is possessing a core narrative and a clear sense of direction. When this sense of inner unity is clear, then the forces of the personality have no natural inclination to scatter themselves in unproductive directions. Being virtuous means finding your truth and finding the purpose that holds you together. If that purpose is not yet clear to you, then the next best thing that you can do is to dedicate yourself to the principles of balance, equilibrium, and harmony. In this case, the goal of simply *becoming whole* is itself the life purpose.

This is by no means a small goal to pursue. It is in fact far more valuable and productive than most of the life goals that people set for themselves. And the interesting thing about this goal is that it is abstract enough that one does not have to set difficult or onerous milestones. It is a purpose that one can attend to in the smallest details of everyday life. If we strive to act in every moment with a mindfulness toward balance and harmony, then every interaction is a step toward wholeness. With this mindset, the pursuit of virtue is no longer seen as something painful or difficult. One could certainly choose to look at the whole thing as a struggle and a moral battle to contain unruly energies, but this would be going about things the hard way. The easy way is to simply *not feed* the false self, and to not buy into the illusions that attempt to define who we are. It is largely a matter of *letting go* of what is not real. The Yellow Sphere is fundamentally an energy of *ease*, in which things flow naturally because they are not misaligned with their true nature.

Astrologically, the Yellow Sphere is the Sun, and one of the principal attributes of the Sun is *unconditional love*. The job of the Sun is to radiate vital energy. And it does this in all directions, indiscriminately. The sun shines alike on the rich and the poor, the wicked and the just, the strong and the weak. And for a Sun, it feels *great* to radiate that energy. Because when you allow that life-energy to flow through you, some of it always remains with you residually, bathing the cells with its vitality and power. It does us much good to emulate the Sun, emitting an unconditional radiance in all directions. It is not an energy that exhausts itself. Rather, it replenishes itself the more that you allow it to flow.

This attribute of *radiating* energy is especially important to grasp, because we need to understand that vice and degeneracy originate from an underlying feeling of *lack*. They represent a kind of desperate but morbid attempt to stimulate the vital energies when a sense of emptiness has taken over. And so an essential feeling of *fullness* must be in place to be able to act with equilibrium. To this end, it is helpful to reflect on the fact that there is a power that sustains your existence at every moment. The very fact that you are *here right now* is a testament to the truth that there is a reason for your existence at this time and place. There is a universal power which decrees that you be exactly who you are, where you are, from this point until your purpose in this life has been fulfilled. If you can tune in to this power that sustains your existence from one moment to the next, then you will feel that this power emanates from the heart of all existence, and therefore its capacity to emanate *through* you is limitless and inexhaustible.

This feeling of inexhaustible energy renders a quality of *uprightness* to the Yellow Sphere. It embodies a plenitude of creative power that translates into a standing-tall and a standing-firm, but with a healthy degree of flexibility and adaptability. To truly understand this idea of uprightness, you must think of it not as an ethical imperative, but as a personal health imperative.

Uprightness is not a matter of dutifully adhering to a set of rules because one "has to". It is more like a balloon that is filled with warm air, and therefore it naturally stands up straight and rises. As Nietzsche rightly observed, it is a mistake to think that virtue leads to happiness. Rather, the reverse is true. The joy that comes from a sense of wholeness leads naturally to upright and wholesome behavior.

So where does one acquire this feeling of personal fullness? It all comes back to having that sense of *purpose*, from the conviction that one's life is held together by an overarching narrative. The power of the Sun is knowing what you stand for, and what your goals are. If you find yourself asking "What is my purpose in life, and how do I live my purpose?", then it is the energy of the Sun that you must tap into, as this is what integrates your life as a whole and brings the synchronicities that you need. The Sun is what gives you the feeling that your life *makes sense*. It brings focus into your existence. Where there is focus, and commitment to a purpose, then that is where the individual shines and stands out. When you are certain of what you stand for and what your purpose is, then there is an inherent knowing of what the right course of action is in any circumstance, and this knowing manifests as charisma. One who does not know what he stands for is like a person who is constantly grasping at straws, acting with uncertainty and usually awkwardly. Such a person tends to guess at what the appropriate response would be in any context, very often guessing *against* what the natural instinct would declare to be the right course. The person who knows what he stands for does not have to guess. The internal coherence of a strong sense of purpose instantly calculates the right action.

This underlying sense of purpose is what makes the Sun a symbol of self-unfoldment. It has a natural tendency to radiate outward into the world, and to make an impression upon the world. And it makes this impression through the process of creating a story in which it is the center and the protagonist. The Sun is associated with radiance, prominence, being seen, and being well-known. This is a natural consequence of having a strong and coherent personal narrative, a coherent sense of purpose. This results in a personality that naturally projects influence. Certainly, one does not gain renown without having a clear and guiding narrative that brings one's life together into something remarkable. The Sun is all about embracing your destiny. In a certain sense, we could say that the Yellow Sphere reflects the clarity of the Diamond Sphere. When you have that pure clarity about your personal destiny, then everything just comes together. It is the clarity of the Diamond Sphere that gives it such power and intensity. That clarity eliminates everything that is not a part of one's core truth. And so when we have such clarity, there is no longer any doubt about either one's will or one's purpose.

Symbolically, the Sun is associated with Christ and the Logos. This Greek word *Logos*, which is used in the New Testament to designate Christ, is typically translated into English as "word". The actual meaning of the term is however far more complex. *Logos* in Greek philosophy was used to signify reason and order, especially in the sense of a cosmic reason that organized the universe and gave it structure. To speak more esoterically, the Logos may be thought of as a natural harmony that binds all things together into a unified whole. Science speaks of a principle that it calls *entropy*, which means a natural tendency of all matter and energy to wind down into disorder and disorganization. Logos is the opposite of entropy. It is the universal tendency to bring matter into organization. If entropy is the force that makes things fall apart, Logos is the force that holds things together. In that respect, the Logos represents salvation and redemption, as it is the force that can clarify the personality and unify it into a coherent whole. The Logos is the essence of wholeness, which is the same thing as *holiness*. Indeed, the very etymology of the word *holy* is from the Old English word for *whole*, from which is also derived the word *hale* meaning robust, vigorous, and healthy. To be holy is to be *healthy* at all levels of one's being.

In summary, then, the Yellow Sphere is the energy that holds your life together and makes sense out of it. Again, this is not something that we can simply intellectualize. It is not so much a matter of *thinking* order into your life, but rather of *feeling* what it means to be whole, and then allowing that wholeness to sort things out naturally. A good way to get a sense of what this means is to engage in some form of creative activity such as art, music, writing, and so forth. When putting something together of creative output, one has to develop a feel for how the parts fit together into an organic unity. This is not a unity that you can codify with a set of rules. It is simply an energy of holding together gracefully. This natural grace that shapes any creative activity is the same Logos that gives structure to your life and makes it meaningful. As you learn to feel into this organic harmony, you develop a sense for what does and doesn't fit into your life, and you then begin to sense the *insubstantiality* of all the petty concerns that merely distract from your true purpose. Feeling into the Yellow Sphere gives us a keen sense for what is part of the plan and what is not. When you are in this place of wholeness, you will possess a natural sense for what the next move should be. Most importantly, you will know what is appropriate *for you*, with no inclination to impose it as a standard for anyone else. The Yellow Sphere is not a set of rules that can be applied universally. It is a balancing energy that applies uniquely to each individual.

If you would therefore resolve to stand in balance, and to examine each thought and impulse that comes into your awareness, asking yourself "How does this fit into the whole?", you will see that a great many of your thoughts and concerns simply drop away. A natural tendency when moving toward wholeness is to jettison the dead weight and discard those things that are no longer useful to your true purpose. The end result of this mental and spiritual hygiene is a most refreshing *lightness* of being - the lightness of freeing yourself from that which is inessential.

The Green Sphere

Below the Yellow Sphere, we enter the realm of material reality. The Orange and the Green Spheres represent *form* and *essence* respectively. By form, we mean that which is measurable and delineable. By essence, we mean that which is qualitative and therefore non-quantifiable. By way of illustration, let us picture a red square that is two inches across. The form is its geometric shape, which can be measured on each side and which occupies a certain portion of space. The color is its essence, which *qualifies* the form but is not a quantitative or measurable attribute in itself. We could imagine a blue square in its place, and it would have the very same form but with a different essence.

At the simplest level then, we can think of these principles as matter and the perceptible qualities of matter. Thus, every type of inherent sensory quality is an essence - color, odor, flavor, etc. Essence is the inherent energy of the form. Emotion is also essence, as is passion. It is essence in exactly the same sense as color and odor are essence. Redness is the passion of the rose, and sweetness is the passion of the honey. Esoterically speaking, there is no conceptual distinction between them.

What we are pointing toward here is the idea that there exists a kind of *inner fire* within all material form which gives it its diversity of sensory splendor. Without this inner fire, all of material existence would be of a dull, monochrome uniformity. It is this scintillating fire of essence, vibrating and radiating from within the heart of matter, that gives to material things their unique energetic signatures which we experience by means of physical as well as non-physical senses. Furthermore, this principle of the *energetic signature* is the same category of experience, whether it be sensory or emotional. The experience of redness, or of the taste of cinnamon, is analogous to the experience of joy or excitement. They are all experiences of a *non-quantifiable* and *formless* energy or essence. What we experience internally as various forms of emotion is, for all intents and purposes, equivalent to what matter experiences as the inner fire which it radiates as its sensory signature.

Modern science does not register this idea of *essence* as part of its paradigm. It sees matter as possessing both form and force, but nothing in the way of an animating inner fire. To the extent that we actually experience sensory qualities in the things around us, the scientific paradigm renders the opinion that these qualities exist entirely within our central nervous system as mere *subjective interpretations* of the material world. That these sensory qualities could actually exist *within* the material things themselves is not recognized. Orthodox science therefore reduces "objective" material reality to a kind of monochrome dullness. The idea of essence is noticeably lacking in our physics.

This is of course precisely what leads many to feel as if there is something *missing* in this orthodox scientific paradigm. There is no admission of a tangible reality to the vibrancy and emotional brilliance of what we experience as our world. There is only a conceptual framework of cold, dead particles knocking about and registering as impulses in our brain cells. This has not always been the picture of reality that human beings have subscribed to. Theories of the universe prior to the modern period postulated the existence of innate and hidden "virtues" within herbs, stones, and animal substances. These "energetic signatures" of various material substances were believed to have the capacity to impress their unique powers upon human beings who made use of them. It would be fair to say then that this concept of the Green Sphere belongs to that realm of theory which is now called "magic". Many would of course argue that what we mean by this term "magic" is in actuality simply a *higher* science, above and beyond the limited paradigm which now commonly goes by the designation of science. In the mindset of this contemporary science, the notion of a kind of *life-energy* that permeates and animates matter is incomprehensible and thus utterly fantastic. Such a concept must therefore seem to be *pure magic* with respect to the monochrome and mundane "realism" of the orthodox scientific worldview.

The Green Sphere

The Green Sphere corresponds astrologically to the planet Venus, which is associated with such things as love, passion, art, beauty, and luxury. All of these ideas can be tied back to the concept of essence or inner fire. If we reflect simply on the idea of *joy* or *passion*, these can be described as a fire that stirs inside of us, and which radiates light and warmth to those around us. The joyous passion of the Green Sphere can be imagined as a kind of *green fire* that envelops the body like a brilliant aura. It is a *clean fire* that does not burn, a fire that is rarefied and volatile, stimulating us with life and a quickening vigor. When this fire radiates from within us, it makes us feel lighter, swifter, and pleasantly warm. It is a characteristic of this energy that it generates *mobility*. It stimulates the free movement and circulation of the physical, mental, and emotional fluids. As Mercury is a reflection of the Black Sphere, Venus is a reflection of the White Sphere. But whereas the White Sphere and Black Sphere are at a very abstract level of being, the Green Sphere and Orange Sphere are tied much more closely to the material world and material things.

Essence is what gives one *charisma,* or the power of fascination. A sparkling jewel has the power to fascinate and hypnotize. Passion has the same power of fascination. Just as fire spreads and generates more fire, so does passion spread and generate more passion. Pure essence is *innocence*. It is essence without any layers of interpretation to distort it, childlike in its truth and simplicity. At its most fundamental form, the Green Sphere is purified and rarefied emotion. We are speaking here not of the heavier forms of emotion, but the kind of emotion that vivifies and stirs one to life. Purified emotion always possesses a brilliance to it, a shining quality that sparkles and scintillates. It never *overcomes* us, but rather *empowers* us.

The passion of the Green Sphere is the creative force that births all forms of art. It is an essence that seeks to express itself and to materialize itself in some way, and through the agency of the Orange Sphere that essence is embodied in a form that speaks, that has life, and that utters the message of the essence. In itself, the material substance of Mercury is passive. The vivifying power of essence is required to mobilize it, like wax that becomes liquid and malleable from the application of heat. Venus is the *animating* force to Mercury. It is a phallic, fertilizing, fructifying energy. From passion comes a movement, swift and nimble, that shapes the substance of Mercury into a form that reflects the essence. This is the alchemy of artistic creation. The essence then *radiates* through the body of the form. The very nature of essence is radiance, and radiance is joy. The infinite living spirit takes pure joy in the breathing forth of luminosity and color and radiance. It is the creative word that says "Let there be light". For this reason, we say that Venus rules art as well as luxury, pleasure, and every manner of *aesthetic* experience which delights in the richness of the senses. It is well to note that whatsoever we find aesthetically pleasing is perceived as having a certain kind of *glow* to it, a radiance or an aura if you will. And that radiance excites precisely the same glow within oneself. And so the aesthetic experience can be described as a spreading fire that quickens and illuminates us with its flame.

Venus is most closely associated with *love*, because love is of course the quintessential state of being aroused into a passionate radiance. To be in love is to feel as if one is quite literally glowing with an ardent flame. Venus is mostly typically associated with romantic and sexual love, but really it applies to all forms of love that inspire us with this feeling of radiance. It could be love for family, friends, pets, community, homeland, a movement - anything that evokes the feeling of *uplifting* and joyous exuberance that we identify as love. Love is the feeling that motivates us to pursue any creative activity through to the end. To create or perform a musical piece, for instance, we must feel the love that the sound evokes in us. And to create a painting or drawing we must love the feeling that the created image elicits in us. It is not enough to simply have a sense of duty or obligation to produce a thing. Love of one's work is the catalyst that unlocks and sustains the flow of energy. Boredom and ennui are the absence of love. Where there is boredom, there is quite literally love for nothing. One can only escape from boredom by finding something, anything, that you are in love with.

The Green Sphere

The power of love has a remarkable capacity for dilating and opening up the energy channels within the physical, emotional, and mental bodies. It is therefore a stimulus for the *channeling* of inspiration and creative energy. Love, like other forms of fire, acts as a source of heat. And heat has the effect of causing fluid substances to expand - becoming lighter, less dense, opening the interstitial spaces and allowing vital energy to penetrate and circulate throughout the particles. Like hot air flowing into a balloon, the heat of love fills us with a feeling of levity that lifts us up, makes us shine, and carries us away. The importance of *forgiveness* becomes much clearer when we reflect upon the vitalizing and invigorating power that love has upon our constitution. The feeling of relentless *gravity* that comes from holding onto a grudge and holding onto judgment is like a palpable millstone dragging down the vital spirits. To simply *let go* of one's anger and resentment is to give those vital spirits the freedom to rise and float on the energy of love. To forgive is not so much a moral obligation as it is a matter of health, hygiene, and personal empowerment. Love opens up the currents of vitality, whereas spite clamps them shut.

In a broader context, it is well to understand that being a species of hidden and interior fire, the Green Sphere possesses certain occult and magical properties. In the symbolism of alchemy, it is represented by the principle of *sulfur*. It is also the primary component of sexual energy, but with the very important distinction that this concept of sexual energy is a matter of far broader scope and application than simply the physical engagement of sex. It is an energy that permeates all matter and which drives the desire of all creative activity, sex being merely one of the many channels through which this force flows. Of this, more will be said later.

The traditional Hebrew name of this sphere is *Netzach*. The word is typically translated as *victory*, but the derivation seems to be from a root meaning *to shine, to be bright, to be brilliant*. Thus, the Hebrew name actually does imply the idea of *radiance,* which is indeed the nature of all things pertaining to the Green Sphere - essence, sensation, passion, and the planet Venus itself, otherwise known as the *morning star* on account of its brilliance. This quality of sparkling brilliance is why Venus was also referred to as *Lucifer*, a Latin name which literally means *bearer of light*.

This may come as a surprise to some, and certainly it raises all manner of interesting questions. The name Lucifer is commonly taken to mean the Devil. But the original meaning actually points to Venus as the herald of the morning light. What has happened here exactly? In what way did Venus become conflated with the Devil? To answer this conundrum, we must look to the one reference to Lucifer in the King James Bible, which is found in Isaiah 14:12-14. These verses, which are uttered as a prophecy about the impending downfall of the king of Babylon, read as follows: "How art thou fallen from heaven, O Lucifer, son of the morning! How art thou cut down to the ground, which didst weaken the nations! For thou hast said in thine heart, I will ascend into heaven, I will exalt my throne above the stars of God: I will sit also upon the mount of the congregation, in the sides of the north: I will ascend above the heights of the clouds; I will be like the most High."

The Hebrew text which is translated here as "Lucifer, son of the morning" is "*Helel, ben-shachar*", of which *ben-shachar* means literally "son of the dawn", and *helel* means "shining one". This utterance is therefore a *metaphor* comparing the king of Babylon - which had conquered and subjugated Israel - to the planet Venus which, as the *morning star*, rises *above* the sun at the break of day. But as Venus orbits around the sun, it oscillates between preceding the sun in the zodiac and following behind it as the *evening star*.

In one sense then, Venus as Lucifer was taken as a symbol of overbearing *pride*, the likes of which would seek to exalt itself above God, only to be cast back down to its humility. There is a deeper interpretation to be taken from this, however, if we look at it in the context of the Tree of Life. Venus, Mercury, and the Moon collectively form the lower triangle which represents the realm of *material* experience. The Sun represents the *Logos*, which is the law of equilibrium that governs the material universe from behind the veil. Venus, being the radiant beauty of material reality, can be thought of in one sense as a kind of siren song, an alluring *temptation* to become completely engrossed in the realm of material experience.

Now of course, this must all be put into perspective. There are certain schools of spiritual philosophy, such as Gnosticism in particular, which would assert that materiality is the polar opposite of spirit, and is therefore inherently dark and impure. This is not at all the perspective that we advocate here. The Kabbalah is a philosophy which maintains that every part of existence, down to the most minute atom, is a manifestation and expression of spirit. So there is no taking seriously here the notion that the material world is evil in any way. There is, however, a state of *limited consciousness* that sees materiality as the *only reality*, and this state of unenlightenment is what is represented by the Devil. We must be clear therefore that it is not in the nature of the Green Sphere to obfuscate spiritual awareness. Rather, the failure to perceive spiritual reality lies entirely in the fault of human awareness in its unevolved state. But to those who *are* less spiritually evolved, the radiance of material things can be a very shiny distraction. And so just as the sparkling light of Venus lifts itself above the sun in the morning sky, the myth of the Devil attempting to usurp the throne of God becomes an allegory for the temptations of the material world outshining spiritual wisdom.

There is one remaining point to make about the Green Sphere, which is not often touched upon. It is the observation that essence is a form of *nourishment*. We are all aware that food, water, and air are necessary for the maintenance of life. But what is not generally recognized is that the stream of sensory impressions that we consume is just as essential to our physical, mental, and emotional health. There is no question that to be surrounded by beautiful and pleasant sensations does wonders for one's well-being. It is equally certain that dull and squalid surroundings tend to starve and deplete the vital energy. We have an instinctive understanding of this with regard to the foods that we eat. Foods that are fresher, richer, and more flavorful are innately perceived to carry a greater abundance of the nourishing life-energy. The stimulation of rich sensory experience is something that we crave because it is something that we *need* at a very fundamental level.

That essential life-energy that we discover in the world around us stimulates and feeds a sympathetic life-energy within us. This richness of essence is the sustenance of physical vitality, and the more of it that we can assimilate from our environment, the brighter we will shine.

The Orange Sphere

Form in its most basic sense is simply a delineation of space, and so the Orange Sphere can be thought of as a reflection of the Black Sphere on a lower arc, just as essence is a reflection of the White Sphere on a lower arc.

It would be tempting, although over-simplistic, to say that the Orange Sphere represents the idea of *matter* in some sense, but in actuality the subject requires a bit more nuance. What we're dealing with here is in fact a concept that may be somewhat difficult to wrap one's head around, as it introduces ideas that are outside of the common framework of how we understand reality. We know from experience that material objects have a definite form and shape. It is also true that we can form images of material objects in our imagination, and these images likewise have a definite form and shape. Now the common understanding of things would say that the material objects that we see around us are "real", whereas the images in our imagination are "not real". They exist merely "in our head". From the standpoint of occult philosophy, however, the constructions of imagination are *just as real* as the objects of material reality, but on a different level from that of the physical senses. In fact, this philosophy assumes an entire para-physical realm known as the *astral plane*, consisting of a substance that is able to hold shape and form, but which is also highly malleable and plastic. Which is to say, the substance of the astral plane is the "stuff" of imagination. This astral plane is also the landscape of dreams, the abode of ghosts and phantoms, and the realm of what is called out-of-body experience, or astral projection.

So we have before our understanding an *astral* substance that can assume a definite form and shape, and a *physical* substance that can assume form and shape. But from the standpoint of esoteric philosophy, these are in fact essentially one and the same. That is to say... *form is form*. What differentiates physical substance from astral substance is that the former is simply astral substance that has acquired a certain kind of *density*.

Now before we go any further, it is necessary to clarify what exactly we mean here by "density". We are not speaking of density in the strictly scientific sense of a quantity of particles per unit of volume. Rather, we are speaking about a certain *force* that substance has which is capable of impacting things around it. I can visualize a hammer in my imagination, and I can even project this image externally into the space around me. But I cannot impact things around me with this imaginary hammer. A physical hammer, on the other hand, would have a very tangible impact on other physical things. This attribute of *having impact* is the domain of the Purple Sphere.

So here we have the nuance that really distinguishes this occult and esoteric framework of thinking. There is no single element on this Tree that corresponds to "matter" *per se*. Materiality is rather the *combination* of form, essence, and force. Or to express it in the symbolism of alchemy - mercury, sulfur, and salt.

In this context then, the Orange Sphere stands for form in its primary manifestation, apart from the attribute of possessing forceful impact. That is to say, Mercury principally represents *astral* substance, the substance of thought and imagination.

In astrology, Mercury represents communication and thought processes in general, especially that type of thinking that we typically call "left brain". It is the process of giving shape to thoughts and ideas. Mercury is particularly noted for the *fluency* with which it can manipulate thought-forms. In mythology, Mercury was the messenger of the gods, and he was depicted with winged feet to illustrate the ability of thought to move swiftly, nimbly, and effortlessly. This is a defining characteristic of astral substance in its pure form. It is remarkably plastic and easy to manipulate in comparison to physical substance, which demonstrates a stubborn resistance and inertia. Thought is capable of traveling light-years, and constructing enormous edifices in the blink of an eye. Like the elemental quicksilver which shares the name of

The Orange Sphere

Mercury, thought is an elusive liquid that evades capture, darting this way and that. It is impossible to nail down quicksilver just as it is impossible to nail a thought to the wall. The fluency of Mercury in manipulating thought-forms lends itself to intelligence, adaptability, and quick thinking, as well as all facility for mathematics, science, engineering, and systems thinking. It is also adept in verbal skills and communication, all of these being the astrological virtues traditionally ascribed to Mercury.

The fluency of Mercury in formulating words and ideas makes it especially clever and crafty. It embodies the archetypal figure of the *trickster* which is found in so many mythologies. This trickster archetype is an aspect not only of the facility for manipulation which Mercury possesses, but also its *superficiality*. This aspect of Mercury's nature should not be underappreciated. The Orange Sphere is entirely the realm of *appearance*. It is all about the projection of image, not profundity. The Black Sphere represents the transcendent *depths* in which all things merge into The One. The Orange Sphere, on the other hand, represents the kaleidoscope of fleeting images which form the *surface* of reality. It has no desire to occupy itself with anything other than the manipulation of these surface phenomena.

This in itself should not be thought of as a necessarily negative attribute. It is in fact this very lack of *depth* and *gravitas* which gives Mercury its freedom to be so agile and prolific. It does not care to be burdened with ruminating over the weighty questions of existence. It is much more comfortable to skip like a stone over the surface of things. And indeed, Mercury is at its best when it is mobile, because then it can generate new ideas and new forms and new patterns. The *power* of Mercury is in its fluidity and adaptability. It is endlessly adept at creating images, spinning out thoughts and ideas and words, and finding just the *right* words and the right modes of expression for any given idea. All of this it does effortlessly, and to be able to do this so effortlessly it must stay out of the deep water. Mercury does not care to go deep into the heart and soul of a matter, because that is the nature of essence rather than form. In a certain sense, we could say that there is a kind of spiritual wisdom to Mercury's superficiality, because Mercury realizes that all of the vast picture-show of life is nothing more than a phantasm, a dream within the mind of God, and so there is no real reason to take it all that seriously. The superficiality with which Mercury dances across the surface of reality contains a lesson in *non-attachment* to that world of illusion and maya.

It would seem to be quite a paradox, to think that this very lack of depth that Mercury typifies could be a type of wisdom. One has to be at a certain level of insight in order to make this work well. When a strong center of gravity has been established, as embodied by the Yellow Sphere, then one can afford to assume a certain attitude of levity toward mundane affairs. Where spiritual insight is lacking, however, this Mercurial mindset can of course express itself in negative ways. There is rarely any element of malice to Mercury, but it does have a distinctly *amoral* quality by virtue of its attitude of not taking anything very seriously. The infatuation with surface appearances, along with the effortless ability to manipulate such appearances, makes Mercury a master of deception and trickery. This deception can be aimed not just at others but at oneself as well, as Mercury is more than practiced at constructing rationalizations and specious arguments in order to justify questionable decisions, or to mask dubious motives. There can also be a tendency, in the absence of any spiritual instinct, to take appearance to be the *only* reality. This mindset of *philosophical materialism* has a certain appeal to it, for all of the reasons that we have already described. It has a reductive, almost elegant simplicity to it. There is less that one has to burden oneself with emotionally, and so there is a feeling of unencumbered freedom that comes with this way of thinking. It is a very *flat* way of experiencing reality, however, and it is not by any means the only way of attaining mental freedom. One can assimilate the benefits of Mercurial awareness, and yet subsume it within a wider and more multi-faceted model of reality. To the spiritually developed, the Mercury way of seeing is a *tool*, but not a complete worldview.

The Hebrew name for this sphere is *Hod* which means *glory* or *splendor*, so called because the shining-forth of material existence is the manifest glory of Ain Soph. The Orange Sphere governs the *spectacular*, which includes the plastic arts and all manner of performance. To create a glorious spectacle is to revel in the appreciation of the boundless creative power of the Limitless Light. The Orange Sphere represents a mode of consciousness that tends to view existence as an *aesthetic* phenomenon. The world is appreciated as a work of art. Broadly speaking, art is the translation of *essence* into *appearance*. The artistic form is the encapsulation or the incarnation of a certain essence. This is why Mercury is said to rule the arts as well as communication. It is the shape-making capacity in the broadest sense - sculpting, articulating, and formulating. Speech and writing are forms of expression that convey abstract ideas in the same manner as painting, design, or music. There can also be an emphasis on the dramatic element with Mercury, but not in the manner of drama that takes itself seriously. It is more in the style of drama for entertainment's sake, dramatic *flair* so to speak.

The Orange Sphere is also the realm of prophecy, as it is the *substance* from which visions are made. This is a much more obscure topic, but suffice it to say that one can *accumulate* astral substance just as a rechargeable battery can accumulate electrical charge. When this accumulated astral fluid reaches a critical mass, and is activated with vital essence, it begins to assume an aura of inspiration. It is then capable of forming images in the imagination which seem to dance with a life of their own. Many of the traditional scrying techniques involve gazing into a luminous point of concentration such as a candle flame, or a reflective surface such as a crystal or mirror. In early practices of hypnosis, the subject was frequently asked to gaze at a shiny object. The point of this is not to actually see things *within* the point of focus. Rather, the action of the light upon the optic nerves stimulates the accumulation of astral substance within the viewer, which eventually takes on a life of its own. The principle of sympathetic vibration is at work here. The act of gazing into a source of *living light* activates the living light within oneself, and it is within this *interior* living light that the visions are seen. The endless fascination that *fire* has had over mankind, since the dawn of history, is a testament to this deeply-ingrained instinct for inspired, visionary imagination.

The Purple Sphere

To truly understand the three lower spheres, it is necessary to wrap our heads around the idea that everything in physical reality is simply a thought-form crystallized. At the cosmic level, the universe itself begins as a thought in the mind of God. At the individual level, our thoughts condense into manifested reality. This can take place through a consciously applied effort - as for example when you decide that you need a cup of coffee, and so you go through the activity of brewing the coffee in the coffee-maker, pouring it into the cup, and adding the cream and sugar. The thought of a cup of coffee has been translated into the physical manifestation of a cup of coffee. On the more esoteric side of things, there is also the *unconscious* application of subtle energies which cause manifestation without apparent effort. Medicine knows this phenomenon as the placebo effect, in which a patient's *belief* in his or her own health or lack of health manifests in the physical body. But the application of this subconscious force extends much further into one's personal reality, and this is what is called the *Law of Attraction*, which states that the thoughts that we habitually focus upon will eventually manifest into our personal experience. The underlying idea behind this law is that reality *is* thought-form.

This is the key to grasping the three lower spheres, because they are all understood in a dual sense. The Orange Sphere for example is *form*, which is expressed on the one hand as thought-form, and on the other hand as physical form. And though we may be tempted to think of these as two separate principles, fundamentally they are the same. Likewise, the Green Sphere is *essence*, which can be expressed *objectively* as the sensory qualities of physical things, or *subjectively* as feelings, passions, and so forth. And again, these are not really separate phenomena but rather two sides of the same fundamental principle.

The Purple Sphere

So now we arrive at the Purple Sphere, which represents *force* in both its physical and non-physical aspects. Physical force is simply the capacity of physical things to exert an influence upon one another. Non-physical force is that mysterious, esoteric force which drives the Law of Attraction, and which drives the manifestation of thought into physical form. This is what we call the *Magical Agent*, and the subjective experience of it can best be compared to a kind of *hydraulic pressure*. Perhaps the clearest way to understand what this force feels like is to try to push the similar poles of two magnets together. When enough of this hydraulic force is accumulated, then its natural inclination is to exert itself and manifest itself in some manner. This Magical Agent is especially concentrated in the *sexual drive*, and the hydraulic nature of the Purple Sphere can most easily be understood through the feeling of sexual arousal. It is of a similar quality to the pressure that pumps blood into the sexual organs during excitation, but we would do well to recognize that subjectively, this feeling of enhanced pressure during arousal is experienced throughout the entire body.

It is worth pointing out here that traditionally Venus is the planet that has been most closely associated with sexuality, and indeed we spoke earlier of the Green Sphere as being the primary component of sexual energy. In actuality though, Venus, Mercury and Luna are *all* connected with sexual energy in different aspects. Venus represents the *pleasure* aspect, as well as the *excitement* that is felt. It is the warm, radiant, tingling glow that one experiences during sex, as well as the feeling of passion that one has for another. Mercury, being the *formal* aspect, represents the body itself, and more precisely the perception of desirable physical features which trigger sexual arousal. The Moon, on the other hand, represents the *compulsive force* of sexual energy. It is the feeling of *wound-up* energy that seeks resolution and drives the sexual act itself like a coiled spring.

In one sense, we could say that the entire physical universe is built upon sexual energy, but with the understanding that this energy is far broader in scope than the mere sexual act itself. What we are calling sexual energy is a generic currency that expresses itself not only in physical intercourse but in *every* creative act. The principal reason why we choose to characterize this universal force as *sexual energy* is because our subjective understanding of it is most readily comprehended through the feeling of sexual arousal, in which it is experienced as a type of compelling subterranean pressure that pushes toward an outcome. This is the universal force of manifestation, and magical work is the mastery and channeling of this force. The ability to *abstract* the compelling force of this energy from the sexual expression itself is in fact the key to understanding how this works. Nature has directed this force most pointedly toward sexual reproduction for the perpetuation of the species, but sexual intercourse is merely the tip of the iceberg in terms of how this force operates universally.

The Purple Sphere presents to us as a feeling of fullness, substantiality, potency, and *intensity*. All of these are feelings that we experience during states of sexual arousal. Anything that delivers intensity is expressing the compelling, forceful energy of the Purple Sphere. It is that force which we call *personal power*. It is also any force by which we feel *overpowered*. It is the magnetic current felt in a charged crowd, such as a musical concert or a political rally. It is also the force exerted by physical magnetism, gravity, and electrical attraction and repulsion. There is a distinct *density* to the Purple Sphere, and of all the spheres on the Tree, it is by far the most dense.

The Purple Sphere represents the *subjective* side of experience. It reflects that awareness of things that is much deeper than a mere mental understanding. It is the *felt experience* of the forces that drive material reality, as opposed to the kind of superficial "book learning" which is entirely in the head. The Purple Sphere must be engaged if one is to grasp metaphysical principles in their *potency*. Otherwise one has only an abstract, intellectual connection. One can have thoughts and words, but lack the corresponding feelings, and without the feeling there is no real power. Esoterically, the Sephirah of Yesod has been associated with what we call the *subconscious*, and the structure of the Kabbalistic system is in fact geared toward activating this level of consciousness, which is more symbolic in nature than intellectual. The function of religious and esoteric symbolism is precisely this - to bypass the intellectual understanding and tap directly into the felt experience of the principle which is being interrogated.

Astrologically, the Purple Sphere corresponds to the Moon, which is said to govern the *feelings*. This should not be understood merely in the sense of emotional reactivity. It also means feeling in the sense of the subjective *grasping* of the world around us. It means a mode of consciousness, a mode of awareness of other things and of other people that is tactile, direct, and immediate rather than filtered through the intellect. This realm of feeling and felt experience is closely attuned to the watery realm of Neptune and the Black Sphere, because to feel deeply into one's surroundings is to be enmeshed with one's surroundings at the level of underlying oneness. It is a mode of *feeling into* one's environment. Feeling is not just excitability. It is also *impressionability*. It is the visceral experience of things around us.

The concepts of feeling and emotion need to be carefully dissected here, as they tend to overlap between the Green Sphere and the Purple Sphere. They are however two very distinct principles. The Green Sphere is a kind of fiery, passionate energy that emanates from within and which radiates outward, whereas the Purple Sphere is an intimate, impactful mode of experience that occurs between oneself and one's surroundings. It may be difficult at times to separate the two when we are talking about feelings and emotions, but it is important to draw the distinction. A good way to understand the difference between them is by their subjective signatures - the Green Sphere is fiery, radiant, and ethereal, whereas the Purple Sphere is dense, fluid and *palpable*. Another way of looking at this is to say that the Moon defines the *intensity* of emotional experience. It is the *amplitude* of the emotion rather than the *quality*. The Moon is the engine that drives the tides, and it is universally understood that the full moon has the power of activating intense and sometimes irrational emotions.

An important thing to bear in mind is that we are impacted by the world around us in the sense of how it makes us *feel*. Feeling is *direct experience*. It is the most fundamental form of experience.

And so the key point to grasp here is that physical experience is *emotional* experience. It is the experience of being moved and impacted by the *otherness* of existence. Physical reality is fundamentally emotional. There is a conceptual equivalence here which is difficult for us in our modern society to wrap our heads around, because we have been conditioned by a worldview of dry scientific materialism to believe that the underlying "stuff" of our universe is fundamentally dead, dumb, and lifeless. But the esoteric worldview is quite the opposite. This view asserts that the stuff of reality is alive and pulsating with feeling. It thrusts this feeling upon us, and we receive it with that which is our own capacity to feel and to project feeling. And so if we pull away the veil of intellect which clouds our vision, we see that in fact there is no "dead matter" but rather a universe of living substance, engaged in a constant fluid exchange of feeling and being felt.

We come back then to the standpoint of Berkeleyan idealism. The feeling and the being felt *is itself* the essence of material reality. The key takeaway, therefore, is that the commonly accepted idea of "matter" - that is to say, the concept of a dead, inert substance which underlies the world of our experience - is simply a mental construct. Only the felt experience is real. The notion of a lifeless substrate on which to hang that experience is a conceptual fiction. What we characterize as physical reality, or the quality of *elemental earth*, is the combined influence of the Moon and Saturn. Saturn is the sense of permanence that elemental earth exhibits. But the Moon is intimately connected with sensory experience and the impactfulness which material things impose upon us. That which feels most "real" to us is that which has the most impact upon us.

It is a curious fact that in an age of digital media, more people still prefer to read a physical book rather than a digital one. Why is this so? The physical book has a tactile quality that is soothing and gratifying. Its heft and its texture make us feel as if it is more than just information. It is something that we are connected to on a visceral level. This is a key feature of the Purple Sphere - it represents the tactile nature of experience and what that means to us emotionally. That which is tactile makes us feel *grounded* in our experience. We know where we are in the world by what we can feel around us. Here we come to a very significant aspect of the Moon astrologically speaking. The Moon is said to represent the mother, as well as our early childhood experience, and the degree to which our early experience makes us feel emotionally secure. The touch of the mother early on is what makes the infant feel grounded in its world. Touch is a form of *validation* which tells the child that it is connected with its surroundings. Contact is the most universally understood form of communication, and the most primitive form of validation. Psychologists tell us that children who do not receive human touch and mothering early on usually have difficulty feeling emotionally grounded in adulthood. Many children will demonstrate this need for touch by developing an attachment to a comforting physical object such as a stuffed animal or a "security blanket", the tactile experience of which serves to ground the child emotionally. To be in touch with one's physical surroundings is to feel connected, and in that connection is found a sense of *belonging* in the world.

The Moon, therefore, represents a very sensual level of experience, and it embodies the feeling of *intimacy*. By this we mean not just romantic intimacy, but any relationship of being close to someone or something in such a way that it has a physical or emotional impact upon us. Intimacy is what anchors us in a sense of *reality*. To experience just how real something is, you must become intimate with it. You must feel it and be impacted by it and be moved by it. To feel the reality of a stone wall is to place your hands upon the cold, hard surface and feel its rough texture on your fingertips. When people say that they crave something real, what they mean is that they are looking for something that makes them *feel*. The Moon has to do with *how* we experience intimacy, with *whom*, and with *what*. It is how we experience closeness and how we situate ourselves within our environment. It is how we establish contact with our surroundings.

Intimacy can be experienced through both love and hate. Either experience is a form of emotional entanglement, and what you hate is just as much a part of you as what you love. Some people have ways of experiencing closeness with others that reflect a dysfunctional upbringing. But even a dysfunctional mode of relating to other people, if it makes one feel real and alive and grounded in the moment, is a form of intimacy. This is why for certain people, it is better to be hated than to be ignored. Under normal circumstances though, discomfort tends to generate an impulse to disconnect from one's environment, and so ideally the Moon embodies the type of sensual experience that makes us feel comfortable and therefore grounded in our surroundings. It is no wonder then that the Moon is said to rule the sign of Cancer, which is the sign of domestic life and "creature comforts", and of knowing where one's place is.

In one respect, the Moon can be described as that quality which we call *presence*. This is a word which in itself sounds rather nebulous, but we must think of it as the degree to which someone or something makes itself felt. The Moon is what gives "body" to something. Without body, a thing will seem abstract and tenuous, as if lacking in actual substance. In physical terms, we experience this as the concept of *mass*, as it is the massy quality of something that has the most impact upon us. In terms of sensual experience, it is the richness and depth of the sensory quality, as when we say that a wine is *full-bodied*. Musically speaking, body is felt in the deep bass sounds which we experience in a very visceral way. To say that an individual has presence, therefore, means that they project a kind of emotional impact in whatever space they are in.

Presence is what makes something *real* to us. Our principal metric of distinguishing reality from fantasy is that reality has a direct impact upon us. The Moon is therefore connected with how you grasp the reality of the world around you, and how you make yourself real within that world. It represents groundedness in the sense of getting a feel for your environment, both in terms of how it impacts you and how you impact it. The Moon represents *immersion* into one's experience, and it is integrally tied up with the concept of *manifesting*, which is the act of making one's presence felt. That which manifests becomes tangible and palpable. And so the work of the Moon is to take an energy or an idea and render it as a palpable reality. In one sense, the Moon can be thought of as the innate understanding of how to actualize the vision of the Sun, and so it tracks to what we call *common sense*. Common sense is what anchors you in the world, and what anchors your goals and objectives into the world.

As we have said, the Moon is intimately connected to that mysterious part of the personality known as the *subconscious*. The Kabbalistic term for this sphere is *Yesod*, which means *foundation*, and it is quite correct to say that the subconscious is indeed the foundation of the personality. It is that which grounds you in your physical reality. The subconscious is the set of instinctive drives and energies that anchor the animal organism in its physical environment. We interface directly with our environment by way of *feeling*. We feel into our surroundings, and we feel into other people. We use our sense of feel for everything around us to navigate through the world. This manner of feeling into things is an ebb and flow of energy. It is liquid in its mode of operation. There is also a distinct characteristic of *impressionability* to the subconscious. It is remarkably adept at absorbing and retaining impressions that can be repurposed later on. In this respect, the Moon is deeply connected to *learning* - not in the sense of book-learning, but in the sense of *experiential* learning. It is the kind of learning which forms the habits that allow one to be perfectly adapted to one's surroundings. The impressionability of the subconscious is responsible for what we call *muscle memory*. That is to say, absorbing and assimilating something by feeling it directly, by direct immersion into it, so that it leaves an *impression* upon your soul. This is perhaps a key insight into understanding why we are immersed into physical reality in the first place. The experiences that we absorb at the physical level are assimilated in such a way that is much deeper than can possibly be had from any abstract mental comprehension. What we learn directly through felt experience can never be replaced by dry intellectual theory.

The subconscious can be described as the pre-verbal level of consciousness. This also makes it the seat of the intuition, insofar as by "intuition" we mean that which is known or communicated without words. The intuition is developed by quieting the verbal chatter of the mind, because then we take in information via direct experience. The Moon represents that more primitive but more "real" way of knowing the world that lies beneath the intellectual, rational mind. This is the most primitive layer of the personality. It is the level of animal consciousness, being the mode of interfacing with reality that we share with the most primitive of creatures. It is also the infantile layer of consciousness. The infant does not know how to formulate words and sentences and concepts with which to order its experience. It knows only what it feels, and how to express those feelings emotionally. And so the Moon represents the infantile part of the personality. To speak of this level of understanding as the infantile consciousness is by no means to denigrate it. It is a layer of the personality that we all possess, and it serves a very important purpose. The primitive layer of consciousness is the very foundation of the rational consciousness. Without direct experience of reality and the instinctive mode of processing it, there is nothing upon which to build a rational narrative.

This intuitive level of consciousness, the *lunar* consciousness, represents your ability to feel the mood around you, and to gauge the temperature of your surroundings. It is a *receptive* faculty. The Moon represents sensitivity in the way of picking up signals, and it would seem to have some bearing on how we blend in with the collective. How well do you *fit in* with the pulse of the world and the society around you? How well do you adapt to your surroundings? A certain amount of fluidity and malleability allows you to blend in and harmonize with the collective mood. In a certain sense, the Moon stands for the common denominator of experience that all are capable of understanding, no matter what their level of wealth or status or education may be. The Moon resonates with the "common man". It represents *street smarts* as opposed to intellect. It is the capacity to pick up on non-verbal cues, to feel out a situation and to feel out other people. It is also the ability to establish empathy and rapport. Skilled politicians use this ability to feel into the mood of the crowd, and those who have their finger on the prevailing zeitgeist are the most adept at manipulating public opinion.

The Purple Sphere

In a society that is increasingly disconnected from natural reality, the lesson of the Purple Sphere is to get out of our heads and get grounded in our material existence. The physical body, and the subconscious intelligence that resonates with it, is far more than just a wheelbarrow with which to carry the brain around. It is an instrument of remarkable sensitivity, attuned to signals and vibrations of deep import if we learn how to listen to it carefully. The key to using this instrument is to subdue the chatter of the mind and engage the ability to *feel*. To become a *simpler* being with a simpler way of looking at things may sound to some like the opposite of evolution. But the over-complicated individual who over-thinks everything is most certainly not the way of the future. The essence of elegance in all things is simplicity, and he who can clear the mind of its clutter and tap the most primitive energy of existence is indeed the template for the new humanity.

Part III
The Tree of Life Understood Holistically

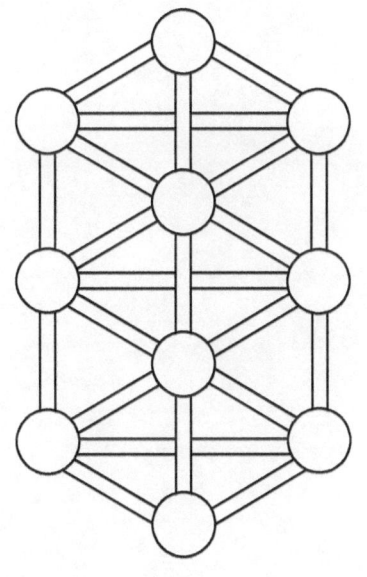

The Psychological Study of the Tree

As a map of human experience, the Tree of Life lays out the fundamental components of human psychology in a way that is both elegant and illuminating. The symmetry and the balance of the diagram seem to point to a sort of ideal template of the perfectly realized individual. Each sphere represents a facet of human expression in its pure state, and meditation upon any one of these spheres allows us to immerse ourselves into the refined essence of that particular mode of expression. If we look to the symbolism of alchemy, we could say that humanity in its unrefined state represents the prime matter of the Philosopher's Stone - a jumbled mass of confusion without proper focus and clarity. To transform raw humanity into the image of the perfected human being, we must follow the alchemical formula of *solve et coagula* - dissolve and coagulate. This means that the hodge-podge of jumbled elements must be broken apart, separated and purified, and then joined back together in proper balance and proportion. With the Tree of Life, we see the elements of the human microcosm separated, clarified, and arranged in a harmonious order. As an object of meditation, therefore, the diagram is in itself a valuable tool for transformation. The structure and the elegance of the Tree impresses upon the subconscious, by way of suggestion, an image of internal balance and harmony.

In broad outline, the three lower spheres represent the *personality*, which is to say the outward-facing part of the individual that presents directly to the world. This is the part of the individual which Jung called the *persona*. In more esoteric terms, we could describe it as the *mask* of the self. The Orange Sphere represents the faculties of formal thought. The Green Sphere represents the passions and the aesthetic sensibilities. And finally, the Purple Sphere represents the basic drives and instincts by which we engage directly with physical reality. In a purely psychological context, the Purple Sphere represents consciousness at its most primitive level, what Freud referred to as the *id* and what Jung described as the *shadow*. The Purple Sphere is the *infantile* level of consciousness, which is focused on self-gratification and the appetites. The infantile consciousness is inherently self-centered and self-serving. And to be clear, there is nothing fundamentally wrong with this. This is what drives the survival instinct, after all. Without a self-serving instinct, we would not know how to maintain our place in the world. This infantile or animal layer of consciousness is an integral and necessary part of every one of us, but it is a force that we must learn to harness and regulate.

Taken on their own, these three lower elements of the personality do not constitute a whole individual. They are simply the constituent parts of an individual - the sulfur, mercury, and salt in alchemical terms. In order to form a complete human being, these elements must be joined together by a unifying force, and this unifying force is the Yellow Sphere. The Yellow Sphere is what holds the personality together. It is the force that binds all of the physical, mental, and emotional components into a coherent whole. The Yellow Sphere is also what creates a sense of narrative, the binding together of events into a meaningful story. It is that which synthesizes all of our thoughts, perceptions, and experiences into a cohesive worldview or philosophical outlook. Most importantly, the Yellow Sphere is what gives us our *sense of self*. A strong sense of self means knowing who you are. That is to say, what you stand for, what you believe in, and what your goals are. Those with a strong sense of self tend to have more influence than those without a strong sense of self. Like the Sun, they become a center of gravity. They pull the forces around themselves into their orbit, synthesize those forces, and make things happen. An individual without a strong sense of self is more prone to drift along in life and to be buffeted about by external circumstances. In psychological parlance, this is referred to as *locus of control*. The individual with a clear sense of self is said to have an *internal* locus of control, which means that he takes responsibility and agency for the outcomes of his own existence. The person with an *external* locus of control sees his life as simply a series of events that happen *to* him, and all of his misfortunes and disappointments are therefore attributable to other people or to society.

Without a strong sense of self, there cannot be a strong sense of personal agency, and so one's life is necessarily perceived as being shaped by outside forces.

The Yellow Sphere represents what is referred to as the *ego* in the psychological sense. This is not the same as the more common and somewhat disparaging sense of the word, as when we describe someone with an over-inflated sense of self-importance as having excessive ego. That type of personality is more characteristic of the *id* or infantile consciousness. Rather, we are using the term *ego* here in its original sense as the Latin word for "I". The ego is the center of the personality that acts as the locus of identity. It is the binding force that *creates* a sense of identity. It is worth noting here that the Yellow Sphere is very much supported by the Indigo Sphere, insofar as the Indigo Sphere gives *stability* to the sense of self. The Indigo Sphere provides steadfastness and resistance to the more disorganized influences of the personality, as well as to social influences which would unseat us from our center of balance, or persuade us to deviate from our core values. The Indigo Sphere above all represents the virtue of *discipline*, without which one can never have true freedom. It also gives us the virtue of *resilience* and stoicism, which means not allowing one's sense of self to be undermined by outside circumstances. Together, the Yellow Sphere and the Indigo Sphere form a *double center* of the Tree of Life. Jointly, they hold the entire structure together.

Clearly, then, the Yellow Sphere is the key principle of mental, spiritual, and physical health. In addition to holding the elements of the personality together, it is also the principle that puts these elements into equilibrium, harmony, and balance. It therefore serves the function of moderating and measuring out the proper proportions of every force and energy within the overall economy of the individual. This includes discriminating between what does and does not belong within that overall economy. And so the Yellow Sphere can also be understood as the principle of mental and emotional *hygiene*. It is a sanitizing energy that ejects all discordant thoughts, feelings, and impulses from the psychological system. Negative thoughts can be especially pernicious and clinging, because they have a peculiar skill of persuading us to *identify* with them. They ply us with subtle reasons why we *ought* to be angry, or despondent, or bitter. And so we may end up convincing ourselves that there would have to be something wrong with us if we were *not* angry and bitter. We might even have other people telling us that we are somehow *out of touch* if we are not sucked into negativity. This is why negativity is so hard to shake off, both from an individual and a cultural standpoint. And yet the cleansing energy of the Yellow Sphere has a very *clear* instinct with regards to negative thoughts and feelings. It spits them out as decisively as one would spit out rotten meat. It has no tolerance for that which is impure and which would disturb the balance and equilibrium of the soul.

The Yellow Sphere is not concerned solely with the *internal* equilibrium of the individual, however. It is also concerned with the equilibrium between the individual and society, and so in this respect, the Yellow Sphere is the domain of *ethics*. This is of course a very complex area of inquiry which we will not attempt to cover extensively. Rather, we will present a very high-level outline of ethical theory. To begin with, we must first recognize that different levels of consciousness have different standards of ethical judgment.

From the standpoint of the primitive or infantile consciousness, *good* is simply that which gratifies one's personal wishes, and *bad* is that which frustrates those wishes. These judgments of good and bad are strictly childlike *emotional* responses, and they are completely *subjective* insofar as the standard of judgment revolves entirely around oneself. Though it may sound somewhat like a paradox, the primitive consciousness actually has the most intense and pronounced feelings for what is good and what is bad. But this moral sense of the primitive consciousness, if one could call it that, is entirely self-centered and self-serving. And yet despite the self-centered nature of this mode of judging things, it is actually the foundation for all of our moral reasoning, because we can't have a proper sense of how to behave toward others without first knowing how we would prefer to be treated ourselves. This is commonly understood as the Golden Rule, and its effectiveness lies in its simplicity. We simply take our own self-centered mode of judging things and project it outward in our behavior toward others. The principle is so simple that it is in fact the baseline of all ethical philosophy. It would be quite a mistake therefore to think that complete selflessness is the basis of morality. One has to be grounded in self-interest in order to comprehend the impact of one's behavior on others. Empathy toward others is derived entirely from our own self-centered point of view.

Where ethical considerations become complicated is when two people have objectives that are at cross-purposes to one another. Then there is a question of whose self-interest will take precedence. To the primitive consciousness, the answer is that one's own self-interest always takes priority. This is not an entirely illogical standpoint, given the limited perspective of the primitive consciousness. At this level of awareness, one cannot fully feel the needs or desires of other people, and therefore they are simply not as *real* as one's own needs. There is only the visceral feeling that whatever frustrates one's own wishes is *bad*. The primitive consciousness is therefore habitually in conflict with its environment, and its primary means of handling conflict are aggression and manipulation. This however is not a particularly healthy and effective way of being in the world. The Yellow Sphere must therefore intervene with a higher perspective. From this higher vantage point, we see that the ability to make compromises at the individual level translates into a smoother functioning of society as a whole, and this leads to better outcomes for both ourselves and others in the long run. The Yellow Sphere is therefore a regulating influence that tempers the impulses of the Purple Sphere, and channels them into constructive resolutions. At the integrative level of consciousness, we learn how to adapt our personal self-interests to harmonize with the greater good.

This tempering function of the integrative consciousness involves a number of different skills. There is first of all the ability to delay the gratification of our impulses, as we must sometimes allow others to take precedence in order to ensure a smooth and orderly flow of things. Waiting at a traffic light is a perfect example of this.

There is also the understanding of where to set boundaries, so that we do not infringe upon another's autonomy or permit our own autonomy to be violated. Then there is the skill of knowing how to respond when we feel that a boundary has been violated, which is by far the most difficult and most fraught of circumstances to navigate. In these situations, it is very easy for the primitive consciousness to take over. The primitive consciousness tends to view things in very black and white terms, and so its native impulse is to annihilate any perceived threat. The integrative consciousness must therefore strike a delicate balance, determining just the right measure and direction of force in order to rectify a situation without going too far.

At this point in the discussion, the key theme that we have explored is a dichotomy and tension between the Yellow Sphere and the Purple Sphere. This is a deeply archetypal relationship which has been expressed in many different ways throughout all cultures. It is sometimes framed as the struggle between good and evil, or between reason and the primal instincts. The archetype abounds in various forms of religious symbolism. In Christian iconography, we have the image of archangel Michael vanquishing Satan, and the legend of Saint George slaying the dragon. In Mesopotamian mythology, it is the Sun-god Marduk who conquers the dragon Tiamat. Egyptian myth gives us the story of Horus defeating the sinister god Set to avenge the murder of Osiris. And of course, the most contemporary solar archetype in Western society is the figure of Christ, who overcomes the curse of *original sin* which represents the primitive instincts with which we are all born. In all of these narratives, there is an implicit association of the primitive consciousness with the forces of evil and darkness. In some sense, there is truth to this, but it is essential to understand that the Purple Sphere is neither *explicitly* nor *inherently* evil. It is simply the blind and raw force of nature which we must learn to harness and channel constructively.

It should go without saying that as a society and as a culture we have not yet fully learned how to integrate the primitive consciousness. This is why the archetype of the Devil continues to have such a morbid but enduring fascination. As a projection of the most primal instincts, it represents a part of ourselves that we fear, but which we also cannot do without. Our relationship with this symbol is full of ambiguity. On the one hand, the Devil is looked upon as the personification of all evil. At the same time, it is seen as a symbol of great power that lures us with the fruits of worldly gain and pleasure. It is true that the primitive consciousness is a source of tremendous personal power, especially with regard to the manifestation of material things. To stigmatize it as evil is a bit more complicated, however. It is somewhat like saying that electricity is evil. Electricity is certainly dangerous, and it can easily kill you if it is not managed carefully. But electricity is not evil. It is simply an energy that can yield tremendous benefits if handled with care.

This recognition of the primitive consciousness as a source of power is illustrated in the lore of magic and witchcraft. Folklore has it that witches gained their magical power by forfeiting their souls to the Devil. But there is also a tradition in the literature of the medieval grimoires which held that a true magician could bind the demonic spirits in the holy names of God and Christ, and compel them to do his bidding without the sacrifice of his soul. There is a deep symbolic truth in both of these ideas. A person who lacks the self-integrating influence of the Yellow Sphere may seek to establish a sense of his own reality by delving into the primitive consciousness. Such individuals have what we would call an *unbalanced* personality. It is a peculiar fact though, that these people tend to have a disproportionate impact on the world around them. They frequently project a more pronounced sexuality, or pronounced aggression, or both. They will also typically be seen to have a keen instinct for manipulation. While their patterns of behavior are generally destructive over the long run, they often display a remarkable capacity for getting what they want in the short term, which is really what they care about the most. Immediate gratification is their primary focus, and they have little capacity for impulse control. These individuals are also notorious for creating drama around themselves. Given that they do not have a clear and coherent sense of who they are, this is understandably the only way that they truly know how to feel *real*. All of this is characteristic of someone who is *given over* to the primitive consciousness. Psychology describes these individuals as having a *personality disorder*, but it is an undeniable fact that the raw animal energy which such individuals exude can exercise a powerful fascination over others. They are disproportionately represented in positions of power and notoriety, and every cult leader is an example of this type of personality. It is also without question that they are disproportionately represented in the creative arts. History is indeed full of creative geniuses of the most base and unhinged character.

To the average person, who has learned to suppress this primitive animal energy, these individuals can be tremendously alluring. The Purple Sphere is the source of magnetism, libido, and sexual potency. Those who are governed by the primitive consciousness will therefore seem to possess an intoxicating power that inspires both fear and awe. This power is in a certain sense illusory, however. As they have no real stable center of self, the forces that they channel invariably spiral out of their control. And so eventually the Devil takes his due in this symbolic narrative, which represents letting oneself go to the intoxication of energies which one is not prepared to handle.

There is, however, a third way between being out of touch with the primal instincts and being consumed by them. This way is symbolized by the magician, who is able to both summon the Devil and also command him with the power of light. The magician stands on a level above the individual who has simply numbed his sensibility to the primal forces within himself. The person who is thoroughly tamed and domesticated by society occasionally indulges in a vicarious taste of these forces from the more unbalanced elements of society. But ultimately his instincts are to keep these forces at arm's distance, and so he is not sufficiently *tapped in* to these energies to wield them to any effect. The magician is one who, having mastered the science of equilibrium, has the fearlessness and the willingness to *engage* the primal forces of creation and wield them as the artist wields his brush.

To be clear then, the truly whole individual is not someone who has a weak connection with his primitive nature. Nor is he someone who is merely a well-tamed social creature. The whole individual is someone with a strong core of integrity that is tapped into a vibrant animal energy. Most importantly, he is centered in his *authenticity*. This means that a good part of his integrity lies in knowing when to *resist* society. In addition to the id and the ego, Freud posited a third aspect of the personality which he called the *superego*. One might initially assume that this word indicates a part of the self which operates at a higher level of consciousness than the ego, but this is not actually what Freud had in mind. What is meant by the superego is more along the lines of *social conditioning*. It is a set of internalized expectations placed upon us by social influences, primarily the parents but also other forms of authority as well as peer groups. The superego is not the same as the integrative consciousness of the Yellow Sphere, but it attempts to operate in somewhat the same way. It represents the collective efforts of one's social environment to establish a stable and harmonious order. In a normally functioning society, the superego will do a more or less reasonable job of this. But because it is a collective rather than an individual product, its norms are very abstract, and therefore not particularly tailored to any given individual. It therefore tends to be more rule-bound than organic.

The superego is therefore a Saturnine aspect of the personality. It is a structure of thoughts and belief systems that tends to be somewhat rigid, but it has a certain utility insofar as it gives us the sense that our social environment has a stable structure that we can navigate successfully, so long as we observe the rules and protocols.

The rigidity of the superego is also its downside, however, and so it constitutes the chief component of what we call the *false self*. The false self is like a mask which we have forgotten that we are wearing. It is this *unconscious* aspect of the false self which robs us of our authenticity. We fail to recognize our true self because we have ceased to notice that we are wearing a mask. To be perfectly fair, the false self does not consist solely of the superego. We cannot blame our lack of authenticity entirely on society. The false self is also constructed of our own rigid belief systems, derived from faulty and reductionist logic, as well as personal compromises based on assumptions about what we can and cannot realistically accomplish. All of this is patched over with defense mechanisms to conceal the gaps in our own expectations, as well as the expectations of society.

In one sense, the false self can be looked upon as a marvel of adaptation. Its chameleon-like facade acts as a protective shell for the most vulnerable parts of the primitive consciousness. At its peak performance, it can bury the most profound pain deep beneath the most convincing veneer of aptitude. This adaptation comes at a price, however. It is a form of slow suffocation. The false self essentially fills in the gaps where the Yellow Sphere fails to flesh out a complete narrative. But unlike the Yellow Sphere, it constructs an artificial order as opposed to an organic order. The false self is built upon the simple premise that every individual feels an underlying need to *make sense* of their existence. This need is the core drive of the Yellow Sphere, but if the individual's latent integrity is not strong enough to construct a coherent story, then the mind will piece together some kind of patchwork from borrowed sources.

This shell then becomes something of a walking prison. In most cases, the individual settles into a strained but stable relationship with the false self. There may be a vague underlying sense of malaise that one is not living one's true life, but part of the job of the false self is to keep such feelings below the surface of awareness. In some cases though, the feeling of discomfort becomes too urgent to ignore. At that point, one has essentially two options. One response is, paradoxically, to double down on the false ego. This generally leads to bad outcomes, but it is a predictable reaction when one begins to feel desperate. If the mental labyrinth which the false self has constructed is consistently leading one into dead ends, then the feeling of being hopelessly *trapped* becomes increasingly palpable. As one reaches for more extreme measures to try to construct a meaningful narrative out of one's existence, the contradictions that have to be covered over become ever wider, and the lies and the distortions become bigger and more stubbornly clung to. The worst aspects of human nature usually emerge from this condition of a mind that feels trapped and desperate, in which case any sense of meaning at all will be grasped at, even if that meaning is nothing more than the waging of pure spite against God or society.

The other option, when we have begun to sense our own imprisonment, is to deconstruct the false self. This is where the Diamond Sphere comes into its key role. Authenticity requires self-awareness, and self-awareness requires clarity. The clarity of pure consciousness acts as a kind of universal solvent, dissolving every aspect of the personality that is not real. This is the process that Jung referred to as *individuation*. It is the process of making conscious what is unconscious, so that one can separate the wheat from the chaff in one's own psychological makeup. It is the shedding of light and truth on the internal landscape of our psyche, and looking at everything with complete honesty. The process of purification is necessarily a process of simplification. The purified product is always simpler when the extraneous and inessential elements have been filtered out of it. And so the authentic and individuated personality will always appear simpler, because it is clearer of purpose and unadulterated with all of the dead weight which comes with the false self.

The Diamond Sphere is so effective at deconstructing the false self because it gives us the ability to *disidentify* with the contents of the personality. Consciousness has the unique quality of being able to step outside of any system that it is observing. This is its transcendent nature. It has the ability to see outside of the box, and this gives us a degree of freedom that we would not otherwise have. Identification forces us to make certain mental and emotional transactions unconscious. By not identifying with the various parts of our personality, we do not suffer from the panicked impulse to deflect and obfuscate when these parts are subjected to the light of scrutiny. We are no longer emotionally invested in them. This allows us to pick them apart and discard the elements that are not serving us. To be clear, the goal here is not to strive for complete detachment from all thoughts and feelings. The goal is to get to a place where we can embrace a much *purer* experience of mind, heart, and body. To become like a surfer riding the waves, rather than being dragged beneath them, is the ideal state of mind to be in. This entails jettisoning the dead weight. The standard of what to keep and what to discard is generally quite simple when we begin to see ourselves with clarity. That which is authentic gives us energy, and that which is inauthentic takes it away from us. We would go a long way simply by keeping this one formula continually in mind.

This function of the Diamond Sphere is extremely powerful, which is why the influence of Pluto has such an ambiguous influence in astrology. Pluto is the illuminating ray that deconstructs the superego, with a resulting liberation of tremendous energy. This can go well, or it can go very poorly, depending on the underlying structure of the personality which is revealed. If the influence of the Yellow Sphere is well-developed, and has put together a strong core self with a strong sense of integrity, then the authentic self is free to unfold in all of its brilliance. If there is not a well-developed core ego, however, then what is exposed by the dissolution of the superego is simply pure *id*. It is generally fair to say then that the influence of Pluto can be positive or negative depending on whether the individual is ready for it or not. The essential action of Pluto is to illuminate and bring to awareness that which has been hidden. This makes it extremely effective at releasing repressed material, which can be immensely disruptive if one is unprepared. Pluto is also intensely involved in breaking down a false ego that is no longer viable. When one has become enmeshed in a false personality that is so devoid of authenticity that the spirit is suffocating to death inside of it, it is Pluto that will engineer a means to split the straight-jacket wide open. In some cases, this can manifest as a mental breakdown, or it can be projected outward in the form of external catastrophe.

Pluto is often associated with death. Esoterically speaking, death represents the dissolution of a way of being which has outlived its purpose, in order to liberate the inherent energy to a higher way of being. This does not necessarily mean physical death as we know it. In the context that we have described so far, Pluto precipitates the death of a false self so that we may be reborn to an authentic self. If one is not ready for this kind of transformation, then the Pluto influence may translate to a radical dissolution of one's external circumstances, or possibly even physical death in some cases. The impact of Pluto's influence can be softened however by our own state of mental preparation. Broadly speaking, the chief reason why people construct a false self is because human beings do not like contradiction. In particular, they do not like the contradiction between self-expectations and reality. They are also especially uncomfortable with what are seen to be contradictory desires and contradictory feelings toward a single person or subject. The subsequent impulse is to then bury one side of the contradiction from awareness. For instance, it is never comfortable to feel both love and hate for the same individual, and so either the love or the hate will be buried. The stronger the contradiction, the more rigid must be the thought-structure that is tasked with concealing it. These buried tensions conspire to create cracks over time, though. To liberate the consciousness, the first step must be a willingness to embrace contradiction.

This is not a position that most of us would think to consciously assume, because we are accustomed to thinking about reality in terms of logical, binary truth statements. The traffic light is either red or green. It is either day or night. I am asleep or I am awake. This is of course a completely valid means of processing reality on one level. But it is also true that countless aspects of our existence are driven by opposing forces that either balance each other out in a state of equilibrium, or create a dynamic imbalance that evolves into a new order of things. As a purely physical example, we can observe the opposing electrical forces of repulsion and attraction which govern so much of our physical phenomena. We can also point to the opposition of centrifugal and centripetal force which keeps the planets in their orbits. In the realm of ethics, there is the opposition between my rights and your rights, or between the rights of the individual and the rights of society. Politics is an ongoing tension between opposing ideas. Our goals are an opposition between our present state and our ideal future. And our evaluation of other people usually encompasses an opposition between their strengths and their flaws.

These contradictory forces will always create a state of tension, and that tension will either be a static tension or a dynamic tension.

Every stable system is held in place by a static tension, whereas a dynamic tension transforms the situation into something new. Psychologically, the tension between opposing thoughts and feelings can be very uncomfortable, and so there is a natural human tendency to want to resolve that tension into a binary outcome. We want to come to a clear decision that this person is either good or bad. That I am right and they are wrong. That we belong to this tribe or to that one, and that our feelings toward another person are either love or hate. The desire to resolve these contradictory feelings can compel us to adopt a final judgment that sounds convincing on paper, but which does not actually acknowledge the truth and the validity of both opposing forces. The result is an apparent stability which is actually an illusion. One side of the opposition is denied and exiled out of awareness. But it does not on that account cease to exert its influence. It has simply been repressed, and a layer of falsification is required to pretend that it no longer exists. Nevertheless, it does still exist and will continue to affect the balance of things in a manner that is unconscious rather than conscious.

To embrace contradiction is to recognize that every aspect of our existence is in a state of either static or dynamic tension, and to learn how to be comfortable with that. It is a recognition of the fact that to eliminate the tension of opposing forces would be to eliminate the motive power of life itself. By accepting these tensions, we are no longer looking for binary judgments, but rather for balances of power and states of equilibrium. One also understands that the balance of forces may be fluid and fluctuate over time, leaning more to this side one day and more to that side the next. The willingness to embrace contradiction undoes the stuckness of rigid thinking, and gives freer scope for new solutions and new possibilities. By allowing the opposing motives to stand together face-to-face, we give them the latitude and the flexibility to feel each other out, to probe the boundaries between them, and to shift the vectors of force into unexpected resolutions. By holding the contradiction in awareness rather than burying it under subconsciousness, we allow it to play out the creative dialectic of thesis, antithesis, and synthesis.

What we are talking about here is a loosening of the fabric of the mind, which ordinarily would be considered the definition of insanity. But the nature of the Yellow Sphere is to hold the elements of the personality together not in a rigid structure, but in a fluid and organic confederation. The Yellow Sphere is a coherence of a much higher order than the rigid structure of the mind, and so it is capable of holding together contradictory forces. The Yellow Sphere is the *natural order* of things, whereas the mind tends to create structures of an *artificial order*. This artificiality of personality is what happens when one's sense of self is rooted too much in the Orange Sphere rather than the Yellow Sphere. It is the state of being "stuck in one's head". The influence of Pluto is to unstick what is stuck. As an archetype of both illumination and death, it disintegrates the structures that stand in the way of clear-seeing.

At the end of this process, we ideally come away with a personality that is an authentic and genuine expression of the true self, a clear lens through which to focus the ray of the essential will. This is not to say that there won't continue to be compromises and adaptations to the social system that we live in. It is not realistic or even necessarily desirable to attempt to dispense with the mask or the superego altogether. But any adaptation that we make should be conscious rather than unconscious. So even when we must make an adaptation that does not reflect our authenticity, we should at least strive to play the part with self-awareness. To believe that the mask is our true identity is to wear it poorly. One could go so far as to say that in self-awareness there is a more authentic way of wearing the mask. It goes without saying that having a sense of humor and a keen sense of irony takes us a long way toward holding together the contradictions within our own existence. Indeed, an appreciation for the implicit absurdity of it all is a distinctly Plutonian perspective which celebrates contradiction as the basis of all creative tension. The fact that life can defy all of our so-called rational expectations with such audacity inspires a certain kind of admiration, if seen through the lens of irony. It reminds us that whatever kind of order our logical mind attempts to impose on the world is ultimately subsumed within a much wider circle. But there is an even grander audacity in our ability to embrace the absurdity, and to laugh at it. With that kind of gesture, we out-circle the circle, and this is Pluto at its most sublime.

Magic and Manifestation

Much attention is given nowadays to an idea popularly known as the "Law of Attraction". This idea is based on the theory that all of physical existence begins from thought, and precipitates from the realm of pure thought into concrete reality. Implicit in this idea is the notion that the universe itself is but a grand thought-form in the mind of God. But the human mind, insofar as it is a reflection and a *fractal* of the mind of God, also has the power of turning thought into reality. Modern theories of magic are grounded firmly on this idea. This contemporary conception of magic began to crystallize in the mid-19th century with the writings of the French occultist Eliphas Levi, but the concepts articulated by Levi can be seen to evolve out of the theories of mesmerism and animal magnetism which began to circulate in the late 1700s. The mesmerists observed that a patient with a physical malady, when placed into a hypnotic trance and given the right suggestions, could undergo miraculous healing. This capacity of the mind to affect the physical body is not at all controversial. It is recognized by medical science to this day as the placebo effect. The theoretical leap from mesmerism to magic is a much bolder hypothesis, however. It is based on the assumption that if the mind can have an impact on the physical body, then perhaps it can impact physical reality beyond the body as well.

This idea that physical reality proceeds from thought has produced a vast literature and philosophy around the theory of *manifestation*. This theory suggests that the mind is constantly spinning our thoughts into the reality that we experience, every second of every day. The critical question is whether this process is happening *consciously* or *unconsciously*. Or to put it another way, is the process of manifestation operating intentionally or mechanically? One would have to argue that for the vast majority of people, the majority of the time, this law operates mechanically. When one has become set in an established pattern of thought, then the thought-pattern precipitates into a reality which reflects that belief. This reality then validates the thought-pattern and solidifies it into an expectation that this will continue to be the reality that we experience, day in and day out. And so the manifestation becomes mechanical and self-sustaining. As long as we do not question the belief that *this* is the reality which we have been dealt, it will continue to run off of its own inertia.

Magic, by contrast, would be the conscious and intentional application of the law of manifestation. It is the deliberate focus of thought and will in order to precipitate the outcome that one desires. Over the centuries, magic has been associated with various forms of outlandish ritual and spell-casting. All of this needs to be put into the proper perspective. Technically speaking, no form of ritual is necessary in order to make manifestation work, nor can the mechanical application of any ritual effect results. The use of ritual magic should instead be thought of as a focusing technique. Its purpose is to enhance the power of the operation by activating the subconscious mind, which engages with reality both *symbolically* and *theatrically*. This mode of operation is observed in dreams, in which the underlying concerns of the conscious self are expressed every night in a form of symbolic theatre. The use of spells and rituals engages a similar mode of symbolic expression in order to shift the consciousness into that dream-like state in which the subconscious is more fluent and familiar. It is well to understand that the effectiveness of this method depends on the ability to allow oneself into the hypnotic state that the ritual is designed to invoke. A spell that is performed mechanically or begrudgingly is worse than useless. One must have the full engagement of the subconscious in order to bring power to the operation. In this regard, it is best that the ritual be customized to one's own personal symbolic map. If the symbolism involved lacks personal meaning or *fails to excite*, then the engagement of the subconscious will be weak.

The realm of manifestation involves primarily the three lower spheres, each of which represents a principal component of the process. The Orange Sphere is the most obvious element in all of this, as all of the literature on manifestation focuses on the need to form a *clear mental image* of the desired outcome. The

Magic and Manifestation

importance of visualization is stressed so consistently that it does not require much elaboration here. What is less obvious, but equally important nonetheless, is the *quality* of the visualization. It is not enough to simply *picture* the desired outcome, one must also *feel* the emotional excitement of experiencing that outcome. In other words, the mental image must be *animated* with the energy of the Green Sphere.

This angle on the matter is easy to overlook but vitally important, as without this understanding we are going about the whole thing from the wrong direction. That is to say, one could easily formulate a mental image that has no animating force behind it, because it does not map to a genuinely felt desire. In the natural order of things, *form follows essence*. When form gets ahead of essence, then we have artificiality and inauthenticity. So in the realm of manifestation, we do best to first understand the essence of what we want. In the clarification of that essence, the appropriate form will emerge. The essence is what *gives life* to the form. Without it, the form is dead. This is exactly what artificiality is. It is *dead form*.

Manifestation must therefore begin not with the mental image but with the *essence* of what you desire, and the essence of the desired outcome can best be described as how it makes you *feel*. This essence should be reduced to something very simple, as the purest essence has the most potent animating energy. Freedom, love, joy, security, fun, serenity, creative power - these are some of the characteristic emotional states that people desire to bring into their lives. Fundamentally, the essence of what we desire can universally be boiled down to a feeling of *excitation,* which may come in many different flavors. Even feelings that we would normally consider passive, such as serenity or security, if we allow ourselves to really sink into the essence of the feeling, can be felt to resonate a low-key hum or vibration. It is this latent excitation that provides the animating energy.

When you are clear on the essence of what you want, the next step is to formulate the image of the desired outcome, and the best way to approach this is to *allow* the form to follow the essence.

This is best achieved by settling yourself into a hypnotic state. Auto-hypnosis is really the key to manifestation, as it is the key to unlocking the power of the subconscious. In the hypnotic state, the critical faculty of the everyday consciousness is relaxed. This allows a number of important things to happen. First, it allows the purity of the essence to reveal itself, because the mind is not trying to overlay it with false narratives and presuppositions. Second, the image-forming capacity of the mind becomes far more fluid and labile. It responds readily to the essence that you have captured and begins to generate the images that *most appropriately* symbolize that essence. This is much like the manner in which the subconscious generates dream images in your sleep. The hypnotic state is in fact a condition halfway between waking reality and dream. It is a state in which the imagination has the freedom to form the correct symbols of the desired outcome, and it is important to *not question* those symbols as they are being created, as well as to give those symbols the time and the space that they need to fully evolve. Finally, the hypnotic state allows the subconscious to become *fully invested* in the image that is created, thus throwing the full force of the Purple Sphere into its manifestation.

This is the element of *desire* that is so often talked about as being essential to the process. Intense desire is the hydraulic force of the Purple Sphere that drives manifestation. But this force of desire must be understood clearly, otherwise it acts counter-productively. Manifestation is driven by a gap between the desired outcome and the existing reality. This creates a dynamic tension, a contradiction. The impulse to bridge this gap is the force of desire, but if one doesn't know how to achieve the outcome then that impulse can devolve into frustration, bitterness, and self-pity. These emotions will turn the focus of attention to the feeling of lack, which will only act to manifest more lack. The force of desire must be kept completely pure and free from any adulteration of frustration or self-pity. This means that you must be capable of experiencing the contradiction not as a frustration but as a *voltage* of potential energy. In electronics, voltage is the force that is generated when two powerful but opposite charges are attracted to each other, but there is no closed circuit to allow the movement of electricity between them. The opposite charges have a strong desire to come together, but the gap between them creates an intense potential energy. If the charge becomes strong enough, it may even create a spark through thin air to bridge the gap. This force of voltage is the power of the Purple Sphere. If you allow it to leak into emotions of frustration and self-pity, then it will work self-destructively and tear you down from the inside. But if the voltage is kept pure and focused then it generates a strong potential energy in the form of *personal power* which will work to crystallize the desired outcome.

There is another aspect to how the Purple Sphere plays into this, and that is the condensation of the mental image into something that *feels real*. This is a point that is often touched upon in the literature of manifestation, but it needs to be contextualized in order to be fully understood. We have spoken of the Purple Sphere as being that attribute of substantive force by which we impact our surroundings, and by which our surroundings have an impact on us. It is the quality through which things become *real* to us, as opposed to those things which have a negligible impact upon us and are therefore *less real*. This is typically how we distinguish "reality" from "imagination". Reality impacts us in a way that imagination does not. With regard to manifestation, we are frequently told that we must invest the mental image with enough sensory clarity and detail that it begins to blur the boundary between imagination and actual lived experience.

This points us back to the hypnotic state as being essential to the process. In a deep enough state of hypnosis, a subject can lose the distinction between reality and imagination. We can think of this as an enhanced state of the *suspension of disbelief* that we adopt whenever we watch a film. As we engage with the narrative of the film, we allow ourselves to be temporarily immersed into an experience in which we *accept* the reality of the story that we are watching. The sights and sounds of the experience are allowed to impact us and to elicit emotional reactions within us *as if* we were actually living them. The hypnotic state is a suspension of disbelief in which we produce the desired outcome in our imagination and then *allow* ourselves to be immersed into it to such an extent that we no longer draw a distinction as to whether it is real or unreal.

This ability to inject the visualization with enough substance to make it *seem* real must be thought of as in some sense catalyzing the manifestation process. The element of *faith* is often mentioned as an essential ingredient to manifestation, however this word is not always clearly understood. Most people think that it simply means believing strongly that the desired outcome will eventually become a reality. This is not really the correct mindset, however, because it still places the outcome somewhere in the future. The secret to manifestation is not really about believing that something *will* become reality. It is more about the suspension of disbelief in which we embrace the outcome as if it were *already* reality. It is about creating the simulation in your imagination just for the present moment, establishing the energy of what that feels like, and living it as if you were actually in it. This is also why we are consistently advised not to invest any mental energy in imagining *how* we will get to the outcome. Because trying to picture the *way* that you get from A to B simply materializes the space between A and B, whereas picturing yourself *at point B* short-circuits that distance. The focus should always be on the end result, not the process.

Having outlined the theory of how manifestation works, there is just as much theory around what causes it to *not* work. The short and comprehensive answer to this question is internal psychological resistance or friction, but we will need to elaborate on the causes of this friction.

The first principal cause of friction would be a lack of clarity as to what we actually want. This usually comes down to not being focused on the essence of what is desired. The result is that we instead formulate a mental image of something that seems like what we *ought* to want, because it fits the standard profile of what society considers to be indicators of success or happiness. But if it is not true to our innate desire, then it will not have the animating life-energy and will merely be an empty shell. The most important question to ask yourself in order to get clarity on this issue is whether the desire is driven by *love* or by *fear*. If the outcome that you picture fills you with a genuine feeling of excitement, joy, or empowerment, then it is a *living* image with motive energy. If instead, it feels like something that merely fills an emptiness, then your heart and soul are not genuinely invested in it.

The best example of how to think about this is in the manifestation of wealth. The primary question should be, what do you actually want wealth *for*? Is it simply because you are afraid of poverty? Is it because you feel stuck and are looking for a way out? If that is the case, then fear or stuckness is the essence of what you will attract. To truly tap into the essence of abundance, you must frame it in *positive* terms. We could say then that the essence of wealth is the freedom and empowerment to go wherever you want to go and to do whatever you want to do. This is a much more powerful force than fear or frustration. If you examine any negative emotion, you will see that it is actually the flip side of some positive impulse. The negative emotion represents the frustrated desire for something good. So the first important step of manifestation is to trace back to the *impulse of love* that is behind your desire. This will be the secret to moving things forward. The key indicator to look for is that positive emotions will make you feel buoyant, radiant, and expansive, whereas negative emotions will make you feel heavy and constricted. If you are visualizing something that does not put you into that radiant and expansive state, then you must take a step back and figure out what will actually get you to that place.

It should become clear from all of this that the better part of manifestation is self-awareness and self-discovery. This demands the type of clear-seeing that cuts through any false narratives that we may have been telling ourselves about what we want. It is a long-standing axiom of magic that the *word* has power. To speak your intent carries magical force. But there is a very important qualifier to this - you must *speak the truth*. This means that you must first of all be honest and clear with yourself about your true will, and not speak something that falls flat. You will recognize the truth as being that which comes out of your mouth most naturally, without resistance and without friction. It will roll off of the tongue with its own sparkle and its own momentum. To uncover this truth means peeling away the social conditioning which has layered upon us all of those ideas that are not our own about what it means to measure up in the world. For most of us, there is nothing magical about the fear of not measuring up in other people's eyes. Magical power comes from *being who you are*.

Another source of friction, and the one that is most commonly addressed, is *doubt* about the possibility of achieving the desired goal. The emphasis on faith in manifestation is all about overcoming doubt, but we need to analyze the substance of doubt more closely in order to truly come to terms with it. More often than not, this source of friction is not truly a belief that we *can't* reach the goal, but rather an apprehension of what we would have to give up in order to get there. This could be an investment of time and resources that we can't get back if the venture proves unsuccessful. Very often it is a sense of security that one would have to sacrifice in order to leave the familiar and step into unknown territory. If we really drill down into the underlying premises of our doubt, it is not so much a conviction that we are simply incapable of accomplishing the goal. If we invest enough time, effort, and patience, most of us are capable of achieving any outcome. The sticking point is more typically the *opportunity cost* of giving up one thing that we value to pursue another thing of value.

There is a key lesson to take away from this, and that is the importance of grasping the overarching vision of your life, and what you want it to look like as a whole. Indeed, you will have to figure out how your life fits together as a unified vision before you can introduce any new elements into it. Simply having an objective that is detached and devoid of meaning does not carry much weight. It is necessary to reach an understanding of why the desired element *needs* to be a part of your existence. You must figure out what essential space it fills as a piece of the overall puzzle.

In a sense, this requires us to have a *growth plan* for our existence. This is a truth of the matter that is not typically at the forefront of people's minds when they think about manifestation. There is usually a tacit assumption that one can simply visualize

Magic and Manifestation

and manifest an entirely new circumstance in life, and yet still be the same person that you were before. On reflection, this makes no sense whatsoever. Your circumstances will always revert back to the essence of who you are. *Something about you must change* in order to manifest a dramatic change in the direction of your life. With this in mind, it becomes clear to us that the objective of manifestation should not be limited to simply concrete outcomes in life. You should also aim to manifest yourself developing the talents, capabilities, and attitudes that are necessary to realize the changes that you seek.

At a deeper level, this growth of self is really the whole point of manifestation. The outcome is simply a *symbol* of the unfoldment of the inner potentials. Once this is recognized, the limiting attitude of doubt can be seen to be irrelevant. If we think of the outcome as an end in itself, and the failure to achieve the outcome as an absolute loss of time and resources, then there is logically a cost-benefit analysis to be had with regard to whether we make the attempt or even acknowledge the desire. But from a higher perspective, we know that a repressed desire is not a healthy thing, and that it is not going to just go away quietly. It represents something that we recognize deep down as essential to our growth as a creative being. If we look at it from this perspective, then giving up on a desire because it feels unattainable does not actually resolve the contradiction that we are trying to avoid. Nor is the attainment of the desire the ultimate end goal. It is far more useful to hold the contradiction in our awareness in such a way that we allow it to *transform* us at the most fundamental level.

In this respect, the practice of visualizing a desired outcome in a way that evokes the essence of what we desire brings its own benefits. If it allows us to activate the positive energies that we are trying to feel, then we are already at a higher place than we were before. And if we can sit still in that higher energy for its own sake, and be open to the transformation that it works upon us, then that is time that we have *not* spent engaging in negative thoughts and emotions. To fret and worry over the fact that we are not yet seeing actual results would therefore be missing the actual point. The inner transformation is the deeper objective, and when that transformation is complete then the results will crystallize spontaneously.

We'll conclude this chapter by touching briefly on the distinction between white magic and black magic. There have been differing perspectives on how exactly to define this distinction. Traditional folklore would say that white magic invokes the aid of angelic spirits while black magic invokes demonic spirits. This, however, is perhaps best thought of in symbolic terms. Others have defined black magic as any magic that aims to harm or control another individual, which would seem to be closer to a meaningful definition. Some would assert that any magic for personal gain is black magic, but one could argue that this is coming from a moral standpoint that is much too simplistic and puritanical. If we try to frame the question within the context of our Tree of Life, then a useful way of looking at it would be to say that white magic is guided by the influence of the Yellow Sphere, and in that regard, its ultimate aim is a higher state of growth and awareness for either oneself or other people. To the extent that the realized end goal fits in with some overall vision of harmonious development, it can be seen as an application of white magic.

Now insofar as the Purple Sphere is the primary driver of manifestation, this guiding influence of the Yellow Sphere is not at all necessary for magic to actually work. The unadulterated energy of primal instinct is intensely magical in its own right. For the individual who is driven primarily by the *id*, this raw energy of the Purple Sphere is their default mode of being in the world, and when they bring that energy to focus they can be remarkably effective at manifesting results. These results will be found to be consistently self-serving. While this in itself does not qualify as black magic, the fact that these individuals lack an underlying sense of coherence means that their ways of manifesting results will tend to be out of harmony with their surroundings, and destructive to those around them. It is especially notable that the results which they achieve will not involve any kind of personal growth. They will be acts of either vindictive malice, immediate gratification, or superficial self-aggrandizement. Another notable characteristic of such people is that despite their seeming ability to make short-term gains, they tend to eventually self-destruct in the end. Without the unifying sense of coherence and purpose that the Yellow Sphere brings, there is nothing to hold their life together in the long run. And so the essential nature of black magic is that ultimately everything falls apart, because there is no underlying rhyme or reason. It is unchecked primitive instinct operating without the benefit of a unifying vision or insight, and in that respect, it can be summed up by the word *entropy*.

Part IV
The Twenty-Two Paths

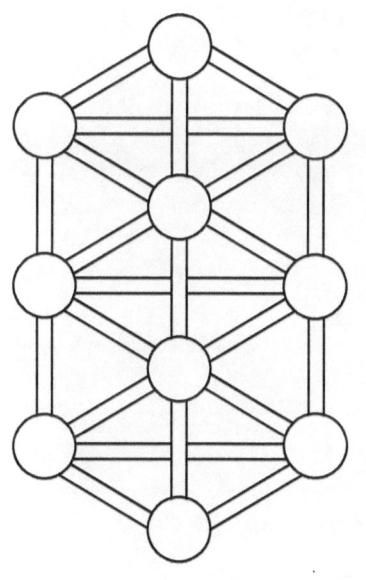

Judgment
Diamond Sphere to White Sphere

We have established up to this point that the Diamond Sphere represents consciousness, and the White Sphere represents the universal life-energy. One of the main facets of the White Sphere is the idea of *freedom,* insofar as the abundance of life-energy gives us a capacity for mobility, adaptation, and creative power. The interplay of these two spheres, therefore, presents us with a theme of *liberated consciousness,* which can also be described as *awakening* or *illumination.*

This key is represented by the Tarot card of Judgment, which has obvious symbolic references to the Book of Revelation. The card depicts an angel in the heavens sounding a trumpet blast, while three figures - a man, woman, and child - rise from their sepulchers to new life. The title of the card makes reference to the final judgment of the Apocalypse, in which the world is destroyed by fire, but in its place there emerges a new heaven, a new earth, and a new Jerusalem. The principal archetype depicted in both the card of Judgment and the Book of Revelation is that of *resurrection.* But the resurrection symbolized here is not a rebirth from physical death, but rather a liberation of the mind from a state of being buried under ignorance, illusion, and *limiting belief.* When the chains of limiting belief have been burst asunder and cast aside, then the consciousness is not only *clarified,* it is also *energized* by the influx of new possibilities that have opened up before it. We can therefore say that this key represents the fire in the mind of God. It is the active side of consciousness, as opposed to the passive side of consciousness which is represented by the High Priestess. This is the universal creative power of existence, which brings forth new ideas, new visions, and new potentials. Thus we have here the central motif of *renewal* as represented by the three figures rising from the grave.

The essence of *fire* is a central theme of this key, and in a dual sense. On the one hand, Judgment represents the *alchemical fire* that separates the pure from the impure, the subtle from the gross, the wheat from the chaff. This is the fire of illumination that burns away the bonds of illusion and self-imposed slavery. In the symbolism of Revelation, it is the fire which consumes the corruption of the existing world order, leaving space for a new world to rise up like the phoenix from the ashes. On the other hand, we have the primal creative fire which *must rush in* to fill the vacuum when the mind is clarified. Because this is in fact the fundamental nature of purification: when that which is dead weight and non-essential has been cleared away, it creates a space into which a higher order of energy can and will flow. That is the *raison d'etre* of the purification process. Just as a purified crystal transmits light, the purified consciousness transmits the creative power of limitless possibility.

The experience of illumination can be characterized as the "aha" moment... that flash of realization in which things suddenly come together and start to make sense. In a more radical sense, it can also be experienced as the moment in which one realizes that one has been needlessly laboring under false beliefs and false values. This is the state of mind that Nietzsche described as "beyond good and evil", in which all values are re-evaluated, and the old order is turned upside-down. Astrologically, the Diamond Sphere and the White Sphere correspond to Pluto and Uranus. The one embodies penetrating insight, the other unbounded energy. Both of these planets are associated with revolutionary upheaval. The synthesis of their energies brings about a radical clarity that leads to radical transformation and paradigm shift.

In the card of Judgment, as with that of The Sun, we have the image of a child. In each case, the symbolism is derivative of the White Sphere which represents newness and freshness. In this card in particular, it represents a state of innocence, seeing with a fresh pair of eyes, in which the mind becomes a *tabula rasa*. In traditional Kabbalah, the White Sphere is called "Wisdom" and the Black Sphere "Understanding". Both of these names describe states of consciousness, and in both cases, the designation

Judgment

is derived from the connecting path to the Diamond Sphere. Understanding is the passive side of consciousness, the path of the High Priestess which empathizes and merges into the Other. Wisdom is the active side of consciousness, the path of the dragon that lives and breathes the fire of creative transformation. It is well to note that this aspect of consciousness is key to unlocking the power of the Red Sphere, because the clarity of awakening and the ensuing influx of energy actualizes the authentic will.

The word that perhaps best describes the essence of this key is *illumination*. But what exactly does this indicate? There are actually multiple layers of meaning to the idea of illumination. In the narrowest sense of the word, illumination could mean a new piece of knowledge, a new discovery, or the revelation of something that we were not aware of before. At this simplest level of interpretation, the synthesis of the Diamond Sphere and the White Sphere manifests as a shift in awareness or consciousness of something new. But this in itself does not fully capture the essence of illumination. We learn new things and make new discoveries every day, however most of them are not particularly meaningful or transformative. For a new awareness to be truly illuminating, it must open up a new realm of *possibility*. Illumination in the larger sense is therefore an experience of *epiphany*. It is a renewal of consciousness that radically changes the existing order of things, a consciousness in which it is possible to make *great leaps* in understanding.

It is impossible to grasp the full meaning of this kind of illumination without exploring the subjective experience of it. Illumination quite literally feels like a state in which the consciousness is "lit up" with the fire of *all possibility*. When the light bulb goes on and shakes apart the old limiting thought-patterns, the energy that is released is more than just metaphorical. It is a state of *mental excitation* in which the consciousness is propelled forward with rocket fuel. If we equate energy quite literally with possibility (which is truly the key to understanding the White Sphere), then the breaking apart of limiting beliefs unlocks a whole new scope of possibilities. This manifests as a lighting-up of consciousness with the sparkling scintillation of all those possible futures. This is precisely why the White Sphere is represented by the color white. Because white light is the sum of all possible colors and all possible frequencies, coalesced into a single cloud of luminosity.

An illuminated consciousness is therefore an *energized* consciousness. But we must understand that this energy is a very real and palpable energy, as real as the energy that drives an internal combustion engine. The state of illumination is not just an abstract concept of the scope of possibilities. It is a state in which you actually *feel* and *experience* the energy that is humming and whirring within that cloud of possibilities. And that humming energy *propels* the consciousness forward into new frontiers. It *animates* and *enlivens* the consciousness with creative power. Only when we feel this animating energy come to life inside of us can we say that we have truly grasped the infinite potential.

This state of awareness is likened to awakening, because it is to the ordinary waking consciousness what waking consciousness is to sleep. We generally think of sleep as a profoundly dull and limited state of consciousness. When we dream, we move through the dream like a robot, possessing little in the way of autonomy or self-awareness. We have no real willpower, and the events of the dream simply happen to us as if we were puppets on a stage. When we awaken from sleep, the illumination of our consciousness puts us on a whole new level of being, in which we are capable of a spectrum of choices and potentials that we were incapable of in the sleeping state. The illumination represented by the card of Judgment is like awakening to an even brighter level of awareness, compared to which the ordinary waking consciousness seems like a dull sleep-walking trance.

Metaphorically, this is like being raised from the dead, in which death is likened to a state of the most limited possibility and the most limited mobility of creative thought. A truly illuminating realization, a "revelation" so to speak, is one in which the mind is flooded with a whole vista of new possibilities. This is what makes it a "flash of light" as opposed to just any other mundane realization.

Judgment

In quantum mechanics, the electron orbiting an atomic nucleus is described not as a discrete particle with a distinct location in space, but rather as a cloud of probabilities. The consciousness of the White Sphere can be likened to seeing into the quantum cloud. Which is to say, seeing into all possibilities at once. This has also been described as the state of "thinking outside the box", in which we look past the self-imposed blinders of limiting assumptions and see into the range of endless possibilities. It is in that higher state of energized awareness that we are able to create something new. When the fire of illumination fills the mind, then the mind is impelled by this energy to go exploring in all manner of directions, to find new truths and new possibilities. When the consciousness is propelled with rocket fuel, then it is able to make breakthroughs. In this active mode of being, it is not just a passive awareness but rather a *creative consciousness*. One of the clear signs of this illuminated mode of consciousness will be spontaneous laughter. Depression, after all, is nothing more than the overwhelming sense of a lack of creative drive and potential. The White Sphere inspires above all the spirit of playfulness, and the influx of the energy of limitless possibility invariably triggers the urge to laugh out loud.

At the highest level, illumination is experienced as the awareness of that universal field of limitless potential which has been characterized by mystics as the presence of God. This can only be described as a singular cloud of omnipotence that pervades all of space. It is every possibility, everywhere at once. It saturates the emptiness of the void and animates every molecule with the vibrancy of the *One Life*. Those who have experienced this illumination have been of the single opinion that it cannot adequately be put into words. The best that we can say about it is that one is filled with the undeniable realization that all things are possible, and the power of this realization is felt as a transforming luminescence that penetrates down to the cellular level.

The High Priestess
Diamond Sphere to Black Sphere

Whereas the key of Judgment represents the active and creative side of consciousness, the High Priestess represents consciousness in the mode of the passive observer. It is consciousness that is able to sit still and *listen* to its surroundings, to tune into the world around oneself and pick up the signals at all levels of perception. This capacity to tune in requires the ability to empty the mind of all distracting thought. It demands that we *make space* in our awareness in order to be receptive to that which we are perceiving, to allow it to speak to us and to reveal itself in its own voice, without imposing our own filters and preconceptions upon it. This ability to be a clear lens is essential to understanding the power of the High Priestess. Whereas the White Sphere is a transforming fire, the Black Sphere is a perfect stillness that is able to absorb everything into its depth.

The Black Sphere is the fabric of space itself, and despite the apparent separation that we experience, the underlying reality is that all beings are woven together into this one unifying fabric. Everything communicates therefore by means of vibration through this fabric. And so the path of the High Priestess represents a state of attentiveness to the fabric, and to the vibrations circulating throughout it. This pertains not just to sense perception as it is commonly understood, but also to intuition and extra-sensory perception. It is important to understand however that these faculties are simply sensory faculties of a higher order. That the intuition is spoken of as a "sixth sense" represents more of a literal truth than not. In order to develop the so-called extra-sensory faculties, you must therefore first learn to develop the sensory faculties, as the principle is all one and the same. Which is to say, you must learn to *listen* in every way. You must learn how to be still and empty so that the information is allowed to flow in. You must learn how to see, hear, taste, smell, and touch. It is all about opening up and making space for the impressions to enter into your awareness.

The High Priestess embodies the Plutonic capacity of *seeing deeply* into the essence of things, seeing into the core, and penetrating into the heart of the matter. This is typically thought of as a very feminine type of intelligence, because it represents the skill of feeling into a situation, feeling into others, reading a person, reading the room, and being sensitive to what is going on around you. Whereas the traditionally masculine type of intelligence is flashy and creative and innovative, this type of intelligence is quiet but deeply penetrating in the most Pluto kind of way. It is the intelligence of sussing things out and sniffing out the truth. The feminine facet of Pluto is that part which sees right through you. In that respect, it represents the skill of psychoanalysis *par excellence*. This ability to see into the heart of things and to see into other people is why Pluto is associated with great power, especially *covert* power. Real power comes not from brute force, but from having enough understanding of how the system works to know what buttons to push. This type of understanding is leverage, and *secret* knowledge is the greatest form of leverage.

This power of the High Priestess comes not so much from an intellectual grasp of things, but more from *feeling into* one's surroundings, and so this aspect of Pluto has a strong resonance with both the Moon and with Scorpio, which is expressed as intensity of feeling. It is not the Mercurial "left-brained" consciousness of words and numbers and theories, but rather the consciousness of "vibes" and essences that are communicated back and forth through the ether. A certain kind of dissolution of boundaries has to take place for this mode of communication to occur, and this requires an attitude of profound openness that is characteristic of the Black Sphere. Openness to experience and openness to the world at large is what allows us to be receptive and tuned in to our surroundings.

This radical openness also comes with a deep sense of vulnerability that we must be willing to face in order to experience the *intimacy* of this mode of understanding. The Black Sphere represents the experience of being *thrown into the world,* of being immersed into the dark waters of existence. From the moment of birth, we are tossed into the deep end of the pool, so to speak. As much as we try to fortify ourselves and erect our defensive structures, our lives are inextricably bound up with the world around us. To successfully navigate this existence, we must be willing to some extent to merge and blend with our surroundings. We must be willing to merge emotionally and psychologically with other people - enough at least to get an understanding of the inner workings of the systems and the people that we are intertwined with, so that we may know how to manipulate the psychological currents toward our survival. This also requires us to expose certain facets of our own inner workings however, and so there is a delicate balance between intimacy and security, all of which are deeply Scorpionic concerns.

The Black Sphere represents what we describe esoterically as *The Void,* which is an emptiness that is also a fullness, because it creates the space for all possibility. With the High Priestess, we are talking about the intersection of consciousness and The Void, and so there is a distinct element of Plutonic *nihilism* to this facet. This is not by any means a destructive or unhealthy nihilism, however. It is rather the creative *deconstruction* of preconceptions and belief systems that allows for a more clear and open assessment of the field of possibilities. It is the dissolution of prevailing mental constructs that allows us to get to a deeper truth. This is the meditative state of simply clearing the mind so that it becomes a *tabula rasa*, a blank slate, thereby allowing us to absorb impressions and assimilate them like a sponge. The consciousness that is not burdened with interfering preconceptions is able to see far and deep. The High Priestess represents a mind like a big crystal ball.

The symbolism of the Tarot card, particularly in the Rider-Waite deck, is quite rich with meaning. Some sources equate the High Priestess with the Virgin Mary. Chapter 12 of the Book of Revelation speaks of a woman clothed in the sun with the moon beneath her feet, who gives birth to a son who will rule all the nations. If we assume this figure to represent the Virgin Mary,

The High Priestess

then the crescent moon at the feet of the High Priestess evokes the same iconography. This would suggest that the Virgin Mary in some sense represents the state of empty mind or empty consciousness that allows access to higher levels of understanding. Like the moon, this mode of consciousness does not emit its own light, but rather absorbs and reflects the light from that which is around it. This gives us the special ability to tune in to the ebb and flow of things, so that we intuitively know the right time to act. The High Priestess above all represents the *psychic* consciousness and the power of channeling, especially channeling of the Higher Self. This is the root of all magical knowledge and understanding, because it is a consciousness that is tapped into the very fabric of creation.

Behind the High Priestess, we see hung between two pillars a veil with a pattern of pomegranates. If we look closely, it appears that beyond the veil and the pillars there lies a sea. Interestingly enough, we see a similar pattern of pomegranates worn by The Empress, who represents the full sensuality of the physical world. The implication here is that beyond the veil of the physical senses lies the ocean of undifferentiated root-substance which is the Black Sphere. The key to all hidden knowledge lies in seeing past the veil and into the fabric of creation. It is the High Priestess who shows us the way beyond the veil.

The Hanged Man
Diamond Sphere to Indigo Sphere

We have seen that the High Priestess symbolizes consciousness which is directed outward, directed at the other, and focused toward the world at large. The path of Judgment, on the other hand, represents consciousness directed toward the realm of possibility, and toward the future. In the case of the Hanged Man, we have consciousness that is abstracted above the realm of time and space altogether, and in that mode it becomes focused back upon itself. That is to say, it becomes *self-consciousness*.

This is an attribute which most people assume that they already have, but few actually do. The reason for this is that their sense of self is tied to the mind-body complex and all its forms of expression, whereas the true center of identity transcends the realm of physical manifestation. And so as long as consciousness identifies with the physical and mental representation of self, it does not actually recognize itself but sees instead the *projection* of itself into material reality, which is in a certain sense the shadow of self. To experience true self-awareness, therefore, it is necessary to attain a point of perspective that stands *outside the system*. Only in this way do we reach the state of independence which genuine self-awareness entails. If we try to represent this by a geometrical metaphor, that point of perspective would be in a direction *perpendicular* to the plane of reference. Imagine if you will, a point on a piece of paper that has miraculously lifted itself *above* the paper. It is then at a vantage point outside and above all vectors of force that operate within that plane, and therefore it is no longer subject in any way to the eddies and currents circulating within that system. From this extra-dimensional perspective, one could observe the vectors of force and manipulate them, while not being influenced by them. It is, in other words, a position of profound freedom and tremendous leverage. Esoterically speaking, this is the lever of Archimedes, the point of stability from which one can move the world without being moved by the forces of the world.

The Hanged Man

The path of the Hanged Man joins consciousness to the Indigo Sphere, which has the attributes of stillness, stability, eternity, and timelessness. All of this points to the *transcendent* nature of self-consciousness. It is essential to understand, however, that transcendence in this context does not mean disappearance from physical reality, but rather a shift to a higher perspective while still remaining connected to physical reality. Self-consciousness anchors itself in the timeless realm, but extends its influence into the realm of time and space. We could say then that self-consciousness is the fixed center around which all of existence revolves. In that respect, it is symbolized by the pole star, the point around which the heavens rotate, also known as the Axis Mundi. When you come to this realization, then you recognize that the world around you is a projection of yourself. But you have to find the center before you can manipulate your projection of the world. Only when you have recognized and established the center can you understand that all actions flow forth from that center. This includes not only physical actions, but also thoughts and beliefs. It is the Axis Mundi that stabilizes this world-projection. By coming to the center of self-consciousness, you bring stability to the world around you. In a certain sense, the Hanged Man is what holds the universe together.

Eliphas Levi described the pentagram as symbolizing the dominion of the mind over the elements, in which the uppermost point of the figure represents Spirit and the four lower points represent Fire, Air, Water and Earth. The inverted pentagram on the other hand, in which the point of Spirit is directed downward and subjugated by the elements, represents the spiritual darkness of bestiality and ignorance. The upright pentagram can therefore be considered the quintessential symbol of all that the Hanged Man represents. In this symbolic map, the transcendent self-consciousness is the point that stands above the plane of manifestation, while the four elements represent the physical, mental, and emotional passions of the personality. Perhaps the most useful metaphor would be to liken the personality to a marionette, and the transcendent consciousness to the puppet master pulling the strings from above the world-stage.

If we analyze the imagery of the Hanged Man, it illustrates quite clearly the ideas that we have been talking about. We note first of all that the figure is suspended in mid-air, above the earth. This describes a state of consciousness that is suspended above the plane of physical manifestation, in the rarefied heights of timelessness and pure self-awareness. Even more curious is the fact that he is suspended *upside-down*. This has been interpreted by many as representing an inversion of the perspective of ordinary human consciousness. The figure has adopted a viewpoint that literally turns the world upside-down, effectively upending every assumption and preconception that the common mass of humanity takes for granted. The result is illumination, as shown by the aura of light that surrounds his head. This is what Nietzsche described as the "re-valuation of all values". It is a state of wiping the slate clean of all that we think we know about reality, in order to see it more clearly and more objectively, free from the value judgments and emotional lenses that we have layered upon it. One could describe it as a distinctly Saturnine perspective of cool, calm detachment. But this cool detachment is necessary if we are to operate from a place of self-mastery.

When we look at the image of the Hanged Man, we are taken by the profound feeling of *stillness* that it seems to convey. We feel as if life is in suspension. The figure appears to hang in a state of meditative contemplation. The higher perspective that he occupies comes from a place of standing above the fray. It is a place of clarity that can only be had by stilling the mind and stilling the emotions. The Hanged Man could also be described, for better or for worse, as a state of *being above it all*. He represents a state of consciousness in which one has gone "beyond good and evil". And yet this card is universally interpreted as a very *sanctified* state of being. How is this so? The truth of the matter is that our convictions about what is right and what is wrong are for the most part very personal. They are shaped by our personal fears and desires, and so they represent a projection of those fears and desires upon a cosmic order. Our moral judgments about the world are effectively our own personal likes and dislikes projected upon God's will.

The Hanged Man

To go beyond good and evil, therefore, does not mean to become self-centered and narcissistic. Quite the opposite. The narcissistic individual in point of fact has a very pronounced sense of morality, but it is a morality that revolves entirely around his own wants and needs. When the narcissistic person does not get what he wants, he feels profoundly *victimized,* and is genuinely convinced that it is all very *unfair*. To such an individual, the frustration of his own personal desires is an indication that the entire universe is out of balance. The Hanged Man, on the other hand, sees the world from the stark recognition that his own wants and needs have no primacy whatsoever in the grand scheme of things. He understands quite clearly that *life does not owe him anything*. And this is a position of *tremendous strength*. There is a great feeling of power and liberation in the realization that you are not owed anything, because then you cannot be a victim.

This is precisely the viewpoint of the Stoic philosophers, who understood that true freedom can only come through liberating oneself from the emotional attachments to how we think life is supposed to turn out. One might be forgiven for thinking that Stoicism is a philosophy of emotional dullness and passivity in the face of life, but this is actually not the case. It is perfectly healthy to be emotionally invested in the *pursuit* of a goal or of a cause, and to prosecute that goal with vigor and energy, as long as one's happiness is not dependent on the *outcome*. To many, this may sound like a paradox, and it does indeed run contrary to the common view to say that we can enjoy and appreciate the things of life without being emotionally dependent on them. But this is the very essence of self-mastery that the Hanged Man represents. The main point of Stoicism is to not put your emotional investment in external circumstances, which ultimately are subject to forces beyond our control, but rather in your own freedom of self-determination. To possess one's free will is above all else the highest goal in life.

And so another seeming paradox of this philosophy is that the first step toward taking control of your life is the *acceptance* of what you cannot control. This stops the flailing. As the Stoic philosopher Epictetus aptly said: *"Why are we enraged? Because we make idols of the things that people take away from us."* The point being that even in the face of adversity, one has a *choice* whether to be happy or unhappy. And to exercise this choice one must operate from a vantage point that is above the attachment to outcomes. Stoicism, very much in keeping with the more mystical-minded philosophies, is concerned with seeing through the world of transitory appearances to that which is eternal. There is a sense that investing too deeply in the pleasures of the world leaves us at the mercy of the unstable ebb and flow of the world around us. And so it is better to be invested in that which is stable and can never be taken away - which is to say, one's core character and autonomy.

Despite the Saturnian side to this key, the Hanged Man represents a state of profound optimism and clarity. One could liken it to the feeling of standing on the top of a high mountain, gazing out upon the wide, sunlit expanse below. In this higher perspective that stands above the world, there is a pleasant and peaceful stillness that grasps the bigger picture in a single glance. We could also say that the Hanged Man represents the discipline of meditation, which is the clarity that comes from stillness. We can only attain true clarity by rising above the perspective of our own self-interests. This is of course an inversion of the common perspective, which is entirely based upon self-interest. But the ability to see beyond one's narrow self-interest is in fact a distinct advantage, because it gives us a much broader perspective, which is in itself a strategic edge.

The influence of Saturn in life affairs tends to be under-appreciated, but it serves a definite function as a teacher of wisdom insofar as it forces us into focus and self-awareness. Saturn is the wall that throws you back upon yourself. That is to say, when you finally hit the limitations of reality and you cannot struggle or flee or fight anymore, what are you then left with? You are forced to sit still with yourself and to become *aware* of yourself. And so Saturn has this potential for forcing self-consciousness upon us, if we can just have the presence of mind to stop thrashing about and simply *be still* in the moment. When you embrace that place of stillness, then you are in a position to see things more clearly.

The Hanged Man

But you must first accept the reality of where you are, which for most people is a difficult proposal. Why is accepting reality so difficult? Because the natural survival instinct is to fight and struggle and thrash around when cornered. But being still in the moment allows you to absorb the contours of reality in such a way that it starts to become understandable.

In psychological parlance, this is known as *radical acceptance*, which is the mindfulness of being present with the limitations around you. Radical acceptance is when you stop flailing against reality, and instead you sit with it and feel into it. A mind that is always wandering is not in the present moment, and a mind that is fighting against reality is constantly trying to jump out of the present moment. It is in fact trying to evade the present moment. But it is only *within* the present moment that the lessons can be learned. Those episodes of intense frustration can be turned into moments of transformation, if we will simply redirect the flow of energy so that it is not grinding against resistance.

From the standpoint of the Stoic philosophers, the limiting influence of Saturn teaches us to appreciate who we really are. When you hit the wall of what you cannot control and are thrown back upon yourself, you realize that the only thing that you *can* truly control is yourself. And so Saturn leads us to the wisdom of self-mastery. You become aware of yourself as an autonomous being, responsible for your own decisions, and responsible for your own choices. You realize that even in the face of what you cannot control, you can choose to confront it with character and with dignity. And so the ability to choose dignity, honor, and integrity in the face of adversity is the ultimate expression of self-mastery. It can therefore be said that Saturn teaches us to rise to our highest level of being.

It is well to understand that this state of being thrown back upon oneself is a profoundly and Plutonically transformative experience if one goes into it deeply enough. It is a common trope that the human being consists of powers and abilities far beyond what we are aware of, and that we don't really comprehend what we are capable of until we are put to the test. What we know of our own potential is but the tip of an iceberg, but when we go deep within and expand the awareness of self, then the full scope of those powers and capabilities begins to emerge. The key point to understand here is that consciousness is more than just what you *think*, it is also what you *feel*. And when you are thrown back upon self-consciousness, you become aware of all aspects of yourself, including the very power of agency within you. At the most basic level, this is felt as an awareness of one's ability to act through the physical body, and to effect changes in the physical world. In the realm of spiritual and metaphysical philosophy, there has often been a bias against the importance of physical activity. And yet, the awareness of that physical interface of the body touches upon a much more core energy than focusing on mental activity. For it is precisely in the *encountering of resistance* that the spotlight is most clearly cast upon our ability to exert and focus our willpower. That is to say, it is in the pressing against reality that one *finds oneself*. Our agency as a creative being comes first and foremost to our awareness in the pushing back against obstacles. It can reasonably be said then that Saturn serves a distinct role in the focusing, concentration, and intensification of self-awareness, down to the deepest level of one's own personal power and autonomy.

The Fool
White Sphere to Black Sphere

In the path between the White Sphere and the Black Sphere, we have vibrant, dynamic energy combined with the limitless possibilities of wide open space. And so the ideas exemplified here are those of *freedom, mobility,* and *adventure*.

To the extent that space is seen as an *emptiness*, we tend to think of it in negative terms. It is regarded as a *mere* nothingness, the absence of anything of value. And yet, insofar as it represents the absence of boundaries and the absence of obstacles, there is a decidedly *positive* aspect to space. Space represents the freedom to move, to dance, to run, and to explore. When the vital energy of the White Sphere encounters the openness of empty space, it manifests as an exuberant impulse to charge forth into the unknown. In purely physical terms, this represents the principle that "nature abhors a vacuum". The attraction of the creative spirit toward the unknown is like the attraction of a gas toward empty space. A space to explore is a space of exciting new possibilities, and so the primal Chaos naturally seeks to expand into the Void. Where there is room to move, Chaos will seek to fill it.

There is a decidedly sexual symbolism at work here, although of a highly refined aspect. The attraction that draws the masculine energy of the White Sphere plunging forward into the feminine depths of the Black Sphere is unmistakably evocative, but it operates at the most fundamental and cosmic level of the Yin-Yang polarity. The same sexual dynamic is reflected in more concrete terms further down on the path of The Empress, in which we have the Yang energy of Venus fertilizing the Yin energy of Mercury, making it fruitful and pregnant with new possibilities. It is important to understand the balance of influence that each principle exerts in this mutual attraction. The Black Sphere is not simply a passive element that is acted upon or acted within. It possesses a mystical allure which exercises a power of drawing-forth upon the creative imagination. At the same time, we must be quite clear that freedom is more than just a *lack of restraint*. It is more than just the empty space to move around in. To be free, you must also embody the energy of Chaos. If you do not have Chaos within you, then you do not have freedom. There is no freedom to speak of without the burning impulse to create and to explore. It is therefore the *combination* of creative life-energy and space to move that defines the experience of freedom. Imagine the feeling of a dog that has just escaped the fence around the back yard. Suddenly, it is all boundless energy. You try to chase after it and catch it, but it is positively overflowing with speed and nimbleness and dexterity. That is the archetypal energy of the White Sphere encountering the Black Sphere. Space in this context represents the taking away of structure to such an extent that the impulse of movement can go berserk and run wild.

Children and pets love nothing more than to run around outside in the wide open. It is appropriate therefore that the Tarot card of The Fool depicts a youth with childlike innocence, accompanied by a dog, going forth into the world oblivious of where his next step may be taking him. Here we see the spirit of an intrepid explorer with the whole world before him. The sense of adventure is palpable as he charges ahead with fearlessness and aplomb. To all appearances, he is about to step off the edge of a precipice. And yet, rather than being alarmed by the situation we find it humorously endearing. Somehow we know that our young traveler will land on his feet, just as we are told by the old saying that God protects fools and little children. From the standpoint of so-called worldly wisdom, stepping into uncharted territory has always been looked upon as a somewhat foolhardy endeavor. Why take a chance on the unknown when there is safety in the tried and true? And yet, the secret that this card teaches us is that the universe has a bias in favor of the spirit of curiosity and fearless exploration. The desire to go forth and experience new things embodies the primal urge of primal energy to find a wide open space in which to enact the creative drive. We could rightly say that The Fool represents the fundamental *evolutionary impulse* that drives all growth and progress. It is the urge for consciousness to expand its horizons, and to seek ever greater degrees of freedom. At the highest level of symbolism, The Fool represents the Yechidah, venturing forth into the realm of experience. Further down he is The Magician, learning to master his creative skills and capacities. But at this level, he simply embodies the soul's journey forth into incarnation, taking life one day at a time.

A key concept of this path is the idea of *mobility*, which is the antithesis of *friction*. Mobility is the very essence of liveliness and vitality. Clear and healthy life-energy is free-flowing and mobile, as opposed to the stagnation of *stuck* energy which eventually leads to sickness and death. Depression, sluggishness, and boredom are all states of the creative energy being unable to move about. This is invariably the consequence of negative and limiting thoughts that restrict the free flow of energy. Examine any negative thought or emotion and you will immediately *feel* the friction that it generates inside of you. It is a palpable feeling of energy grinding against itself, as if the thoughts that you are holding onto are presenting such an obstruction and a resistance that you must try exponentially harder to get anything done. Simply letting go of such limiting thoughts has an immediate effect of "clearing the air". It is an unfortunate truth that many people hold on to dense and heavy thought-patterns because they feel as if they are somehow more profound or more complex for all of their mental churning. They may even fear that without all of their ruminations, they would simply be "superficial" or "shallow". It doesn't take a lot of reflection to recognize the vanity of this misguided pseudo-intellectualism, and once the fallacy of this way of thinking is seen clearly, we immediately recognize that there is a great deal of wisdom in *not taking life so seriously*. Life is simply a lot easier when you don't make it complicated. Think of it as applying the art of Feng Shui to the mind. By clearing your head of all the junk that you don't really need, you create ample space for the creative energy to flow easily and readily. For this reason, the card of The Fool is often associated with the element of Air, which embodies the spirit of *levity*.

Another key realization to be had here is that you must *feel into* the substance of space in order to truly feel the essence of freedom. This is not entirely intuitive, as our normal tendency is to think of space as an emptiness rather than a substance. Nevertheless, we can prove that space is not an emptiness because we can measure it. If you have two cups sitting on a table, you can take a tape measure and measure the distance between them. If space were a *mere emptiness*, a mere nothingness, then there would be nothing separating the two cups. There would be nothing to measure. Anything that can be measured is substantive. If space truly had no substance, then it is a certainty that no one would pay more money for a house with more space. But the value of space lies in the feeling of *openness* that it evokes within us. Being in a place with bigger space instinctively triggers our feeling of freedom. A wide open space naturally arouses the Primal Chaos. This is why we love grand spaces so much. A grand space makes us feel as if our creative energies are expanding, unfolding, and spiraling outward. The having of space is seen as a great luxury, because space is a metaphor for scope of possibility. It is space to move, space to live, space to explore. Having more space is instinctively felt as having the opportunity for energy to circulate and evolve. And so large open spaces are experienced as places where energy can unfold.

To truly experience freedom you must therefore *own* the space that you are in. To own your space means to consume it and to become one with it. A certain Neptunian dissolution of personal boundaries comes into play here. We assume a kind of gaseous and permeable quality in the opening up to space that exemplifies the feeling of expansion and freedom. When you run and dance, there is an exhilaration that is experienced not only in the movement *through space,* but also in the feeling that space is moving *through you.* This blending and integration with the space around you is not only evocative of playfulness, but also profoundly mystical at the same time. It is precisely this playful aspect of The Fool that teaches us the deepest wisdom. The childlike impulse to venture forth and explore the world is, at the most basic level, a journey into oneness with everything.

The Wheel of Fortune
White Sphere to Indigo Sphere

The path between the White Sphere and the Indigo Sphere expresses the idea of *fate* or *destiny*. It is quite simply the principle of inertia applied to movement. A force set into motion maintains the trajectory on which it has been set, and this becomes its destiny. The Tarot represents this as a wheel because the principle is best exemplified by the Law of Cycles, especially the cycles of astrology.

It is important for us to understand that destiny is not something that is absolutely fixed. It is not predetermined or irrevocable. Fate is simply the logical outcome of a movement that continues to be what it is. Destiny is the same thing as *destination*. It is that toward which you are headed. One is always capable of altering the destination through free will. Those with the power of precognition are not witnessing a preordained future *per se*, but rather the trajectory of forces already in motion. The power of precognition in fact gives us an option of altering the outcome. We should not assume that this is always easy, however. Some trajectories are more difficult to alter, because they have more momentum behind them. If an impulse or a movement has been repeated and reinforced and persisted in for a long period of time, then it has acquired a momentum that requires that much more effort to change. To this extent, such a movement with momentum behind it assumes more and more the bearing of a fate that one cannot avoid, at least not without extraordinary determination. This is exactly what the Greek philosopher Heraclitus meant when he said that "character is destiny". What we call character is that pattern of behavior which we have made habitual, and which makes us predictable. It is a movement of the soul that repeats itself over and over again. A movement that you persist in long enough becomes your destiny. To change this type of destiny requires a radical change to one's character, which can only be accomplished by virtue of penetrating clarity and self-awareness.

Another aspect to this, however, is the fact that a movement acquires the sense of fate or destiny to the extent that there is *intent* behind it. This is a very important point to grasp, because it teaches us to look at fate not as something that necessarily *happens* to us or is *imposed* upon us, but as something that we take part in the shaping of, both *before* the coming into physical existence and also during the life-journey, by means of the habits and mindsets and energy-profiles that we cultivate.

When looked at from this angle, the concept of destiny doesn't feel quite as heavy and onerous. We see it instead as simply a part of the fabric of Saturn which holds the universe together in a stable and coherent structure. Without the consistency that the Indigo Sphere provides, there would be no solid ground for our existence to stand upon. And so the world-stabilizing force of destiny gives us a foundation upon which our freedom can be exercised. This perspective is in fact the great power of this key, because when you are able to understand the currents of destiny and stand above them, then you can ride these currents like a surfer riding the waves.

To embrace your destiny is to then ride the wave of your own self-propelled movement. If you can avail yourself of forces that are already in motion, then you can work *with* destiny rather than against it. In a certain sense, this simply means doing what comes effortlessly, because a movement that is already set in motion does not require any effort to sustain it. The Saturnian aspect of this can be thought of as a state of *rest in motion*. That is to say, a sense of calm and stillness as you ride the wave. In the Tarot card, we observe the figure of the Sphinx sitting very calmly atop the Wheel of Fortune, while others are carried up and down by its rotation. Notice how he doesn't have to do anything, or make any effort. He does not have to struggle in any way. He is simply riding the wave. This epitomizes the idea of "going with the flow" or following the Way of the Tao, which simply means following the line of least resistance. This may sound like mere laziness, but there is actually an intelligence to this approach. Laziness is an entirely non-productive state of being, whereas following the watercourse way is more a matter of harnessing the currents that are already available.

The experience here is very much like the feeling of being on a moving train. And the brilliant thing about being on a moving train is that you don't need to move, because the train does the moving for you. You can sit perfectly still, but at the same time be moving toward your destination. There is something immensely gratifying about the sense of movement from here to there with no effort required. It is a sensation of simply coasting into your destiny. When you get into this mindset, you begin to realize that life doesn't really require that much effort. It tends to roll along of its own momentum. And when you allow yourself to be carried by that current, it becomes much easier. This should not be misinterpreted to mean that we should take a completely passive attitude toward life. What we are talking about is rather an *intelligent* application of force that maximizes the result of our efforts. If we attempt to paddle against the natural current, then we are expending a great deal of energy to go not very far. This is the outcome of over-thinking and over-analyzing life, which results in confusion and stumbling along the path. But by taking the watercourse way and moving with the current, we attune to the natural flow of the natural unfolding of who we are.

Another key aspect of the Wheel of Fortune is that it embodies our concept of *time* as a structured framework. Previously, we have spoken of the White Sphere as being the essential principle of time, because our concept of time depends on some kind of movement taking place. If there is no movement or change, then there is no time to speak of. And yet we also know that Saturn has been traditionally associated with time, particularly in his Greek representation as *Kronos*. In the axis of the White Sphere and Indigo Sphere, it is Saturn that gives structure and regularity to time. If we imagine a state of flux that is completely random and chaotic, which is what Uranus represents in its purest sense, this would not fully comprehend our sense of time, because we think of time as *linear*. That is to say, we perceive it as having a somewhat predictable structure. Insofar as we can conceive of such a thing as fate or destiny, it is bound up with the idea of a movement that is projected forward by its own inertia, and this is precisely where our sense of linear time comes from. Now the only way that we can measure time with regularity is in terms of cyclical movements - days, months (which is to say, lunation cycles) and years. We could say then that our concept of structured time is based on the *predictability* of certain movements, most notably the cyclical movements of the heavens.

It is clear then that in one sense the Wheel of Fortune represents our ability to see forward into the future and plan accordingly. This requires us to assume a higher point of awareness above the immediacy of the present moment. From the standpoint of the Sphinx, we observe the broad trajectory of the cycles of time, and this gives us the foresight to plant the seeds of opportunity that will yield fruit later on. As long as a movement continues to be what it is, we can know precisely where it is going to arrive at a certain point in the future. This structural understanding of time is therefore an essential means of adapting to our reality. There is a more esoteric side, however, to our experience of linear time, and that would be that it seems to give us a framework for tracing out the *logic* of our choices and actions.

The concept of logic, in its most abstract sense, is the process of unfolding all the meanings and ramifications of an idea while at the same time preserving it exactly as it is. Logic is a movement of consciousness through various perspectives *around* an idea, while the idea remains fundamentally the same. The most basic illustration of this is the *syllogism*. If we know that Socrates is a man, and that all men are mortal, then we can logically conclude that Socrates is mortal. From a certain perspective, we have made a movement of awareness to a new understanding, even though *nothing has changed* with regard to the initial premises. The entire discipline of mathematics is precisely this kind of unfolding of awareness. Even though our mathematical theorems become increasingly expansive and complex, ultimately they are simply a re-framing and a fresh articulation of what we already knew.

From this angle, we can think of linear time as the logical unfoldment of the decisions that we have set into motion. Were it not for this structural nature of time, every impulse would be realized instantaneously. With the gradual development of our actions through linear time, however, we have the opportunity to reflect upon the process as it is unfolding, as well as the opportunity to change the trajectory at any given moment. We could say then that linear time provides a *narrative structure* to our existence that allows us to consciously process the implications of our choices. Within this paradigm, the notion that character is destiny can be seen as part of the learning process of human existence, because it allows you to follow the narrative arc of the attitudes and beliefs that you have chosen to act out.

When we understand destiny in this way as an unfolding of character, then it is no longer a question of fighting against fate, but rather of *becoming who you are*. With this kind of attitude, we are then eager to unfold the narrative and discover where it leads. Destiny, from this viewpoint, becomes the elucidation and the *exegesis* of what you stand for. Life then becomes a matter of simply letting go and following where the narrative takes you. It is imperative to understand however that this narrative proceeds from the character that you build, which is defined by the beliefs and values that you cultivate. These must be chosen with the clearest of *intent*. When you put enough intent and perseverance behind your values, then your fate becomes like a rolling train, and you are simply riding it to the destination.

In a way, this is a bit like observing one's life as if it were a movie playing itself out. This is a very peculiar state of mind to be sure, but it gives us a certain heightened perspective. By standing above the narrative in this sense, we allow the forces and the vectors of our life and personality to follow their trajectory without resistance or interference. From this perspective, we can observe more clearly what their character and flavor are, how they direct themselves, and how they unfold. And there is enough clarity in this perspective to make just the right corrective adjustments, which in some cases may be very subtle and indirect, and yet may be just enough redirection of force to alter the outcome significantly. This is the position of the Sphinx who sits atop the Wheel, having the wisdom to harness the forces of destiny rather than being carried by them helplessly, hither and thither.

A final side-note to this key is that the symbolism of the Wheel carries the implication that every movement is ultimately a circle, even though from our limited perspective the immediate trajectory may appear to be a straight line going indefinitely forward. From this simple idea, we derive the doctrine of *karma*, which teaches us that every action eventually comes back around to its source.

The Sun
White Sphere to Blue Sphere

If we think of the Blue Sphere as the scope of one's personal potential, then the activation of this potential by the universal creative life-force is experienced as *vitality*. Vitality is something distinct from willpower. The Martian energy of willpower is quite focused and directional, whereas vitality is a more diffuse feeling of personal power, a feeling that one can do just about anything.

The Sun is an appropriate symbol of this feeling because it radiates its vital energy in all directions at once. It embodies a sense of immense power, but without the aggressive pointedness of Mars. It simply showers its light and warmth every possible way, with no discrimination whatsoever as to who or what receives the benefit of its creative energy. There is an extraordinary freedom in this attitude of unconditional radiance, of not having to modulate one's radiance based on judgments of who is deserving of it or not, but of simply rendering equal light to all and sundry. The image of the child riding a horse captures this spirit of unfiltered innocence. The freedom of Uranus combined with the expansiveness of Jupiter represents the epitome of abundant creative energy.

As the sphere of one's personal resources, Jupiter is closely connected with the physical body, and so The Sun therefore represents the source of physical vitality. In a very literal sense, our sun is the ultimate source of all energy and life on the planet. Its rays are the motive force of every physical and chemical process on earth, from the circulation of the winds down to the machinations of the cells in our bodies. In all living things, the energy of the sun is felt at the bodily level as a fire in the nervous system that urges us toward movement and activity and the impulse to make things happen in the world.

This universal life-energy has been designated in various terms such as *prana*, *chi*, and *kundalini*. It is also the fundamental life-energy which alchemists sought to capture in the form of the Universal Medicine. The vitality and health of the body depends on the free circulation of energy, and this is precisely what the White Sphere represents in this context. The creative impulse is the same as the life-force, and it is that very force which keeps us alive and in a constant state of renewal. The creative energy must therefore have the freedom to flow without hindrance, and if the flow of that energy is obstructed then the health will inevitably start to deteriorate.

A key lesson then of The Sun is that the free flow of creative activity is essential to physical health and vitality. Understand that when we speak of creative activity, we are not referring exclusively to activity of an artistic nature. Creative activity can be any endeavor that makes you feel as if you are empowered and contributing something of value to the world around you. This feeling of empowered and effortless productive movement is what we call the *flow-state*. It is a state in which the creative energy is circulating freely, and we are happily in control of our faculties and our potentials. In flow-state, we are master of our domain and the creative juices are swirling. It is also that state of being which we describe as *channeling*. The Tarot card of The Sun has traditionally been interpreted as success, which is the natural outcome of being in flow. The key takeaway here is that the vitality and renewal of the body depends upon the circulation of the creative power. The universal life-force is given to us for a reason, namely that we use it for creative purposes. If we don't use it, then we eventually lose it.

The *mood* that Jupiter brings to this is especially worth taking a look at. Jupiter has a certain kind of homogenizing influence, in the sense that it *smooths out* the energy and evokes an attitude of warm calm. That balmy, temperate atmosphere of being in relaxed control of all one's faculties and energies is the essence of Jupiterian optimism. It is an undeniable fact that Jupiter makes everything seem *easy*. There is a universally smooth and frictionless quality to its influence. To get into the energy of Jupiter, you must therefore get out of the mindset of struggle, because Jupiter represents what is *effortless*. Unlike the Saturnian quality of the external world which offers resistance and friction to your will, that which is in your personal domain of influence is non-resistant. And so there is a very fluid aspect to Jupiter which is the antithesis of rigidity and friction.

This would seem to suggest that the key to having more ease and control over your life, and thereby more success, is to assume an attitude of fluidity and adaptability. There is a universal law of sympathetic vibration which dictates that the energy which you emit will be stimulated and reflected back to you by your environment. This means that if you attack life with an attitude that conflict and struggle are necessary to accomplish anything, then the sympathetic vibration of resistance and friction will be elicited by your surroundings. If, on the other hand, you assume a fluid and adaptable approach to life, then life will itself reflect a fluid vibration that yields gently to your touch.

The World
Black Sphere to Indigo Sphere

This path could best be described with an image of *space freezing,* becoming glassy and dark like obsidian as it hardens and crystallizes. It is a particularly strange image to be sure, but it represents in a very tactile form an archetypal process of fluid substance solidifying into something permanent. The Tarot card of The World is commonly interpreted as representing a state of completion and fulfillment, the bringing together of a plan to a settled resolution. But the completion of any work involves a kind of crystallization and settling into place. Just as the mortar in the interstices of a brick edifice must congeal and harden in order to solidify the structure, the space of any completed work must fixate and congeal in order to bring the work to rest in its final form.

Saturn is traditionally associated with Saturday or the Sabbath, the seventh and final day on which God rested from fashioning creation. In a more contemporary mythology, the imagery would be that of the molten ball of a newly-formed earth gradually cooling into a hardened sphere. The end result of any process that finalizes in a fixed and stabilized structure is a kind of stage on which the drama of life may be enacted. Shakespeare observed that all the world is a stage, and the esoteric truth of this statement is very apt indeed. If the universe were a game of chess, then The World would be the chess board. It is the stable background upon which life plays itself out. If we reflect this idea down to the path between the Indigo Sphere and the Blue Sphere, represented as the card of The Chariot and the zodiacal sign of Cancer, then it assumes the symbolic form of the *castle.* The castle represents the world on a more personal level. On a more universal level, The World represents the architectural framework of reality.

This is a new and somewhat tricky concept to grasp, but in essence it represents the stability of the fabric of space, which in turn lends stability and consistency to the structure of the world. If you can simply imagine a large piece of black fabric with many white stars painted all over its surface, it is the stability of the fabric which holds the stars in their patterns and constellations. The idea also manifests as the *resistance* of space, in the sense that we cannot simply go from point A to point B instantaneously, but rather we must traverse the full distance *through* space and exert energy in doing so.

What we have here then is the concept of *space* evolving into the concept of *place*. What does this even mean? To be a *place* implies two things. First of all, a place is somewhere *in space*. And secondly, the place has some kind of permanence. A place is enduring. You can go away from the place, and come back to the place, and the place is still there. You can stay in the place, and the place stays with you. The place must possess this reliable stability in order to serve as the scene of the drama. And so with The World, we have this idea of the stable and enduring backdrop of reality. The World is a place where life happens. It is the stage on which the drama of life is performed. Implicit in this concept of place is the idea of things standing still, things staying at rest. What is it exactly that imposes this state of rest? It is simply the fact that there is a certain *viscosity* to space. Space has inherent resistance.

This viscosity of space is what keeps us grounded in a sense. It holds The World together. But the viscosity of space also resists our freedom to move. It takes work and toil and effort to move through life. And so The World has a decidedly bittersweet taste for us. It is the foundation of all the beauty and all the wonder that we can experience in life. But it is also a place from which we cannot escape, except through death. Like the crisp air of an autumn morning, The World is both cold and beautiful. In an esoteric sense then we could say that this path, and to a certain extent the path of the Chariot, embodies the symbolism of the *crucifixion* insofar as it represents the soul being nailed to the cross of physical existence.

In the context of the Law of Attraction, this key would seem to be connected with the mysterious process by which thoughts condense into physical manifestation, an idea that we could describe as the *crystallization* of reality. Kabbalistic tradition depicts the Tetragrammaton, or four-lettered name of God (otherwise known as Yahweh/Jehovah), as mapping out a formula for the universal process of manifestation. In this formulation, the first letter Yod corresponds to Fire and Chokmah. It represents the creative drive and will, but also the abstract and archetypal idea of that which one desires to manifest. The second letter He corresponds to Water and Binah, being the universal undifferentiated substance out of which all forms are drawn. The letter Vau corresponds to Air and the six Sephiroth from Chesed to Yesod, but the Sephirah of Tiphareth is especially implicit here. It represents the formulation of the archetypal desire into a specific image which embodies that desire, a formal template to be applied to the undifferentiated substance. The final He of the name corresponds to Earth and the Sephirah of Malkuth. It represents the encapsulation and crystallization of the first three principles into a manifested outcome. It is this final He that is most closely connected to the principle embodied by the Tarot card of The World. The precipitation of physical existence out of the cosmic imagination of Binah is the energy at work here. In terms of human activity and psychology, it represents the instinct for *consolidation*. That is to say, it is the instinct for grounding oneself in one's environment, establishing roots, laying foundations, and fixing the results of one's efforts into a lasting and enduring legacy. In short, it represents all of the earthy, Saturnine, and practical instincts that anchor us firmly to the physical world.

The Tower
Black Sphere to Red Sphere

The Red Sphere is the element of the will, and in a deeper sense it represents the *true will*, which is the pursuit and execution of one's authenticity. The Black Sphere is more complex in its meaning. On the one hand, it represents the root-substance from which all bounded and finite things arise. At the same time, it can represent the dissolution of boundaries and the return of form back into the formless substrate. What does The Tower stand for then? Some interpretations have likened it to the Tower of Babel, which represents the human intellect so flushed with pride and enamored of itself that it seeks to overrun the gates of heaven, and is therefore decisively undone by God himself. In psychological terms, we can say that The Tower represents the ego-structure. But more to the point, it represents an ego-structure that has become much too rigid to effectively serve its own purpose. It is an ossified personality that can no longer act as a lens for the true will, because it has been rendered completely opaque by fixed beliefs, limiting attitudes, and narrow self-interests. The Tower is what psychology understands as the *false self*.

What we see depicted here then is a dissolution of the ego in order to create an opportunity to release the authentic self. In the Tower of Babel allegory, this comes directly as divine intervention, and the Tarot card also depicts what would classically be described as an "act of God". In fact, some of the earlier French versions of the Tarot refer to this card as "La Maison Dieu" (*The House of God*) or "Le Feu du Ciel" (*The Fire from Heaven*). The latter designation is particularly illustrative, as it points to the lightning blast as a decisively Martian energy materializing out of the depths of space itself. While there is a strong element of truth to this interpretation, it is also critically important to understand the degree to which the individual participates, at the subconscious level, with the undoing of the false self. Keep in mind that the Black Sphere represents the merging of the individual with the collective awareness, and when the boundaries between the self and the All become tenuous, then the boundary between the individual will and the will of God begins to dissolve as well. The lightning blast that destroys The Tower can therefore be understood as the true will co-creating with the universe to assert itself against the false personality.

While the imagery of The Tower is quite unsettling, it is essential to keep in mind that despite appearances, none of the Tarot cards have an inherently negative meaning. What is depicted by The Tower represents an extreme manifestation of the underlying principle, a manifestation that tends to appear when the individual has failed to apply adequate self-awareness and insight to the unfoldment of his or her own life. In other words, when one has stopped listening to the inner voice altogether and instead committed to a false path, it may take some form of catastrophic event that shatters the ego in order to reset one's life completely. But this is by no means the only way in which this idea has to be expressed. The collapse of ego-structure may be an entirely internal experience, and furthermore, it can be controlled or uncontrolled.

An example of a semi-controlled dissolution of ego would be the intoxication of alcohol or drugs. This is by far the most common expression of the idea that The Tower represents. People seek intoxication as a means of temporary escape from the self-imposed restrictions of the ego and all of its defenses. Most importantly, there is a dissolving of inhibitions that comes with intoxication that allows a glimmer of the authentic self to shine through. Needless to say, this is by no means a perfect method of finding one's truth, and it can come with much confusion. Oftentimes, the effect of intoxication is to strip away the outer layers of the social mask just enough to expose the individual's unresolved anger and despair. Thus, the intoxicant does not provide a complete understanding of the individual's authentic nature, but in relative terms it may take him closer to the truth than the ordinary state of consciousness, and so in that respect the addicted individual keeps coming back to the drug of choice in the hope that it will eventually take him deep enough to some genuine understanding.

The Tower

Despite the obvious peril of relying on chemical substances for enlightenment, it is nevertheless true that some people are better than others at navigating the effects of alcohol or other intoxicants in moderation, and in the state of loosened expectations and thought processes that ensues, some will experience genuine flashes of insight and creative awareness. This is especially true of many of society's artistic geniuses, although the creative output often comes at a great cost of personal dissolution over time.

A completely uncontrolled collapse of the ego-structure would look something like a mental or emotional breakdown. Broadly speaking, this normally evolves out of an acute feeling that the personality is inadequate to express its higher purpose. If we were to look deeply enough into these feelings of inadequacy, we would usually find that the root of the problem is really a failure to find authenticity, and to focus on it resolutely. But in the absence of such clarity, the subjective experience is that the personality is too dense and too clumsy to be of any real use. What emerges is an urge to go beyond the narrow confines of who one currently is. There is an innate understanding that the expression of the true self is hemmed in by the limitations of one's own mind, and so the personality has to be broken down in order for something to change. This can manifest as all manner of self-destructive tendencies, but at the heart of it is an urge to self-transcendence. The mental breakdown is a natural response when the personality has become inflexible. It is a state in which you are so acutely aware of the limitations of the false personality, that you actively start to take it apart. When you see that the thing that you are is no longer getting you to where you want to be, then a deeper layer of consciousness steps in and attempts to burn it all to the ground.

This less-than-conscious expression of The Tower's core energy is best described as the Neptunian impulse of *self-undoing*. While the process appears wholly destructive in its unfolding, the underlying purpose is to break apart a structure that is no longer working, and to create a gap in which a higher vision can emerge. Another Neptunian word that fits the theme here is *martyrdom*, which describes a state of being so disillusioned with the limitations of the personality that one would gladly sacrifice it for a higher purpose. The impulse to martyrdom is usually seen as the ultimate form of self-effacement, but there is a deceptive element of grandiosity behind it. The element of self-sacrifice is not really a sacrifice when you realize that it is driven by a desire to be relieved of the burden of one's own smallness. Even if one's personal existence feels insignificant, it can assume a greater dignity by being given over to something bigger than oneself.

In point of fact, the self-sacrificer has *gained* a great deal of power. The strength of the will becomes immense when the petty ego is taken out of the picture. Someone who has no regard for self-aggrandizement or ego-gratification is capable of nearly anything. He has the same capacity for fearlessness as one who has nothing left to lose. And the martyr *is* in fact someone with nothing left to lose, as he has given up his sense of self entirely to his cause. This is the most intoxicating kind of power that there is. It is the mental space of both great heroism and great vision. While the higher goal that is pursued may be either spiritual or secular, the urge to transcend the personal ego is at bottom a deeply religious impulse - a desire to align the personal will with something larger and more powerful than oneself. The loosening of the ego in such a context lends itself readily to visionary states, and there is a natural evolution from the martyr to the prophet. This can be an extremely profound transformation, but it can also easily turn into megalomania when the rejection of the personal self is so intense that it unfolds into the assumption of a world-historical mission.

Up to this point, we have focused on the more pathological manifestations of this energy, as that is what the imagery of The Tower would appear to emphasize. To truly grasp what this key represents, however, we must understand that there is a process here which is, in its ideal expression, both controlled and deliberate, not desperate and catastrophic as the blasted tower seems to suggest. It is not a process that is familiar or accessible to our ordinary way of understanding things, and so for most of us the default expression of this energy would appear as an unconscious eruption of self-undoing, whether that be in the form of a breakdown, chemical escapism, or an "act of God". It is possible, however, to loosen the bonds of the personality-structure in a way that is both conscious and regulated. Certain types of shamanic ritual fall into this category, the purpose of which is to induce a hypnotic state in which the normal logical structures of thought are allowed to dissociate and deconstruct. The result is a state of mind that is more liquid and fluid, in which the atoms and molecules of thought can unravel and rearrange themselves into new and novel perspectives. It is a state in which breakthroughs of understanding become possible. In essence, the shamanic ritual is a kind of controlled mental breakdown.

At a deeper level then, The Tower represents the adage that genius is akin to madness, because those who are geniuses in the realm of art or philosophy have found a way to deconstruct the limiting thought-structures in a controlled manner. The Tower represents the *divine madness* from which prophets are born. Those who are *merely* mad have not figured out the control mechanisms by which to hold the liquid waters of Neptune within a containing structure. The visionary and the prophet, on the other hand, have learned how to execute just enough control to gather the visions into a meaningful narrative.

There is a lesson here that shows us how to deal with times of emotional or psychological crisis, and that is to simply *let go* of the rigidity of the ego and loosen the structure of the personality. It has long been understood that flexible structures are more resilient than rigid structures, and the ego is no exception. The blasted tower is an extreme representation of this truth. When the ego is rigid, it will be shattered by the psychological stresses that test it. But a *loosely held* ego that can bend and sway like a willow tree can withstand the gusting storms of mental and emotional turmoil. One could say that every psychological crisis in life is an opportunity to experience the loosening of the ego that The Tower represents. Crying is just such an example of a controlled breakdown of the ego. It is a temporary dissolving of energetic bonds that serves as a release. A healthy and cathartic cry causes the inner structure to loosen up just enough, and just long enough, to allow the emotional body to absorb a new insight and a new understanding of the situation.

There is an important nuance to all of this that demands clarification. When we talk about the loosening of the ego-structure, one could easily assume that a transformation of consciousness is the primary outcome. While there is definitely validity to this assumption, it is principally a transformation of the *will* that is represented by the Neptune-Mars interaction. When the boundaries of the individual personality become hazy, the personal will begins to merge and resonate with the will of the Divine Matrix. There is thus a certain unstoppable aspect to this energy, because it is supported by the Higher Self as well as the wholeness of Binah. The blending of the personal will with the transcendent will is *pure magic*. It is as if the fabric of space itself has its own will, which has been channeled down through the vessel of the visionary. Another angle from which to look at it is to say that the true will, which is in tune with the Divine Will, has taken the decisive action of dissolving the limiting thoughts and beliefs which have held it back. This can be expressed unconsciously as a sudden unexpected disruption, or it can unfold consciously as a deliberate transcending of boundaries and expectations. In any case, the underlying premise is that the stultifying self-absorption of the mundane personality will ultimately give way to a higher calling. One is either *set straight* by the lightning bolt, or one *becomes* the lightning bolt.

The Magician
Blue Sphere to Red Sphere

Jupiter is the archetype of resources, and among the most valuable resources that we have are our *skills*. A skill is any field of activity that we have internalized to the point at which it becomes second nature to us. It becomes effortless. With skill, we can transform our activity into something of value. This includes, but is by no means limited to, things of economic value. Our skills can also provide us with social or even spiritual capital.

Mars is the archetype of action, and combined with Jupiter it represents the *application* of skill. There is much more to this than just doing a job, however. The grandiosity of Jupiter lends an air of theatricality to the procedure, and so the demonstration of proficiency becomes a *feat* of skill rather than just a completed task. In older Tarot decks, The Magician was called The Juggler. Although the latter sounds far less impressive, he nevertheless expresses the same idea. The Juggler's dazzling display of dexterity has a kind of miracle-working quality to it. It appears like magic to those who are not versed in the secrets of the craft, and in a certain sense, any mastered skill *is* a form of magic. To have such complete possession of a thing that you can manipulate it freely and effortlessly is the very essence of magic. There is a sense of *plasticity* here in which a substance or subject matter (Blue Sphere) is manipulated (Red Sphere) with perfect ease. In the hands of The Magician, reality becomes fluid.

So in the most mundane sense, The Magician represents the expression of one's mastery through the manifestation of great power or skill, often in a miraculous-seeming or spectacular way. It is all about bringing one's power to bear upon the world with confidence and fluency. It is about playing to your strengths, and playing up what you are naturally gifted at. Most importantly, The Magician represents the *pleasure* that we feel in flexing our skills and abilities.

This last idea deserves special attention, as it points to the deeper, underlying meaning of the symbol. The pleasure that one feels in exercising one's personal power and doing what one is good at is more than just idle bravado and showing off. It reflects an instinctive understanding of the law of growth, which says that your potential only expands as much as you make use of it. To grow your scope of possibility, you must make something of the potential that you already have. It is like building a muscle. In order for the muscle to grow stronger, you have to use it. You must make something of what you have in order to gain more. That is the law of Jupiter, the law of expansion. Mars is implicit in Jupiter as action is implicit in potential. Action is the *why* of potentiality, and so you cannot comprehend the essence of Jupiter without comprehending, at the same time, the impulse to fashion something of value out of that potential.

Picture the infant who has just learned how to walk on two feet. The child is positively beaming with exhilaration, and he has no reservations whatsoever about advertising his newly-discovered capability, because he recognizes that it opens up a whole new realm of possibility. Walking is now the most important thing ever, to be done as much as possible and wherever possible. Walking never grows old, and the quest is to walk ever further and faster.

This impulse to self-expansion is what Nietzsche described as the *will to power*, which is the sense of excitement that one gets from pushing one's possibilities to the next level. When we speak of "will to power", we must understand this in terms of *creative power*, as opposed to the more negative connotations of power as control and domination over others. The latter does not at all represent power in the Jupiterian sense. Jupiterian power is the capacity to create, and the will to power in its true sense is a desire for mastery of *oneself*. A key point to understand about this will to power is that it is just as excited about helping other people to maximize their own potential and to increase their own creative capability. There is no zero-sum mentality where Jupiter is concerned.

The Magician

Another way to think of this is that it represents the *will to evolve*. The evolutionary impulse is toward ever greater creative potential. The Magician represents someone who has gone to the next level on the evolutionary ladder, someone who has expanded to a wider circle of creative power. And so the essence of this card is the primal urge to acquire new knowledge and master new skills. Life seeks to continually expand its scope of possibilities, and self-improvement in any form is an expression of this impulse. If you make this your pole star, then you will always be moving in the right direction. There is in fact something magical in the *intent* to evolve. The intent works a transformation of the self, not just at the mental and spiritual level, but at a physical level as well. When you commit to the path of evolution, changes begin to happen at the level of the DNA.

There is a distinct mindset that exemplifies The Magician, without which this arc of evolution is impossible. This is the attitude of *taking ownership*. Jupiter represents ownership in a very literal sense, but combined with the energy of Mars it represents ownership in a philosophical sense. This means owning one's choices, owning one's words and actions, and owning one's decisions. Above all, it means assuming ownership of one's outcomes. The lexicon of psychology has a special term for this attitude. It is known as *internal locus of control*. To the individual with an *external* locus of control, life is always something that happens *to* them. They see their outcomes as shaped by forces outside of themselves. If they don't get the results that they desire in life, it is because they were born into the wrong circumstances, or because they never got a lucky break, or because other people failed them. In contrast, the person with an *internal* locus of control operates on the principle that he or she is ultimately responsible for their own destiny.

This way of thinking is indispensable for the evolutionary impulse to work its magic. To expand your circle of power, you must first accept the notion that you *have* power to begin with. Without this basic premise, there is no capacity to launch in the first place. Ownership of oneself is both an existential concept and a magical energy. Are you buffeted about by the winds of fate? Or are you a center from which action originates? Are you driven by environmental influences? Or are you self-driven? Taking ownership of your thoughts, actions, and decisions stimulates the Jupiterian expansive force that takes ownership of ever wider circles of power. It is a magical thing, really. When you believe in your own power, then your power will believe in you. By becoming aware of yourself as a *responsible agent,* you initiate a magnetic field of evolutionary energy that operates at all levels of body and soul, subtly and slowly transforming you into something more. Without ownership of self, one has nothing. But once you claim self-ownership you become a *center of power*. This is the path of all evolving life. The principle of ownership is what distinguishes persons of calibre from those who simply float along on the waves of existence. It is what separates the path of evolution from the path of stagnation.

It is important to recognize that this arc of evolution does not have to start with grand gestures of skill or power. It can start with the smallest of deeds, as long as you take full ownership of it. The consciousness of ownership and the decision to accept ownership is the force that pushes the evolutionary movement forward. This impulse to assume responsibility for one's destiny is self-propelling. It drives us to become more, so that we can do more and create more and experience more. It pushes us to learn new things, to cultivate new talents, and to acquire new skills. Indeed, the key principle to take away from this is that no matter where you are starting from in this very moment, your capacity to evolve is limitless, and it begins right now if you will simply *own* the journey.

There is a Law of Growth at work here, which is also a Law of Abundance, which says that taking ownership in small things will lead to ownership in larger things. As the saying goes: *to he who has, more shall be given; but from he who has not, what little he has will be taken away*. When you recognize and take responsibility for the power that you have, then the evolutionary impulse will expand your circle of power. But we must understand that this law stipulates that power must be used constructively to propel the evolutionary arc forward. Taking ownership of your power means taking responsibility for your authenticity, for speaking your truth, and for being what you truly are. There can be no evolution where there is no authenticity. The Law of Growth does not support that which is false. It does not support that which hasn't the courage to be what it truly is. Every false mask stunts the growth. Responsibility begins with being a genuine actor. If you haven't yet figured out how to do this, then start by taking responsibility for being authentic in some small capacity. Find *one thing* that truly makes you feel empowered, and then do that thing, and see how that makes you feel. Above all, you must dispense with all trace of self-pity, because self-pity is the energy of disempowerment. To see oneself as a victim of circumstances is to believe that life is something that happens *to* you, whereas the attitude of The Magician is that no matter what life throws your way, you always have the final word.

The Empress
Green Sphere to Orange Sphere

The image of The Empress evokes a feeling of *luxury*. The concreteness of Mercury combined with the radiance of Venus represents everything in life that sparkles and glitters with sensual richness. Picture the brightest, most opulent jewel that you can imagine, and you begin to capture the essence of this key. The Empress embodies the joyous world of sense experience and all of the riches that life has to offer. It is the spirit of every treasure and every shiny thing that hypnotizes us, and lures us into the dream-world of physical existence.

Why are humans so attracted to things that sparkle and glitter? The answer is rooted in a law of sexual polarity. While Venus is typically associated with feminine qualities, on the psychological plane it actually represents the masculine Yang energy in relation to the feminine Yin energy of Mercury. As the embodiment of concrete and formal thought, Mercury on its own tends to be dry and sterile. It must be germinated with the vital, creative warmth of Venus in order to yield *fruit*. For the sake of metaphor, let us imagine Mercury as a ball of wax. In its cooled and hardened state, it is pliable, but in a brittle and very clumsy manner. When it is warmed by the heat of Venus, it becomes liquid and lively and dancing with ideas. The liquid imagination that is quickened by the vitality of creative passion is the source of all abundance in both the mental realm and in nature.

The Empress is therefore a symbol of *fertility*, which is only possible where there is a coming together of essence and substance. There must be the fire and heat of essence to create conditions in which meaningful form can come to fruition. But there must also be a pliable, plastic, mutable substance that can receive the impression of that essence. Without Venus, the forms that Mercury manufactures are bland and flavorless. And without Mercury, Venus has nothing to give it body or expression. It is the combination of the two which produces a fertile imagination and a fertile environment. We have to understand that it is the animating fire of the Green Sphere which provides *nourishment* to the soul, mind, and body. The freshness of a food reflects the amount of essence that is still within it, and the essence is what is ultimately assimilated. Food that is lacking in fresh and rich flavor does not have as much of the essence that an organism needs. And though it goes largely unrecognized, the consumption of sensory impressions is just as essential to the vitality of the organism as the consumption of food, water, and oxygen. It is equally essential for one's well-being that these sensory impressions be beautiful, harmonious, and stimulating.

Through the action of sympathetic vibration, this consumption of sense impressions stimulates the *living light* of active imagination. By active imagination, we mean imagery which is *animated* with life and movement. The Green Sphere has a vitalizing warmth which naturally persuades the Orange Sphere to shape-shift and evolve into a *symbol* of the essence. It is like the warmth of the mother hen sitting upon an egg, a warmth which seeps into the plastic substance of the protoplasmic fluid and gradually quickens it into the shape of the baby chick. If we think of Mercury as the domain of the left brain and Venus as the domain of the right brain, then we could say that Venus *informs* Mercury. There is a magical effect at work here insofar as the essence of Venus fashions the pliable Mercury into a *natural* representation or embodiment of the essential quality. Mercury yields to the *implicit* contours of the Venusian essence. To allow this process to work its magic, we must loosen the mind just enough to let it yield to the contours of the animating fire. Without this influence of Venus, any shape that the left brain constructs will essentially be a dead shell, an artificial thing without soul or life. That is to say, the image must embody some kind of *genuine* emotional valence in order to be a thing of creative worth. Venus informing Mercury is the formula for the creative process in the true sense of the word.

The essential nature of this process is both alchemical and sexual. With the combination of the masculine and feminine energies, the Sulfur and the Mercury, a mysterious fertilization and germination takes place, a subterraneous process which the artist would do best not to interrogate or to second-guess. The creative output is not something that can be arrived at through left brain calculation. The form must evolve organically out of the essence, just as a seed planted in the earth evolves of its own natural logic. This requires that the substance of the Mercury-mind take a passive and fluid role. To some extent, this is the very purpose of meditation. It is often assumed that the object of meditation is to empty the mind of all thought, but this is not really the case. The object is to relax one's *grip* on the mind. Meditation trains us to assume a hands-off approach with regard to the wanderings of the imagination, giving it the space to circulate freely and to generate images of its own will. This loosening of one's grip is the real goal of meditation, but it is only half of the equation as far as the artistic process is concerned. The other half is to kindle the fire of passion, and allow it to animate the mind-stuff of imagination.

That the fire of creative inspiration is intimately connected to the fire of sexual passion is hardly a secret. Venus is an energy of fertility in both the mind and in nature. The harnessing of sexual energy is an especially powerful means of bringing the creative fire to bear upon the labile imagination. This formula is particularly relevant to the theory of magic. It is often said that visualization is the key to the Law of Attraction. What is not as well understood is that this visualization must be animated by the fire of Venus to have a *magical* effect. It is the *living imagination* that has real power, and it is from this magical liquid fire that visions and prophecies are born.

So to come back to the question: why do humans love shiny things? It is because they stimulate the liquid fire and fertilize the imagination. Those things that activate the creative juices through sympathetic vibration will always be the most prized and valued. This is the origin of fire worship, and the reason why fire has always held such a primitive fascination. We cannot gaze into the dancing radiance of a flickering flame without feeling both hypnotized and aroused by its primal resonance. It is a universal symbol of the living light that gives birth to all that is fruitful.

The Empress

The same is true of all things that are abundantly rich in sensory stimulation. They strike a chord within our emotional depths that ripples and hums with creative excitement. The essence of The Empress can be encapsulated in a very poignant image. The heat of Venus plus the fluidity of Mercury produces a humid mist, out of which is born a scintillating rainbow – the iridescent symbol of all the treasures that the sensory world has to offer.

The Emperor: Aries
Red Sphere to Yellow Sphere

The Sun represents the unifying force that brings all the parts of oneself together into a coherent whole. Mars represents the will. Together, their combined energies represent *unity of will*, or the single-mindedness that typifies Aries. The keyword here is *alignment*, which means all of your internal faculties pointing in the same direction. Picture the sun's rays focused through a magnifying glass. Aries is a one-pointed focus of intent, a complete uni-directional alignment of all of one's energies. A person operating at this level is exponentially more powerful and effective than someone whose energies are scattered and incoherent. It is like laser light, as opposed to diffuse light. For a person operating in alignment, everything is easy and effortless. There is no internal friction, only forward motion. The movement of Aries is like a battering ram. It is a fire that moves swiftly and decisively, and strikes like lightning.

Aries has a decidedly *external* focus. It is a very outgoing energy. It is not characteristic of Aries to ruminate or self-reflect, nor does it stop to ask the deeper questions. Aries initiates with action. It glides into action so easily because it does not know anything other than immediate action. Aries is forward-moving and to the point. This energy is best understood as a ray or vector that has no direction other than straight ahead, and it can be quite impatient with anything that is not moving things directly toward the targeted outcome.

The key virtue of Aries is *decisiveness*. When it comes to cultivating and strengthening the power of the will, being decisive is the first thing that you must learn. Without a clear definition of what you want, it is impossible to bring together the focus that leads to effective action. The difference between a strong will and a nebulous yearning is that yearning is a vague and wishy-washy kind of desire that doesn't really have primacy over other

The Emperor

competing desires. It is simply one desire in a muddled hodge-podge of desires, in which none of them has the authority to point the entire system toward a single goal. Aries is knowing exactly what you want, and moving directly toward it with conviction. It represents a *purity* of will that is not diluted with ulterior motives, or conflicting feelings, or muddled thinking.

To be divided internally between conflicting desires is truly an unpleasant place to be. It is a frustrating condition of going nowhere because the competing interests cancel each other out. To get around this impasse, it is necessary to make a decision and stick to it with complete commitment. Perhaps the most important lesson that we can learn from Aries is that it is better to make a wrong decision than to make no decision. To make no decision is to simply be inconsequential, whereas a wrong decision at least gives us the focus and the determination to make something happen. The underlying philosophy at stake here is that it is better to be whole than to be divided. When you make a decision, therefore, do not shrink back from it or second-guess it, but move forward with conviction. And if you are faced with conflicting desires, you have simply to ask yourself, which one is the strongest? Then go with that one desire, and do not waste any energy looking back. It is a very simple calculation, really. Do not expend mental or emotional energy on a desire that you are not going to act upon.

Aries is represented by the Tarot card of The Emperor. When an emperor commands his army, the soldiers all move in formation with one direction and one purpose. And so, in its ideal concept, Aries represents the self-discipline of bringing together all of the thoughts and emotions and scattered impulses within oneself into a coherent course of action. This may seem somewhat contradictory, as Aries is not typically thought of as highly disciplined, but rather as impulsive and shoot-from-the-hip, with little thought given toward the follow-through. Nevertheless, there is a clear discipline involved in being able to focus the whole of oneself into a single point of action, even if it is a short-lived burst of lightning. Aries is completely *undiluted* when it makes its move, though it would do well to learn how to maintain that focus over the long term.

This key, above all others, represents the energy of *courage* and conviction. If part of you wants to do a thing but another part is saying no, then that is a divided will, which is lack of conviction. But when every facet of the being is in agreement with one purpose, then the deed is as good as done. There is no questioning or backing down from a single-minded conviction. The special power of Aries is to not really care about the outcome. Which is not to say that Aries wouldn't prefer success over failure. Aries never goes into action half-heartedly. But it is not the nature of Aries to *calculate* the probability of success before committing to the attempt. For Aries, it is a matter of *honor* to act upon what you want, whether it pans out or not. There is a principle of *wholeness* at stake. If you will a certain thing but do not act upon it, then you are not whole inside. And it is better to fail honestly than to not be whole. This is ultimately where Aries gets its courage and fearlessness. It is more afraid of not being whole than of anything else.

There is never a question then of "Is it worth it?" To calculate in such a way is seen as dishonorable and petty. Aries is the aspect of Mars that is most clearly expressed as *authenticity*. That means to express one's will in a true and pure form, without duplicity and without hiding or concealment. To not confuse one's own will with that of other people, or to be subservient to the expectations of other people - that is the Aries code of honor.

There is an undoubtedly *magical* quality to the action of Aries when we understand the core essence of it. When you purify and unify the will for the sake of wholeness, you create a kind of *magnetic field* that influences things around you in unseen ways. A magnet, after all, is formed by all of the atomic electrons in a metallic body aligning themselves in the *same direction*. The uniting of all the elements of oneself into a single focus of will increases the likelihood of success through a type of occult influence. The coherent flow of a decisive will creates a magnetic current that pulls surrounding energies into its stream. Fearlessness is indeed magical, in the most literal sense of the word.

The Hierophant: Taurus
Indigo Sphere to Red Sphere

Taurus represents an application of willpower that stands in stark contrast to that of Aries. Whereas Aries is fiery, energetic, and daring, Taurus is slow, laborious, penetrating, and enduring. The energy of Saturn combined with the energy of Mars gives a *consistency of will* that does not dissipate or wind down over time. It embodies the characteristic Taurean attitude of tenacious determination. Once it is fixed upon a task, it is not easily moved from its course. The Tarot card of The Hierophant has typically been interpreted to represent social conventions and traditions, and the institutions that uphold them. It represents the habits and customs that a society has agreed upon because, in some sense, they have worked. They have served a purpose in holding the culture together. And while the established ways of doing things may seem stubbornly irrational at times, they do provide a solid bedrock on which the wheels of civilization may be relied upon to crank out their necessary work, day in and day out.

Like Aries, Taurus is therefore a sign of *discipline*, but in a different sense of the word. Aries represents the discipline of uniting all of one's energies in a single direction, whereas Taurus is the discipline of keeping the momentum going over the long term. Saturn and the Sun together constitute a double-center of the Tree, and they both carry a sense of "keeping it all together". The Sun embodies the idea of synthesis and focus, while Saturn embodies stability and steadfastness. As they both pivot around Mars to form the energies of Aries and Taurus, the two signs represent the Yin and Yang, the complementary facets of self-discipline.

The best way to understand the energy of Taurus is to think of it as *internalized* will. If you can internalize your goal to the point that every fiber of your being pushes toward it without your even thinking, then this is guaranteed success. Imagine a large stone rolling down a hill. It doesn't have to think about getting to the bottom. It doesn't stop to consider how long it might take to reach the destination, and at no point does it question whether it is even worth it to keep going. The stone is driven down the hill by its own momentum, which is baked into every atom of its mass. The strength of Taurus is its ability to focus in the present moment, and to only worry about what needs to be done *right now*. Taurus is what enables you to practice a thing over and over again until you have mastered it. As far as Taurus is concerned, there is not really a sense of striving toward an end goal, because there is only the present moment. This is the true meaning of patience - to recognize only the *now* and to be fully grounded in it, to be so absorbed in a task that there is no past or future. The persistence of Taurus comes from a deep inner stillness that does not get distracted. It does not allow itself to go wandering off, it just settles into the job that is at hand. For this reason, it is the energy of Saturn that we are aiming for in the practice of meditation, because it is precisely the *stillness* of the mind that grounds us in the present moment.

Taurus has a reputation for being materialistic and sensual, and this is a direct corollary of its being occupied in the *now*. When the mind is not wandering off into the past or future, then the natural focus of attention is upon the objects of immediate sense-perception. And clearly, the Saturn side of Taurus has a natural affinity for the consistency and stability of material things. But there is also a side to Taurus's materialistic nature that has to do with being in one's natural element. Taurus is especially adapted for moving the will through the viscosity of physical reality. It is a fact of existence that we are never able to manifest our will instantaneously. We must move through the natural resistance of the material world. This is endlessly frustrating to those who have no patience, but Taurus has the special ability to move forward relentlessly through this resistance and *not experience it as friction*. We could say then that Taurus feels *at home* in that solid realm of the tangible and concrete. It is like a creature that has evolved to move through molasses. Patient persistence is ingrained into its muscle memory. It knows how to blend in with the here and now. Whereas Aries becomes quickly impatient and frustrated with the environmental resistance of physical reality, Taurus has no issue with taking things slowly and steadily. Subsequently, it has learned to appreciate the journey as much as the destination.

The thing to understand about Taurus then, is that it does not simply represent a grim determination to force one's way through at all cost. If that were the case, it would not be very well adapted. It is rather that Taurus is *acclimated* to the groundedness of the present moment. It draws energy from the here and now, and that is what sustains it indefinitely in its untiring march forward. For Taurus, the journey is like listening to music. No one ever listens to a song that he or she enjoys and thinks, *let's hurry up and get this over with*.

So as a mode of being-in-the-world, Taurus teaches us a valuable lesson. If we come back to the function of the Moon, it represents that which we absorb through direct experience, as opposed to the "book learning" that we gather in a purely abstract and intellectual sense. The lesson of Taurus is that when we try to move too fast through life, we do not absorb the nourishing energies of sensual experience. We become like a plant that has been pulled out of the ground. Though we may not appreciate the limits that Saturn puts upon us, it nevertheless holds the soul in a matrix of experience from which it draws knowledge, wisdom, and understanding. It is this matrix of experience in which the soul grows, just as the roots of the plant draw sustenance out of the ground. To move through this matrix too hastily is to connect with it only superficially. It is to undercut the *osmosis* that naturally occurs between the self and the world. The key lesson of Taurus is that even if we get from A to B in record time, we have not absorbed the essential energies that the journey is meant to provide. We arrive at the destination undernourished. In the overall economy of the soul, sensual experience is an essential nutrient.

Another sense in which moving slowly and patiently is advantageous is that you become *attuned* to the surroundings. You develop a rapport with the environment, and this is always a tactical advantage. Moving at the pace of the environment allows us to pick up the signals around us, and to learn the language of the medium through which we are moving. This can only be possible when we match the rhythms of the surroundings. Trying to push through too fast puts us out of sync with the natural rhythms, and the principle of sympathetic vibration falls apart. Our note then strikes a dissonant chord with the notes around us. Taurus is known to be especially attuned to nature, in part because of its ability to match the rhythms of nature, but also because the movements of nature are driven by the fixed will of instinct that resembles Taurus's mode of operation. Taurus represents action that has been persisted in so consistently that it becomes second nature. It is a will that has become so steeped into the fiber of one's being that it does not even require effort. Nature moves in the same manner, being guided by a fixed, ingrained will of instinctive behavior. It is the slow but steady will that causes the crops to come up out of the ground. It is the tireless, persistent will that causes the heart to beat over and over again, every second of every day of one's life. Nature is driven by a steady and dependable will that never grows weary of its job, and never gives it a second thought.

The Lovers: Gemini
Indigo Sphere to Yellow Sphere

In Western astrology, the sign of Gemini is taken to represent the mythical twins Castor and Pollux. In Indian astrology, however, the name of this sign is *Mithuna,* which conveys something closer to the idea of a pair of lovers. Gemini represents the path between the Sun and Saturn. The Sun plays a role of tying things together. In that respect, it serves both a mental and rational function insofar as it establishes associations, relationships, and webs of meaning between the countless elements that make up our experience. Saturn plays the role of laying down a stable foundation. From the intersection of these two forces we get Gemini, which serves the role of building the *mental structures* that hold our experience together into a sensible narrative.

If the Diamond Sphere is consciousness, then we can think of Gemini as that which constructs a *lens* through which consciousness views the world. It is how we impose order upon our reality. If we try to imagine what the world must seem like to the newborn infant, it would have to be a chaos of sense impressions bombarding the nervous system. Light and color and sound and feeling all flood the brain in a bewildering wash of sensation. Over time, the child learns to piece these sensations together into logical units. The logical units then coalesce into patterns, and from these patterns emerge generalized rules of engagement with our surroundings. Cause-and-effect relationships begin to form out of the web of associations. Eventually, the primordial soup of sensory experience becomes an orderly world that can be negotiated and navigated with relative ease. The waters of experience turn into solid ground.

Astrologically, Gemini and its opposite sign of Sagittarius are both associated with education. There is an important distinction between them, however. Whereas Sagittarius is associated with "higher" education and the loftier journeys of the mind,

The Lovers

Gemini represents the kind of basic education that we receive in childhood. Reading, writing, and arithmetic - these are the foundational mental skills that we require to make sense of our environment and to get around in society. Primary education builds the mental framework that the child needs to construct a functional and workable model of the world around him.

Now the interesting thing about this narrative-building function of Gemini is that it is inherently *superficial*. That is to say, it is a mental layer that we place upon the underlying structure of reality. We all know that every one of us has a different narrative lens through which we view the same set of facts. When Gemini is self-aware, it is fully cognizant of the superficial nature of its narrative structures, and it recognizes that the stories which it creates are merely a surface layer of the truth. And so we observe in Gemini a characteristic detachment toward life, coupled with a sense of irony. It is the nature of Gemini to not take anything too seriously, because of all the signs it is the best equipped to see through the superficiality of its own constructions.

Without this degree of self-awareness, the narrative structure can easily become a trap. It becomes a veil of illusion, the veil of *maya*. The most difficult trap to escape from is of course the narrative structure that has been invested with *emotional* value. The inherent instinct of Gemini however, is to *not* invest its mental structures with emotion. To the contrary, Gemini prefers the light-hearted entertainment of skating swiftly and freely across the surface of its narrative structures, just as one would skate across the surface of an icy lake. Gemini takes a certain quality of aloofness from Saturn. It much prefers cool logic over sticky emotion, and while such a lack of emotional depth may strike others as shallow, to Gemini it is precisely this breezy detachment that allows it to float so swiftly and effortlessly through life. We could even argue that Gemini has an innate capacity for piercing through the veil of maya, and it is well worth considering that this particular path, extended upwards, leads directly to the path of the Hanged Man.

Gemini is often spoken of as the most distinctly *human* sign. This is only natural, as it represents the type of mental activity that imposes a semblance of order and meaning upon the universe. To be clear, Gemini does not embody meaning in any deep or profound sense, but rather it typifies the more mundane associations of meaning that hold one's day-to-day experience together. It is well suited to strategic or systematic thinking, as it has a feel for the interconnections and energy flows between things. Most significantly, Gemini is associated with *communication*, and it is stereotypically regarded as the chattiest of the signs. This is also quite natural, as to communicate is to frame a narrative about the shared reality. Language is in fact the very process of pasting layers of interpretation over our experience.

An important keyword with Gemini is *networking*. Gemini is all about connections. In traditional astrology, Gemini was associated with roads and bridges, trade routes and commerce. In the modern paradigm, it is cables and wires, computers and information systems. Wherever energy and information flow back and forth through channels of exchange, the Gemini archetype is at work. Think of neural synapses and motherboards, algorithms and economics. Gemini has some similarity to the Black-Indigo axis in that they both give structure to the universe. The difference is that Gemini represents the *circuitry* of the cosmos. There is a distinctly electrical quality to Gemini in the way that it darts about at the speed of thought, and the very nature of electricity would seem to suggest that in some fundamental sense, it is a universal medium of communication. Whether we are talking about the flow of information between neurons, or the flow of information through a circuit board, it is the medium of electricity that constitutes the life-blood of the network.

There is an important lesson to be gleaned from Gemini, which has to do with how we fashion our own reality. The mental fabric that Gemini weaves acts as a kind of structural mesh which binds together the gelatinous substance of our subjective experience, holding it together into a coherent story. It is the *connective tissue* of our perceived reality. What is most striking about this mental fabric is that it is completely immaterial, and ridiculously easy

The Lovers

to manipulate and deconstruct. And yet, it holds our entire life together. Without this tenuous web of meaning to bind and shape it, our existence would fall apart. With Gemini then, we come face-to-face with the question of *what is truth?* For something so insubstantial and pliable, our mental structures are profoundly influential. It is the framework of meaning which you put around your life that determines how your life will manifest and unfold. The wisdom of Gemini - which is also its levity - lies in seeing just how thin this layer of meaning is, and how easy it is to redefine.

The Chariot: Cancer
Indigo Sphere to Blue Sphere

The Blue Sphere stands for that which is *our own* - our possessions and the space that we occupy. The Indigo Sphere represents stability. And so the intersection of these principles signifies the preservation and protection of one's personal domain. Cancer is therefore the zodiac sign which is most concerned with *security*. Defending and holding on to what is ours is a key focus of Cancer, and the archetypal symbol of this is the ancestral castle.

The idea of *home,* which is a central theme of Cancer, can mean many things on many levels. In the most literal sense, the home is a protective structure around one's personal space. Like the shell of the crab, the physical walls of the home are a fortress in which we take refuge from the forces of the outside world. The home is where we retain our personal belongings and keep them safely in our possession. It is also a sanctuary and a place of privacy, a place in which we can be alone with our thoughts and introspect in peace. The home is a place of quiet meditation, unmolested by external circumstances or the noise of the world outside.

Cancer has a deep connection with the physical body, which serves as the domicile of the soul. When we consider our personal belongings, nothing is more firmly in our possession than the body itself. While a car or a purse or a phone can be stolen from us, it is unheard of for someone to steal our body and make it their own. The body is therefore the primary example of the Saturn-Jupiter idea of *fixed possession*. Real estate comes close as a secondary example, as it is not the kind of property that anyone could just walk away with, but the physical body is much more aligned to the core concept. While the body can therefore be thought of as the *temple* of the soul, it also serves as the *vehicle* with which we get about in the world. Thus, the imagery of the Tarot card The Chariot is a fitting representation for the sign of Cancer, as we have not only the vehicle as the central motif, but also the armor worn by the main figure, and the walled city in the background.

In a broader sense, the Cancerian notion of home can be defined as setting a boundary around that from which we draw sustenance and nourishment. Thus the attachments to family, tribe, clan, and homeland are all very Cancerian sentiments. Cancer is known for having a nurturing disposition, as well as being fiercely protective of those who belong to its inner circle. Both of these attributes correspond very neatly to Jupiter which provides resources, and Saturn which preserves the integrity of boundaries. The Cancerian bond of kinship and tribe is therefore an instinct for belonging, and for taking refuge in a mutually-supporting group. In terms of our overall strategy for managing and navigating the world, Cancer represents the *home base* of operations. It is the place in which we make plans, consolidate gains, rest from our labor, and explore our feelings in private.

Unsurprisingly, Cancer is known for holding on to things. The grasping claws of the crab are possessive and reluctant to let go. This tendency often reveals itself as nostalgia and sentimental attachment to things of the past. It can also manifest as possessiveness in relationships, and while Cancer is known for being emotionally nurturing and affectionate, this affection can become smothering if the grasping tendency is not moderated. Cancer can also have an unhealthy habit of clinging to its emotional wounds and ruminating over the past. While it is known for being gifted with a retentive memory, Cancer can sometimes benefit from learning how to let go.

This is not to say that Cancer's grip on the past is entirely retrograde. The memory of past experiences creates a behavioral imprint that informs how we navigate the present. This is a natural and useful tool for survival. There is a cultural tendency at present to focus on the negative side of the subconscious, as popular psychology has made it abundantly clear that dysfunctional behavioral patterns tend to be rooted in bad childhood experiences. This bias fails to recognize, however, that our useful behavior patterns - which would be most of them - are also formed from the imprints of past experience. The formative influences that have shaped us should therefore be thought of as largely beneficial. To the extent that they are *not* serving us well, we should aim to dialogue with them, rather than try to fight them or reject them. The subconscious contains far too much valuable information for us to squander on a negative and distrustful relationship. It is the storehouse of what we have learned, both individually and collectively. This includes not only the lessons of our own experience, but also the ancestral memory that has been passed down from generation to generation through the DNA, as well as the racial memory that has been preserved in what Jung has called the collective unconscious.

One of the things that is often noted about Cancer is the seemingly stark contrast between the tough, defensive exterior and the soft, sensitive interior. This character study begins to make sense if we think of Cancer metaphorically as an egg. If the hard outer shell corresponds to Saturn, then Jupiter represents the interior protoplasm, which contains all of the essential resources that the beginning life needs in order to grow into itself. In this jointly Saturnian and Jupiterian role, we see Cancer as both preserving and providing, protecting and nourishing. And what better symbol of this do we have than the mother's womb? As the zodiac sign most associated with motherhood, Cancer protects that which is still in the process of formation. It creates the secure and fortified space in which transformation, growth, and evolution can occur.

Now one could rightfully ask, how is this relevant to those of us who are already fully-formed adults? The answer is that in a deeper sense, we are all undergoing a continual process of growth and evolution. The transformations that we experience in adulthood are not so much physical as they are *emotional*, but much of the symbolism applies just the same. Whether we are talking about the fetus developing in the womb, or the soul evolving within the vessel of the physical body, the process in either case is a state of profound *vulnerability* in which the self is fluid and constantly shifting. We can think of the soft interior of Cancer then as the *emotional matrix* of our being, in which the growth of the self is a constant process of undoing and reintegration.

This process naturally requires a safe and secure environment in which the protoplasm of the personality can undergo its transformations, undisturbed by outside influences.

In the symbolism of alchemy, this is represented by the *athanor*, the hermetically sealed vessel in which the transmutation takes place. The signs of the zodiac are regarded as alternating between the polarities of extroversion and introversion. In a continuous cycle, the extroverted polarity goes forth to acquire new experiences, and the introverted polarity goes inward to assimilate them. Cancer can be seen as the most archetypally introverted sign, as it represents the state of going inward by which to emotionally process and consolidate the experiences that we have gathered.

In the day-to-day sense then, Cancer represents how we make space for our inner growth. This involves creating an environment in which we feel emotionally stable and secure. The Saturn side of Cancer creates an atmosphere of undisturbed relaxation, in which time stands still. The Jupiter side gives us a sense of being provided for, of having the resources that we need to reflect and grow. If we could visualize the essence of Cancer, it would be a place where you can relax by a warm fireplace with a cup of hot cocoa, or a bowl of soup. The words "food and shelter" epitomize the functions of Jupiter and Saturn, and together they provide the *creature comforts* that make us feel warm inside, and which give us the space to become who we are.

Strength: Leo
Blue Sphere to Yellow Sphere

The best approach to understanding the path between the Blue Sphere and the Yellow Sphere is to begin by looking at the character traits that are commonly associated with the zodiac sign of Leo. Leo is generally described as a personality that thrives on being in the spotlight. There is always a *performative* aspect where Leo is concerned. It has a way of seeming larger than life, with a flair for showmanship and theatricality. The mode of expression is often exaggerated and dramatic, but there is a definite entertainment value and uplifting energy that comes from Leo's over-the-top fanfare. While Leo undoubtedly enjoys being the center of attention, it is also known for acting with wholesomeness, good-heartedness, and generosity. Leo is often associated with authority and with being a center of influence, but it is the type of authority figure that inspires confidence and motivation. Leo leads by example, and the charisma that it radiates has, on balance, a vitalizing influence on those around it.

All of these qualities can be mapped to attributes of the Sun and Jupiter. Jupiter is expansive and takes up space, just like Leo's dramatic gestures and rhetoric. The Sun is the center of the narrative, in the same way that Leo is the center of attention and the unifying focus around which things revolve. The Sun is also the source of all life-energy on the planet, and it dispenses this energy unconditionally to everyone and everything. The vitality that the Sun bestows is experienced as a Jupiterian feeling of abundance by those who receive it.

How then do we summarize the core concept of Leo? To fully grasp what Leo is about, we have to understand its principal motivation. Leo's presentation can come across as egotistical, and it can be tempting to take the cynical but somewhat lazy view that Leo's core motivation is simply to consume all of the attention for itself. If this were truly the case, then Leo's role in the world

Strength

would be entirely parasitic. The reality is in fact the opposite, though. Leo's core motivation is to *shine*, and it is compelled to shine because it possesses, from the depths of its being, a *super-abundance* of vitality and energy that it has to dispose of in some way. The fact that Leo *does* attract attention and admiration is *transactional*. Leo can only become the center of attention by providing something of value. It has to radiate light and warmth in order to be seen and appreciated. And because Leo feels deep down in its heart that the energy that it puts forth *is* valuable to everyone else, it *must* of necessity exude this energy to everyone around it. Ultimately, this is not a matter of moral principle. It is simply the *physics* of energetic abundance which dictates that it must discharge its excess generously and unconditionally.

Behind the surface of Leo's radiant persona lies a little understood esoteric truth. Simmering within every infinitesimal point of space lies a source of universal vitality that is both nowhere and everywhere. Described by some as the Great Central Sun, it is a limitless depth of creative fire which burns at the heart of all things beneath the surface layer of reality. To tap into this bottomless energy is to become larger than life. The primal fire fills the personality and expands it like a hot air balloon. When the boundaries of the personality have been overrun, this fire radiates out like a ball of light and saturates the surrounding space. The Leo personality is sometimes described as being "full of itself", and the truth of this is more literal than we realize. The key secret of this energy dynamic though, is that the radiating out of creative power does not deplete Leo of its vitality. In point of fact, the more energy that Leo gives, the more it draws up from the limitless depths of the Central Sun. The giving-forth of vitality acts as a kind of *energy pump* that sustains the flow from the primal source. It is often said that the difference between introverts and extroverts is that introverts recharge through time spent alone, while extroverts recharge through social interaction. As we have described Cancer as the archetypally introverted sign, Leo qualifies as the archetypally extroverted sign. The source of its revitalization is the continual giving-forth of energy. Thus, Leo has an abundance of confidence, optimism, and audacity, because it knows that its source of power will never dry up no matter how much it yields.

It is not surprising then that Leo tends to attract a following. The Yellow Sphere influence that it channels is healthy and organic, wholesome and harmonizing, an energy of building-up and knitting-together. The energy that Leo channels is a creative energy, and so the Leo experience is one of theatricality, splendor, entertainment, and *fun* - all of which inspires people to exercise their creative juices. It is also an energy of physical vitality and physical integrity, and it illuminates the essential connection between creativity and health. When the creative energy is low, the body lacks a unifying purpose, and therefore naturally tends to run out of steam and wind down. But when the Solar creative power is streaming steadily through the cells and tissues, it powers up the harmonic magnetizing forces that hold the body together in a purposeful and coherent organization. It is precisely this organic and *organizing* quality of Leo that makes it a center of influence. The charisma and *performance value* of Leo is not just superficial. It is a type of living poetry that inspires others to model its creative exuberance.

The lesson that Leo teaches us then is that we should not hide our light under a bushel. Modesty is certainly a virtue up to a certain point, but it is also healthy to have a bit of *swagger*. And while we clearly want to be mindful that we are not pushy or overbearing, it doesn't hurt to make yourself a *little bit larger* in gesture and expression. To allow yourself to shine is to spread light and warmth to others, and so despite what our puritanical instincts may tell us, there *is* some inherent value to self-promotion and exhibitionism. Leo challenges us to serve as an example and a role model. Each one of us has a unique perspective and focus to bring to the mosaic of expanding human consciousness, and we must each take the responsibility of *broadcasting* that perspective within our sphere of influence. Leo challenges us to level up our presentation skills. The real thrust of Leo is not simply to gain attention, but rather to dispense some form of Jupiterian, expansive, uplifting influence. It may be wisdom, knowledge, levity, joviality, or artistic expression. Whatever manner of influence we see fit to take, Leo is the delivery system for the unfiltered energy of pure creative abundance.

The Hermit: Virgo
Blue Sphere to Green Sphere

Virgo is perhaps the most deceptive of the zodiac signs. Typically seen as quiet, reserved, and unassuming, Virgo gives a presentation that renders an air of modest humility. This modesty, however, conceals an urge to be completely in control, and Virgo understands very well that real power is found not in bluster, not in sound and fury, but rather in a quiet but firm grip.

The name of the sign is deceptive as well. Virgo is taken to represent the virgin, which would seem to suggest a somewhat sterile and *asexual* disposition. This is also a misconception. Virgo has a way of *sublimating* sexual energy. It channels and harnesses sexuality into a sharper focus. But the sexuality of Virgo is *no less* than any other sign, it is simply more sophisticated and refined, and in that sense it is *more powerful*. Virgo refines sexual energy in a way that makes it more concentrated and more potent. By saying more with less, it exudes a certain kind of alluring mystique which hints at far more beneath the surface.

In similar fashion, the deceptively cool disposition of Virgo hints at a character fiber that is more powerful than it advertises. We have been told that a barking dog seldom bites, and that the individual who speaks softly and carries a big stick is the one that we should be wary of tangling with. Quiet power makes a stronger impression on us than loud gestures, because it indicates a degree of self-control and self-mastery that is to be respected and taken seriously. If there is one thing that we have learned from the movies, it's that the most powerful characters - the hero and the arch-villain - are both cool and calculating in how they get things done, whereas the boorish and bombastic characters are invariably dispatched with surgical precision.

Virgo is perhaps best known for its *perfectionism*, which reflects both the Jupiterian impulse for control as well as the aesthetic

The Hermit

sensibility of Venus. Virgo's principal motivation is to express the essence of a thing in its purest and most distilled form, which is achieved through refinement and precision. One could say that Virgo seeks to extract the Platonic ideal of the matter, and embody it in the most concise representation. The fine-grained efficiency and sensitivity to detail that Virgo brings to the table allows it to speak volumes with the most subtle of gradations. In every craft, there is far more power in nuance than there is in overstatement. Generally speaking, we have the most admiration for art and literature that gives us just enough information to let our imagination fill in the gaps, rather than spell everything out for us. Virgo is masterful at giving us the broadest implications with the most minute of details. To do more with less - the definition of efficiency - is what Virgo excels at. To accomplish this requires that we refine the essence of a thing, that we extract it down to its purest and most *potent* form. The potency of anything lies in its purity. And as potency is an attribute of Jupiter, and essence an attribute of Venus, Virgo is therefore the natural intersection of the two.

As it is often necessary to go inward to find the essence of something, Virgo is a sign of *introspection*. This is the overall mood of the Tarot card of The Hermit - to take a solitary journey inward to a place of silence, in order to feel into the heart of the matter. The inner space of quiet contemplation is where Virgo does its alchemical work of filtering the pure nature of a thing from the non-essential details. The refining focus of Virgo is a process of *intension* as opposed to *extension*. Virgo is often described as *analytical*, but what does that mean exactly? To analyze something means to reduce it to its essence, or to extract its essence. But more importantly, to extract the essence in a way that is practical and useful, to capture the Platonic ideal in a way that can provide value.

When the signs of the zodiac are mapped to the parts of the body, Virgo is traditionally associated with the digestive system. And so we have here, in both the physical and metaphysical sense, an activity of breaking something down in order to distill and assimilate its purified essence. This process of digestion could be described as a *sublimation* - an extraction and refinement of an essential energy in order to raise it up to a higher purpose. Similarly, we can point to a number of practices that involve extracting a valuable essential component from physical substances. Alchemy, chemistry, herbalism, medicine, drugs - all of these are products or processes of a Virgoan nature. Chemistry is all about extracting a pure substance with useful properties, and distillation is the chemical process that exemplifies the action of Virgo most clearly. Chemistry is of course the direct descendant of alchemy, and the central theorem of alchemy was that the Universal Medicine could be obtained by extracting the purified essence of gold from its corporeal metallic body. Herbalism is likewise an alchemy of herbs, in which the healing essences of plants are extracted from their material forms.

This brings us to an interesting point. Virgo has always been regarded as a very practical and earthy sign. And yet at the same time this underlying focus on the intangible essence of things has a magical quality about it. A little-known fact about Virgo is that the ancient Greeks and Romans actually associated the sign with Demeter and Ceres, both of which were goddesses of fertility, agriculture, and harvest. In fact, artistic representations of the constellation typically depicted a woman holding a sheaf of wheat. We could certainly say that few things are more practical and earthy than agriculture. But there is also something mysterious and magical about the natural processes at work in the growth of herbs and plants. Consider the seed, for instance. It is a tiny, nondescript, seemingly insignificant thing. And yet it contains the potential to eventually become something as enormous as a towering oak tree. It is as if the massive oak were distilled down to its most condensed and potent essence. Then there is the germination of the seed underground, in which it extracts and sublimates the organic essence of the rich black soil. Interestingly enough, the theory of alchemy compared the alchemical process metaphorically to agriculture. It was believed that the pure extracted essence of gold - which was called the *seed* of gold - when implanted into the molten substance of a lesser metal, would transform the entirety of that lesser metal into gold itself. And so throughout the conceptual topics of herbalism, agriculture, and alchemy, there runs a common thread around the magical and transformational virtues of the Venusian essences found in nature.

A salient question arises from this. If the sign of Virgo was originally associated with fertility goddesses, then where does the motif of the virgin come from? The answer is that Virgo was also associated with the mythological figure of Astraea, the chaste goddess of innocence and purity. Astraea was said to be the last of the immortals to live amongst human beings during the Golden Age of humanity. As society gradually lapsed into moral degeneracy during the Bronze and Iron Ages, she eventually fled to the heavens, dismayed at the wretched state that humanity had fallen into. This myth clearly illustrates the perfectionist sensibilities associated with Virgo. But the conflation of the fertility goddess and the virgin goddess points to a more esoteric truth, which is that the sexual energy of this sign is deeply powerful, but deceptively covert. It touches upon the magical secrets of *sexual sublimation*. The underlying principle, alluded to in certain mystical theories and practices, is that the directing of sexual energy inward transforms it into magical energy. In a place of quiet stillness, the Venusian sexual fire germinates into profound powers of perception, insight, and influence. This is the secret concealed behind the silent inner work of The Hermit. Beneath the cloak of unassuming obscurity, he is both prophet and magician.

Continuous self-improvement is a decidedly Virgoan pursuit, and it is no surprise that cleanliness and hygiene, both physical and psychological, are top of mind. The perfectionist standards that Virgo strives for can lead to such debilitating self-criticism, however, that it undermines its own sense of self-worth. This is perhaps the chief reason behind Virgo's reputation for self-effacement. It has a tendency to hide out of a sense of not being good enough for its own standards. The obsession with getting everything just right can also lead to crippling inaction. Virgo has a clear path to personal power, however, if it can simply learn how to be a flawed being. The innate advantage that Virgo holds is its ability to command charisma and presence through the natural *gracefulness* with which it articulates itself. Virgo's keen attention to nuance embodies the ideal of *beauty in precision*. The trick is to not get caught up in an uptight pursuit of precision for its own sake, but rather to focus on the clarified *essence* of what it is that one seeks to communicate. The mindset must be changed from finicky to graceful. Once that fundamental essence has been clearly grasped, then Virgo can condense it into a perfect form that sparkles and shines like a polished jewel.

Justice: Libra
Yellow Sphere to Green Sphere

The Sun and Venus are both naturally bright and uplifting energies, and so together they have a signature that is exceptionally radiant and pleasing. With Libra, we have a strong appreciation of *beauty*. In fact, we could say that the principal keyword of this path *is* beauty, but its quality is not nearly as sensual or sexual as that of The Empress. It is a much more refined sense of beauty, light and aetherial. Whereas the watery and contracting nature of Mercury, when combined with Venus, gives The Empress a more earth-bound appreciation of the senses, the aerial and fiery nature of the Sun adds more of a luminous and glowing quality to the Venusian influence. Libra represents the sense of beauty that comes from wholesomeness and harmony, and the essence of harmony is *joy*. Joy is the feeling that everything is in balance, that your experience is bound together by a unifying equilibrium. When the parts of the whole come together in harmonious agreement and balance, there emerges from this synergy a radiant and glowing *aura* of healing energy, which we experience as joyfulness. Just as the Sun emanates rays of light, the harmonizing influence of Libra emanates rays of joy.

Libra is symbolized by the scales, which represent balance. In one sense, we could say that Libra stands for balance in relationships. That is to say, a balance of give and take, a balance of rights and obligations, a balance of right action for each given circumstance. And this is precisely what we mean by *justice* - the balance of power between individuals in a society. But in another sense, there is also an internal balance which we call beauty. When the parts of a whole are in balance, then we say that it is well-proportioned, beautiful, and elegant. The instinct of Libra is to balance out all of the forces and energies in such a way that the resulting whole emanates an aesthetic radiance. The calibration of energies and relationships results in a luminous glow. This is the natural radiance of harmony, and with Libra, the instinct for justice is the same as the instinct for beauty.

One thing that is absolutely essential to understand here is that the idea of justice embodied by Libra is not one of judgment, or vengeance, or punishment, or retribution. Libra stands for none of these things. It is not a vindictive justice that Libra strives for. Libra is simply about putting things back into balance. Anger and vengeance are forces that invariably swing the pendulum too far in the opposite direction, and so their natural action is to *perpetuate* imbalance. Libra sees through to the unbalanced nature of vengeance, and therefore has no desire to have any part of it.

This is not to say that Libra won't fight for what it believes in. It is not an aggressive energy, but it is not exactly passive either, and it *will* take whatever action it deems appropriate to set things aright. But if Libra *does* have to put up a fight or execute justice, it will do so without any feeling of malice or vindictiveness, and it will never take the fight any further than necessary. Libra fights with honor. It will take just enough corrective action to restore things to a healthy balance, and no further will it go beyond that point. It is also in the nature of Libra to temper justice with mercy. Libra does not enjoy holding a grudge or hanging on to resentment, and so it has a natural inclination to be forgiving once the balance has been restored. The idea that anyone *deserves* to be punished is alien to Libra's way of thinking. There is no desire to dehumanize the guilty party or to inflict suffering upon them, as that in itself would have an unhealthy and dehumanizing influence on the punisher as well. Libran justice is simply a system of checks and balances, the aim of which is to maintain a social order of harmonious beauty.

Libra is regarded as an air sign, and so it possesses an inherent levity that comes from letting go of negativity. Negative thoughts and emotions have by their nature a very dense and heavy quality. They drag us down and burden us with a thick and oppressive viscosity. Libra is simply not interested in this. It has no *taste* for thoughts and feelings that would weigh it down, or that would otherwise inhibit the Venusian inclination to shine and to be radiant. The natural disposition for balance makes Libra *allergic* to negative energies. Libra simply can't be bothered with them.

This actually represents a certain kind of willpower on Libra's part. The most insidious thing about negative thoughts and feelings is that they have a way of convincing us that we should interrogate them, and ruminate over them, and feed them our attention. Our negativity has a persuasive manner of plying us with arguments as to why we *need* to stew over the perceived injustices that others have done to us, and why we simply *must* be angry and upset over things that are beyond our control. Our negativity tries to shame us into thinking that if we are *not* wallowing in discontent, then it shows that we simply *don't care* as much as we should. But Libra has the good sense and the conviction to just say *no* to these demands. And so it presents an aerial texture that the dense energies simply can't stick to or grasp hold of. Libra has a certain quality, similar to that of Gemini, of not taking things too seriously. This sense of levity and emotional detachment is what gives Libra the balanced perspective from which it can do that which is *truly* the right judgment in the circumstances. As much as they may try to convince us otherwise, feelings of anger and outrage do not have the insight or the moral clarity to restore things to a harmonious outcome.

Libra is therefore of the instinct that whatever is healthy and balanced will naturally have an uplifting and aesthetically pleasing influence, and anything that has the opposite effect is naturally morally suspect. Another way to describe Libra's perspective would be to say that "by their fruits shall you know them", or "the proof of the pudding is in the eating". Which is to say, the proof of the goodness or fitness of a code of conduct is that it produces a healthy, well-balanced, and aesthetically pleasing outcome. This must not be understood in a superficial sense, however. Anything that is pleasing on the surface but internally corrupt will eventually reveal itself in unbalanced outcomes, and so the harmony must be evident both internally and externally.

By this way of judging things, Libra would give no credence to ideologies that claim a kind of self-righteous moral high ground, but which ultimately leave everyone feeling more unhappy. To be righteously miserable is an oxymoron from Libra's point of view. That which brings joy and elevates people to a higher energy state is the signature of *natural good*. That which brings people to a chronically lower state is the definition of what is unhealthy. A person who is miserable can certainly be ideologically dedicated to helping others, but their misery will nonetheless have an infectious and unhealthy influence. Our ability to have a genuinely positive influence on the world around us must therefore start with finding joy and radiance within.

A useful thing to keep in mind about Libra is that the energetic stimulus between the Sun and Venus flows in both directions. That is to say, harmony and wholesomeness naturally arouse feelings of joy, but the energy of joy also generates a balancing and harmonizing influence. Lightness and laughter are naturally healing energies. They cleanse the cells of the body in a radiant wash. Just as it is easier to be in a good mood when our health is good, it is also easier for our body to repair and regulate itself when we power it with positive feelings. The salubrious levity of Libra is like the energy of a sunrise. Its antiseptic rays dissolve the dark clouds of negative thoughts and emotions, lifting the body's vital spirit to the peak of its creative power.

Death: Scorpio
Green Sphere to Purple Sphere

To really understand the nature of Scorpio, we must compare and contrast it with Capricorn. Both signs make a connection to the Lunar energy, Capricorn from the side of form and Scorpio from the side of essence. Capricorn, therefore, represents the impactfulness of the world through form and materiality. Scorpio is the impactfulness of the world through essence and sensuality. To understand Scorpio then, we must recognize that impact is not just implemented through material means. There is also emotional impact, which has just as much effect *if not more* upon the world. With Scorpio, we have the idea of passion, emotion, and essence projecting force, whereas Capricorn embodies the idea of form projecting force.

The shared connection to the Moon means that Capricorn and Scorpio are both close to material reality, and so they both tend to see the world in "naturalistic" terms, although in a markedly different manner. Capricorn deals with the formal side of reality, and so it tends to take a more scientific perspective, viewing the world as a set of formal rules. Scorpio, on the other hand, sees the world more fluidly as an interplay of power dynamics. Capricorn's picture of the world is that of Newtonian bodies acting upon each other mechanistically, whereas Scorpio has a somewhat more animistic perspective which sees "forces of nature" as driving human and natural events. And where Capricorn tends to think of causality as driven by material forces acting on a subject from without, Scorpio comprehends a type of causality that is driven from within by the essence of a matter.

In this respect, Scorpio deals with a more mysterious and occult side of reality, one which blurs the boundaries between nature and magic. The idea of essence or emotional energy (Venus) as possessing a motive force that can impact reality (Moon) does not fit within the paradigm of orthodox science. Nevertheless, Scorpio is completely attuned to the animating Venusian energies that lie beneath the surface of material reality, and it recognizes them as a natural part of the primal and primitive forces of existence. The fact that they are not subject to scientific measurement or manipulation does not make them any less real as far as Scorpio is concerned. With Scorpio, there is thus an innate understanding that the Lunar force operates not just through physical action, but also through an esoteric and magical influence. This Scorpionic vector of force is a key component of magic and witchcraft, and it can operate completely subconsciously. One does not have to actively believe in magic to exert magical power. It is something that simply comes naturally, especially to those with a strong Scorpio presence.

This last point is important to take note of, as we have been ascribing to each of these signs a particular "worldview" which should not be taken too literally or simplistically. It would be a mistake to think that anyone with a pronounced Capricorn or Scorpio influence is a philosophical materialist or atheist. These individuals could be just as deeply involved in any organized religion as the next person. A more nuanced way of looking at things would be to say that each sign imparts a particular *flavor* in terms of how one is conscious of reality, and which aspects of reality receive enhanced focus. In some cases, this can result in a decidedly one-sided or reductionist view of the world. But more often, the influence of a sign is to simply lend an *emphasis of attention,* whether consciously or subconsciously, to that particular aspect of reality.

With that in mind, we can generally say that Scorpio shares with Capricorn a pragmatic perspective on things, and so Scorpio's mode of reading a situation tends to look beneath the moralistic or idealistic view, and into the primitive drives and power dynamics. Scorpio is not looking at how the world *should* be. Scorpio is looking at the world as it is. This lends to Scorpio something of a reputation for ruthlessness, and in the worst cases this may be accurate. But even the most ethically functional Scorpio can valuably enhance the understanding of a situation with a dose of penetrating clarity and insight. Scorpio's grasp of the underlying *realpolitik* is a critical component of any strategic decision-making, and one would dismiss it at one's own risk.

In sharp contrast to the Sun and Mercury, the energies of Venus and the Moon lean more toward the instinctive and non-rational forces of human nature. Scorpio tends to think of these as more "real" than the rational or left-brained modes of interpreting reality, and so it experiences the world as relationships of emotional power and psychological power. The core idea of Scorpio is the motive force of essence or emotion. When we consider the sexual urge, which is strongly associated with Scorpio, it is basically a Venusian energy that impels us in a certain direction. It has a certain compulsive or obsessive quality which is also characteristically Scorpionic, and we can classify it along with any other subconscious motivation or impulsive behavior that is driven by an underlying emotional energy.

Scorpio has a keen sensitivity to these subterranean emotional energies and unseen forces, and so it is sharply attuned to the subtext and undercurrents of any given situation in a way that could almost be described as psychic. For this reason, Scorpio has often been characterized metaphorically as *deep waters*. The instinct for the utilization of emotional power lends a powerful charisma to Scorpio. It is often known for having a forceful presence which some would describe as *magnetism,* or force of personality. This feeling of unseen but palpable presence is the Lunar influence, animated by the fiery Venusian energy. Scorpio has a natural talent for projecting this magnetism as a means of influence, and it is especially adept at wielding sexuality as a form of power.

One thing to bear in mind is that Venus represents not just emotional energy but also sensory modalities as well, and so the combination of Venus and the Moon can be understood as *saturation* or *intensity* of both sensory and emotional experience. The world feels more intense to Scorpio. It finds *reality* in intensity, and so that is where it feels most alive. To Scorpio, the definition of what is real is that which impacts us emotionally - and this is also the definition of power. This can include the power of the *aesthetic* experience. And so Scorpio is especially sensitive to the power of art, music, and poetry. It values these particularly for the emotional impact that they have, with the arts and literature of the Romantic movement being perhaps the most decisively Scorpionic in this respect.

So far we have considered Scorpio as Venusian energy expressing itself as a motive force. But there is another angle of Scorpio to consider, and that is the manner in which contact with the physical environment stimulates the Venusian energies. Scorpio has a way of being *in the moment*, much like its opposite sign of Taurus. Its enhanced sensory awareness makes it highly engaged with the physical surroundings, and so there is a natural dynamic by which the intimacy of physical contact (Luna) arouses the Venusian fire of passion. This is obviously recognizable as the sexuality that Scorpio is known for, but it also represents a passion for engaging with sensual reality in general. The Moon represents power at the most primitive level, which is the ability to manipulate the world through physical contact. And there is a certain Venusian gratification to be had in grasping things physically and feeling our power over them. But we cannot grasp hold of a thing without also feeling the reciprocal force that it exerts upon us. The resistance of the physical world is gratifying in its own way insofar as it *makes us feel something,* even as we impose our own power upon it. And so the power dynamic of physical contact is bi-directional, resulting in a curious merging and osmosis between the controller and the controlled. This osmosis represents the kind of full *immersion* into an experience that Scorpio seems to thrive on.

What we get with Scorpio is therefore a peculiar amalgamation of power dynamics with intimacy and sexuality. Let us remember that the Moon represents how we feel anchored in the world, and this sense of anchoring comes from the reciprocal balance of power between ourselves and our environment. That balance of power is what we experience as intimacy. So just as much as Scorpio gets satisfaction from exercising power, it is also comfortable with being *subjected* to the influence of emotional power. That is to say, the *experience* of power carries an emotional intensity whichever way it flows. To be deeply moved by a piece of music, for instance, is to be subjected to its power. But we don't mind this generally, because we enjoy the intensity.

The last, but not least, aspect of Scorpio to consider is its *penetrating* quality, as symbolized by the sting of the scorpion. The Venusian energy expresses very differently in Scorpio than it does in Libra. In the latter, it manifests as a warm and diffuse radiance, whereas in Scorpio it is more focused and packs a punch. The passionate desire-nature of Venus, when channeled through the palpable and forceful Lunar energy, is expressed as a determination to get what one wants that will pierce through any obstacle. This could be interpreted in some circumstances as simply a *lack* of boundaries or compunction. But what we have to understand is that it is not the penetrating action *per se* that is Scorpionic, but rather the overwhelming forcefulness of the desire which gives no alternative but to cut through all obstacles by any means necessary. This notorious single-mindedness of Scorpio can go in two sharply different ways. It can manifest on the one hand as a ruthless pursuit of the basest instincts, or on the other hand as a penetrating insight into the highest truths. Whichever direction Scorpio goes, there will be in some sense an elimination - or a *liquidation* if you will - of whatever stands in the way of the objective. Scorpio is marked by a willingness to make sacrifices. In the worst cases, this may be a sacrifice of other people. But even if Scorpio is pursuing completely noble and ethical goals, which it is entirely capable of, it will be perfectly willing to sacrifice the weaker elements of its own nature, if they prove to be a drag or a hindrance. Thus we have the association of Scorpio with the Tarot card of Death, which in the actual practice of Tarot is almost never interpreted as physical death, but more as a symbol of shedding baggage. All of which is to say, the more noble and evolved Scorpio can be quite ruthless *toward himself* in the pursuit of an ideal. In the realm of primitive power dynamics, it is all simply a matter of a strong desire overcoming weaker desires.

Temperance: Sagittarius
Yellow Sphere to Purple Sphere

The image of Sagittarius is the centaur, a curious combination of both man and beast. This symbol is strikingly appropriate, as the Yellow Sphere represents the rational side of human nature, while the Purple Sphere represents the primitive animal instincts. The governance of the animal nature by the rule of balance and harmony is what we mean by *temperance* or *virtue*, and the application of temperance leads one to the state that we call *uprightness*.

Now one thing that we need to be clear about from the outset is that any form of denial or devaluation of the animal instincts, or of the physical body in general, is not in any way part of the Sagittarian ethos. There are some who would think that moral virtue consists of a kind of ascetic renunciation or enervation of the animal passions, as if the animal nature must be struggled against and *defeated* in some sense. This is nothing more than an unhealthy and self-destructive neuroticism. The very idea of temperance means neither too much nor too little of anything, but *just the right amount*. This applies just as well to the animal passions as anything else. The animal side of our nature is the source of our effectiveness in the world. The horse is a strong and powerful creature, and its raw physical strength gives the human rider the capability to range far and wide. When the human rider respects the power of the beast and handles it with gentle mastery, then the symbiosis between the two is profoundly constructive.

It is just as important to understand that when the animal instincts are properly balanced, there is no sense of struggle. It is not a matter of fighting with an unruly part of oneself, and if that is the feeling that is experienced then one is going about it in the wrong way. The sense of struggle is itself a symptom, as well as an exacerbating factor, of the unbalance. True balance is not obtained by matching an unruly force with an equal and opposite force. Balance is a *state of mind*. It is a respect and appreciation for a kind of natural order and harmony. The love of harmony generates the influence which naturally and effortlessly sets the animal passions in equilibrium. The sense of struggle, on the other hand, is itself an indicator that the element of love is missing. If one does not love and appreciate the animal side of one's own nature, then there is no question but that it will rebel and make itself difficult.

There is another angle to all of this which is seldom recognized, but critically important nonetheless. It is the understanding of the extent to which the animal vitality in itself *contributes* to a posture of moral uprightness. What does this mean, exactly? Sagittarius embodies an idea of *rectitude*. The very word "rectitude" - from the Latin word "rectus", meaning "straight" - connotes an image of standing upright, standing straight and tall. That which is well-balanced and well-proportioned assumes a straight and upright posture. It does not lean or sag to one side. But there must be something to *hold up* this posture against the force of gravity, and that is the raw elemental force of the Purple Sphere. The Moon is that element of *fullness*, heartiness, strength, and animal vigor that gives one the support to maintain a state of rectitude and balance. Let us illustrate the principle with the metaphor of a hot-air balloon. If the balloon is filled with warm air, then the force of that air will expand the balloon to its full shape. It will stand upright and eventually rise into the air. But if there is insufficient inflation, then the balloon will sag and slouch. It will wobble over to one side, and it will lack the energy to get off the ground. It is much the same with human beings. One who lacks the force of the animal spirits will lack the strength to maintain a posture of uprightness.

This may not be altogether obvious, and one might argue that a person lacking in animal vigor is simply harmless and therefore morally benign by default. But if we think into the matter more deeply, this is often far from the case. A condition of ill health is well known to induce a state of emotional dysregulation and irritability. When the life-forces are out of balance, this is experienced as a vitiation of energy, which the weakened psyche tries to counter-balance through abnormal forms of stimulation. Attempts are made to jolt the system back into a sense of liveliness. Physically, this can take the form of alcohol, drugs, or unhealthy foods, or in some cases impulsive sexual behavior. Psychologically, it assumes much more insidious forms. The unbalanced need for stimulation can manifest as self-destructive behaviors, or it can present as behaviors that are cruel or destructive toward others. Moral depravity is therefore rooted in a feeling of *powerlessness*. The unbalanced person acts out this sense of existential insecurity through an over-sensitivity to perceived threats, and through over-reaction to the presumed threat. Vindictiveness and cruelty can therefore be seen as a manifestation of an underlying feeling of ineffectiveness. It is an unbalanced and desperate attempt at restoring a sense of personal power. Another way of looking at this is to say that people are more liable to make ethical compromises when they feel as if they haven't the ability to function *without* making compromises. And so what we call "moral weakness" correlates to a deficit or a perceived deficit in one's own personal effectiveness.

So we could say then that the sense of personal power, which is represented by the Purple Sphere, is a key component of uprightness, balance, and fortitude, because personal power is needed to uphold one's boundaries. Without the power to maintain boundaries, one is governed by a constant state of irrational fear. The Moon is our sense of effectiveness in the world, from whence we derive a feeling of security. Insecurity is the driver of malicious and underhanded behavior. It is also the driver of malice disguised as self-righteousness. A noble, well-balanced, and cheerful disposition comes from having a sense of personal effectiveness in the world, combined with an appreciation of natural harmony.

The well-balanced life-force puts us into an instinctive understanding of the back-and-forth of energy between self and others, and so the balanced individual has a *natural* sense of justice and upright behavior. This is altogether different from a rule-bound sense of justice, which can be overly abstract at times and not properly tuned in to the nuances of the given moment. The Moon represents the push and pull of natural forces, of boundaries coming into contact with each other, testing each other in an ebb and flow to establish a balance of power. The solar influence feels into this ebb and flow and feels out a natural and wholesome balance of boundaries. With Sagittarius, we have a natural feel for the equilibrium of the elements - knowing when to advance forward like Fire, and when to give ground like Water. When to stand firm like Earth, and when to dance like Air. Altogether, Sagittarius carries a flavor of *wholesomeness* which comes from an ideal of balance and harmony that is grounded in the physical side of existence.

Sagittarius is often associated with law, religion, and philosophy, all of which represent the delineation of some kind of moral order. As the image of Temperance suggests, the implicit ideal of Sagittarius is a regulation of the brute force of the animal nature into something harmonious. The connection of Sagittarius to teaching is also appropriate insofar as the teacher instills the student with an understanding of the social and moral order. If we see the student, especially a young child, as representing the raw state of humanity that the Purple Sphere connotes, then the teacher is the influence of the Yellow Sphere molding that raw substance into a paragon of balance and harmony.

In this respect, Sagittarius has an affinity to its opposite sign of Gemini. There is some contrast between the two, however, insofar as Sagittarius integrates the intuition to create a more holistic synthesis, as opposed to the purely intellectual synthesis that Gemini constructs. The intuition is that which we understand from our *felt* experience, and so Sagittarius aims to integrate worldly experience with the more abstract and philosophical ideal of a rational and harmonious moral order.

This inclination of Sagittarius to expand its worldly experience can be seen as an aspect of its Lunar side. The Moon represents the essence of experience, because every experience is something that leaves an imprint upon us in some way. Our experiences make an impact upon us that we can absorb and assimilate to our advantage. The reaching out and grasping for new experiences is therefore a reflection of the wholesomeness and physical vitality of Sagittarius. It manifests as a robust drive to get up and go, to use the legs and the feet to reach out into the world and discover new things. This urge to sally forth is not just an indicator of vitality but also *conducive* to vitality. To go for a walk in the fresh air, to circulate and oxygenate the blood, to be active and engaged with life - these are all essential to balancing the life-forces. The natural tendency toward physical fitness, therefore, goes hand-in-hand with the Sagittarian proclivity to *engage* with the physical world.

To summarize the essence of Sagittarius, we have to recognize the profound *optimism* that it embodies. The harmonious and bright disposition of the Sun, combined with the animal vigor and vitality of the Moon, cannot result in anything other than an energy of supreme confidence and exuberance. Sagittarius has an innate sense of balance and rectitude, as well as the personal power to back it up and to take a stand for what it believes in. As the union of the Solar and Lunar principles, it is also the archetypal template of both physical and psychological health. The wide-ranging tendency of Sagittarius to explore and to become intimate with the world is well represented by the metaphor of archery. If we take the motive force of the bow to represent the Purple Sphere, and the mental focus and aim of the archer to be the Yellow Sphere, then together they send the arrow flying on a straight and direct path to the target. This robustly direct projection of oneself in all things is the clearest depiction of Sagittarius's mode of engagement with the world at large.

The Devil: Capricorn
Orange Sphere to Purple Sphere

The path between the Orange Sphere and the Purple Sphere is the most closely connected to material reality. Mercury represents form and shape, while the Moon represents forcefulness and impact. Their intersection, therefore, represents the impact of matter and material things. It is the force of a hammer driving a nail into wood. It is also the force of a wall pushing you back when you try to walk through it.

This combination of force and form is what defines *boundaries*. Every solid object delineates a perimeter around itself which resists intrusion. Ultimately, this sets limitations on what we can and cannot do. Boundaries delineate the formal parameters in which we can act. They define the scope of our freedom. The sign of Capricorn is therefore characterized by a recognition of the limits that the world imposes upon us, and the practical understanding of how to work within those limits. In this respect, it is worth noting that boundaries are not just defined by physical constraints, they are also defined by rules and regulations. While one could argue that these rule systems are socially constructed, they are also enforced by the threat of material sanctions, and so ultimately they carry the same impact as physical boundaries. Whether we are talking about society at large or an organization in which one works, the rules and protocols can be seen as a system that gives form and shape to the collective structure, and that system is enforced by material means.

The archetypal image of the *labyrinth* is an especially strong and resonant symbol of this idea. In the physical world, as with any other rule-bound system in which we operate, we have a limited number of moves at any given moment. Our success in the world, therefore, depends on learning how to navigate the literal and metaphorical walls which define the structure of reality. Capricorn's primary focus is on coming to grips with the rules of material existence. Its mindset is worldly and pragmatic. There are many who will rage and shake their fist at the labyrinth, complaining that it is unjust and oppressive. To Capricorn, this is simply an exercise in futility. It does not see a winning strategy in fighting against what we cannot change. Capricorn recognizes that the only way to beat the system is to embrace it. To win the game, you must internalize the rules forward and backward. By engaging, understanding, and mastering the rule system of material reality, Capricorn aims to manipulate its environment to achieve effective and lasting results.

Given the effort that is put into mastering the system, it is not surprising that Capricorn tends to have a strong sense of *investment* in rules and structure. This can sometimes lead to the criticism that Capricorn is perhaps *too* comfortable working within limitations, and may have difficulty thinking outside the box. From Capricorn's perspective however, the rules and the structure give one a sense of being firmly grounded, because if you understand clearly and unambiguously how the system works, then you can leverage it to your advantage. This may at times result in such a pronounced tendency to see only the limitations, that one labors under self-imposed blinders. There is a certain logic to it all, however, when you consider that Capricorn's underlying philosophy is that "the devil you know is better than the devil you don't know".

As Capricorn measures reality in terms of its material impact, it is focused on making its presence felt through material contributions. This is accomplished through *work*. Work is the practical business of making an impact on the world. Capricorn aims to make a *visible* and *measurable* impact, which means an impact that can be grasped formally and concretely. We should recognize that work in the most concrete of senses means a re-shaping of material structures - moving things around and re-arranging them, taking things apart and putting them back together. In the terminology of pure physics, work is defined as force applied to mass through distance, or displacement of matter to put it simply. Whatever form it takes, however, the work that Capricorn does is intended to leave a lasting impression that one can point to and say "I did this".

The Devil

In this regard, Capricorn has a very externally-oriented focus which makes an interesting contrast to its opposite sign of Cancer. Whereas Cancer represents the security of one's home base, Capricorn represents the broader environment "out there" which one must learn to negotiate in order to survive. Capricorn is about "making it" out in the world, and making your mark upon the world. The broader lesson of the Cancer-Capricorn axis is that you cannot survive by simply shutting yourself off within the confines of your castle. The necessities of life will eventually run out. It is necessary to engage with the outside world to maintain the upkeep of the home base. So one must periodically venture forth to obtain the things that one needs to secure the home front. This involves staking out a secure position in the world at large. One aspect of this survival imperative is the ability to earn a livelihood. To primitive man, this would have meant the ability to hunt and forage. To modern man, it means the ability to hold down a career. Whatever the context, Capricorn represents the ability to demonstrate personal effectiveness and competency toward material ends. This demands a dedication to learning the tools at one's disposal, and to mastering the skills required to shape the world around us. It requires that we develop an intuitive feel for "how the world works" both socially and materially.

The Tarot card of The Devil would appear on the surface to stand for something objectively bad, but we have to keep in mind that none of the elements of the Tree are fundamentally negative. Some of them have more complex shades of meaning, however, depending on how we approach them. The symbolism of The Devil seems to represent a more pessimistic attitude toward physical existence, based on the fact that it *does* limit our freedom and potential in so many ways. The image hearkens back to the philosophy of the ancient Gnostics, which was strikingly similar, in mood at least, to Buddhism. The Gnostics asserted that the physical world was not created by the highest God - the true God - but rather by a malevolent lesser deity which they called Ialdabaoth. This Ialdabaoth, who was functionally equivalent to the Devil, was thought to have fashioned the material world for the express purpose of ensnaring and entrapping human souls. And in the same sentiment as Buddhism, the Gnostics believed that the goal of wisdom was to escape the perpetual rebirth of the soul into the prison of material existence.

Implicit in this belief system is the idea that it is *ignorance* of one's own spiritual nature which keeps the soul trapped in the physical world. The Rider-Waite version of The Devil hints at this idea very subtly. The card shows two human figures chained by the neck to the Devil's throne. Despite their predicament, these figures do not appear to be overly concerned with the situation. In fact, their expressions seem to indicate that they are perfectly content with their lot. And a closer inspection of the image reveals that the chains hang so loosely around their necks that they could easily be removed at any moment. This symbolism would seem to convey the idea of material reality as a veil of illusion, concealing the deeper spiritual truths which we can only approach by turning our awareness inward. Capricorn's outward focus toward understanding the mechanics of physical reality would make it arguably the most *materialistic* of all the paths on the Tree.

To paint this as entirely negative would be deeply unfair, however. Indeed, the Gnostic perception of physical reality as an unmitigated evil is not the only way of looking at the narrative of human existence. There are other perspectives that view the challenging and rigorous nature of physical existence as a type of *advanced school*. Rule-based systems often get a bad rap. They tend to be thought of as a hindrance to creative freedom, and Capricorn's attention to the rules can be seen as somewhat "square". But there is something to be said for the focus of creative energy that a rule set provides. Without a set of rules to give structure to one's creative efforts, the results will typically be shoddy and unremarkable. Music, for instance, is defined by a certain set of rules. The notes will be restricted to a particular scale, and a regularity of rhythm is maintained throughout the piece. Now certainly, one can break these rules arbitrarily to make an artistic statement, but this type of experimental music tends to function more as an intellectual exercise than as actual music. It will not evoke the same kind of feeling and emotion that more carefully crafted music does. To put it all more succinctly, most of our rules have been created for very good reasons. Some of course have not. It

The Devil

is incumbent upon Capricorn to understand how to discriminate between the two.

From a more esoteric perspective, we can imagine that in a similar way, the limitations of physical existence force the soul to master certain skills. There is something to be said for the focus of consciousness that one finds in limitation. It brings one back upon oneself in a way that clarifies self-awareness. Being in limited circumstances compels us to look deeper inside of ourselves for answers and for resources. There is indeed a mysterious sense in which the containment of consciousness within the three dimensions of space forces it to go further into a higher dimension of spiritual truth, just as the explosion of gunpowder has to be contained within a rifle barrel to send the bullet flying through the air. At some level, we have to admit that a game with no rules is not very interesting to play, and that the whole point of the game is to sharpen our faculties. Mastery in any sense of the word demands self-limitation. To excel at any given discipline requires us to focus inordinate hours of practice and study on that one thing, to the exclusion of everything else. The ultimate reward of such discipline is an enhanced awareness of one's own personal agency. To fully master a craft within the limits of a rule-bound system brings the individual deeper into his own resources and willpower. The rigor of physical reality sharpens us like iron sharpens iron, which ultimately is the reason why Capricorn is so willing to embrace the challenge.

The Star: Aquarius
Yellow Sphere to Orange Sphere

The Orange Sphere represents the world of appearance in all its richness of diversity and multiplicity. The Yellow Sphere stands for the principle of integration and unity. The path between them, therefore, represents a hidden and underlying unity behind the apparent multiplicity of all things.

Aquarius presents an interesting contrast to Capricorn. Both are focused upon the realm of form and appearances, but Capricorn is more concerned with the raw impact of the material world and how to manipulate it, whereas the insight of Aquarius is to look *through* the veil of materiality, into the abstract patterns and harmonies which give rise to its manifold expressions. Aquarius aims to comprehend the *Logos* - the sacred geometry of the cosmic order behind reality.

In this sense, Aquarius is a bit more detached from the concreteness of physical existence, tending to immerse itself into an abstract realm of Platonic ideals. It sees past the representations of sense experience into the underlying *rational* pattern that ties them all together - gazing, so to speak, into the pure mathematics behind the perceptible world. We could say then that Aquarius is a profoundly *metaphysical* sign. Which is not to say that it is or ever could be completely detached from the material world. Indeed, it is only *through* the observation and comparison of the multifarious objects of sense experience that Aquarius is able to arrive at the generic principles that bind them all together. Nevertheless, the realm of abstract principles that Aquarius arrives at is a place *beyond* the realm of physical appearances.

It is fair to say that this urge to dive into the metaphysical layer of reality expresses a deeply spiritual and inspirational impulse, as it represents an intuitive feeling that there is a universal unifying principle behind the multiplicity of all that we see. It is equally true to say that Aquarius represents the driving impulse of *science*, because it seeks in all of the different realms of experience to find the universal principle that encapsulates each of the individual cases. It seeks the mathematical formula for a triangle that describes all triangles, or the chemical formula of water that describes all water. Science is, therefore, fundamentally a metaphysical endeavor.

It may sound to some like a contradiction to conflate science with metaphysics and spirituality, but this is simply a bias of our modern culture, which tends to draw a sharp line between science and religion. For the Galileos and the Newtons of several centuries ago, there was no contradiction whatsoever in seeing a divine cosmic order in the laws that govern the physical universe. Unfortunately, the hostility of the Church toward the challenges that science presented to its monopoly on truth has led to a widening and hardening opposition between the two. The outcome of this is an implicit cultural assumption that empirical and intuitive ways of understanding reality are somehow incompatible. The essence of Aquarius is to transcend this duality, merging the empirical and the metaphysical into two sides of the same experience.

This may not be obvious for every individual expression of the Aquarian energy. Given the cultural bias that tends to separate science and religion, the contemporary Aquarian may come down on the side of a purely secular scientific worldview. Nonetheless, the underlying impulse behind this worldview is a quest for the *Logos* that binds reality together into an organic whole. Whether consciously or unconsciously, Aquarius seeks to discover a unifying spiritual principle *within* the world of form and within the diversity of material reality. Aquarius believes in a *grand design* in a way that is not all that different from religious faith. How this is defined philosophically may be colored by the cultural and historical narrative, but at bottom, it all amounts to the same thing. The search for a "grand unified theory" is simply a search for God framed in different terms.

This *vision of unity* that Aquarius projects into the world is so profound and so deep that it can't help but evoke the most idealistic and aspirational feelings. Aquarius holds a deep-seated conviction that there is an underlying rational order to the world which acts as the engine of human progress. This conviction is felt at a fundamental level whether it is framed in spiritual or secular terms. It must be noted, however, that whereas religious philosophies tend to focus on the world beyond, Aquarius focuses on the unifying principle as expressed through the domain of form and appearance. Aquarius is therefore primarily concerned with realizing the vision of unity within the material world, and so its vision tends to be *utopian* in nature.

We can think of Aquarius then as aspiring toward some form of perfect harmonious order here on earth. This will typically take shape as some kind of movement for political, social, or scientific progress, but with a quasi-religious fervor as most idealistic movements tend to have. The principle of *synergy* - the belief that the whole is more than the sum of its parts - plays a tremendous role in Aquarius's way of thinking and doing. The concept of *Logos* compels Aquarius to bring diverse ideas, diverse resources, and diverse talents together into an organic collective endeavor. The notion of congregation, community, and coming together for a shared goal is perhaps the most archetypal expression of Aquarian synergy. It has often been observed, however, that the emphasis on the collective can assume such overwhelming importance with Aquarius, that the individual is lost within the bigger picture. To have a profound love for humanity as a whole, and yet fail to see individual human beings, is often perceived as a fairly typical Aquarian shortcoming. And so one of the potential downsides of the Aquarian vision is that the vast utopian brilliance may reduce the individual to a mere cog in the machinery of the grand narrative, as we have seen in various idealistic but totalitarian societies of the past and present.

One thing that can be said for Aquarius's breadth of vision, however, is that it has a certain genius for innovation and *synthetic thinking*. Because it sees all things as ultimately connected in some deep sense, it can gather diverse elements that most people would consider unrelated or incompatible, and synthesize them in creative ways. Aquarius possesses an eclectic way of seeing that can take seemingly disparate things and envision the unity between them. It would seem that there is a natural architecture to the Aquarian mind in which everything finds its rightful place, like puzzle pieces coming together into a grand tapestry. There is a remarkable beauty to be found in the way that Aquarius is able to assemble an elaborate clockwork of ideas, but it is more of an intellectual beauty than the kind of aesthetic beauty that one finds with Libra. Aquarius is especially emblematic of *technology,* because technology more than anything else represents the synthesis of formal relationships into a unified and harmonious design. Picture the gears of a finely crafted clock, how they all interconnect in a symphony of mathematical ratios. There is indeed a profound sense of the *organic* in the way that Aquarius puts things together, even when it comes to technology. Because after all, the parts of a machine fit together in a purposeful fashion just as the parts of the body fit together with an overarching end in view. From this organic and technological outlook comes the utopian vision that society can be engineered like a well-oiled machine, running with a perfect efficiency to maximize the greater good.

When we look at the Tarot card of The Star, the connection to Aquarius is clear from the central figure of the woman pouring water from two vessels. But what symbolic meaning do we read into the star itself? In one sense the star is a sun, the same as our own sun, and so it represents all of the attributes of the unifying energy of the Yellow Sphere. If we take materiality as representing the night-side of existence, then The Star becomes the essence of the Logos shining through the veil of the physical senses. While its presence is nowhere near as brilliant as the sun during the day, its sparkling beauty in the dark of night leads our imagination toward an ideal of perfect harmony beyond the world of appearances. There is also a sense in which Aquarius represents the force of *gravity*. On one level, we can understand this quite literally as the physical gravity that causes a vast cloud of atoms to coalesce into a shining star. At another level, we can think of Aquarius as the social gravity that brings human beings together into groups and tribes and movements. But at the highest and most abstract level, Aquarius is an *intellectual* force of gravity that pulls diverse parts together into a synthesis. The essence of Aquarius is a mind that works like the gravitational pull of a star, drawing all aspects of existence into its orbit and weaving them into a grand design of unity and scintillating beauty.

The Moon: Pisces
Red Sphere to Orange Sphere

Pisces is typically seen as the most empathetic, compassionate, and easygoing of the zodiac signs. It may seem strange then to associate Pisces with the Martial energy of the Red Sphere. To understand this connection, we have to recognize that the core energy of Mars is not aggression or belligerence. Those are the expressions of Mars in a less developed state of awareness. The purer expression of the Red Sphere is rather a quality of boldness, daring, initiative, and authenticity. When this energy is combined with the fluid, image-forming capability of the Orange Sphere, then we have the power of *imagination*, which is the principal keyword of Pisces.

We could say then that in the realm of dreams and visions, Pisces has a boldness and a daring to go in directions that others would not think to explore. The imagination and the dream realm are a place in which reality becomes fluid, and so it is a place in which we can begin to embrace new possibilities outside of the rule-bound existence in which we normally live. Pisces is at the vanguard of exploring the limits of what we know to be possible. It is a creator of worlds, and a prophet of the future. It is true that Pisces often takes criticism for not being fully grounded in reality, but someone has to have the *audacity* to dream big and dream wide in order to show humanity the significant leaps forward. Someone has to take the questionable step of seeing past the currently accepted limits, in order to find the way to the future. Imagination is the driver of evolution, and Pisces has the ability to envision boldly where others can only think inside the box.

The relationship that Pisces has with reality goes much deeper than mere daydream however, and this brings to light a very mysterious and occult side to Pisces that is little understood. At an instinctive level, Pisces feels a very Martian conviction that reality is fluid and malleable. In practical terms, this means that Pisces is the operative principle of magic and witchcraft. The entire philosophy of magic and manifestation is based on the premise that imagination, shaped and driven by the force of focused will, fashions the template which eventually crystallizes into reality. Will and imagination, the core components of Pisces, are the occult building blocks of the world that we see.

Furthermore, the philosophy of magic declares *faith* to be an essential element of manifestation, and faith requires a certain Mars-like *defiance* in the face of what are commonly taken to be the cold, hard facts of reality. To look past the prevailing picture of what is real and deny its power, to create an alternative vision of reality and stubbornly maintain the conviction that it takes all precedence over what the physical senses say to be true - that is a level of audacity and will that transcends the very fabric of physical existence. Magic is an operation of the will that burrows down into the deepest layers of the root-substance of reality, shaping and impressing it into the image of one's desired end goal.

This instinctive feel for the fluid malleability of reality is what gives Pisces a tendency to idealize and romanticize. Pisces has the boldness of vision to see past the here and now into a *potential* future. It is a strong believer in the latent potential within everyone and everything. This is largely what accounts for its empathetic and humanitarian disposition. Pisces has a belief in the perfectability of humanity and the perfectibility of each individual. It sees in every man, woman, and child a source of limitless radiance waiting to be opened up. Pisces can imagine each person as the best version of his or her self. And because it inherently knows that reality is malleable, it sees the potential for evolution in every individual and every situation, despite the surface layer of flaws that may conceal the underlying spiritual perfection.

This allows Pisces to see possibilities in people where others with less imagination would simply be cynical and jaded. It also lends Pisces more of a readiness to forgive, because the whole point of forgiveness is to allow others an opportunity to move past the limited awareness from which their shortcomings arise. How is it possible to truly forgive after all, if we don't believe that people are capable of change and growth? Mutability is a key characteristic of Pisces, and mutability means the ability to evolve. And so Pisces will stand up for the right of every individual to expand into their fullest potential.

Now strictly speaking, the imagination is endlessly versatile, and could be used to fashion any kind of image whatsoever. It can conjure up a vision that is completely banal or mundane, or even ugly. But that is not really the point of imagination. The vivacity of the Red Sphere strives for something more exciting. The underlying *why* of the faculty of imagination is to articulate a vision of something *ideal*. If you can fashion your own reality, then why not make it as glamorous and beautiful and romantic as possible? It is not insignificant that Pisces is on the same axis as Virgo, as they both seem to be striving toward something pure and idealized. And while Pisces often takes flack for being overly romantic and seeing the world through rose-colored glasses, it nevertheless plays an essential role in seeing through the surface reality to a deeper and more essential truth. Pisces is not altogether misguided in its romanticism. It is simply ahead of the curve, and seeing things from a higher plane.

This is why art is always an idealized representation of something. In a story, for instance, the characters are crafted with just the details necessary to give an ideal depiction of what they represent. We don't need to see the more mundane details of their existence, which contribute little to the symbolic role that they play. The characters, settings, and events in a story are all fashioned to represent a theme or a set of ideas, and to that end, they will be constructed with a deliberate clarity. This idealizing glamour is true even for unpleasant or horrific characters. To the extent that they symbolize something unpleasant, their representation as such makes them an ideal example. The visual and plastic arts function in the same way. A picture that we hang on the wall in our house will likely depict a place where we would like to be. Likewise, a portrait of someone will try to capture them from the most flattering angle, and in the best light. Whatever representation Pisces fashions, it will have a symbolic value that points us toward something of deeper significance.

While Pisces is much-extolled for its emotional warmth and inspirational influence, it is also notorious for its more challenging aspects. The fluid nature of Pisces is often associated with dissolution, and an inability to get grounded in material reality. It is also deeply connected with the collective unconscious, and so there may be some difficulty in forming a clear and stable identity. Pisces embodies the mercurial archetype of the *trickster*, which excels at all manner of prestidigitation and legerdemain. The ability to shape-shift and manipulate appearances comes so naturally to Pisces, that it has a reputation for being inveterately deceptive and chameleon-like. This deceptiveness is not necessarily malicious, or even consciously deliberate. It simply represents a blurry boundary between fantasy and reality. A lack of boundaries tends to be a common concern with Pisces, which can lead it into all manner of self-destructive entanglements. The challenge of Pisces is to bring enough focus into its life that it can build a bridge toward the realization of its ideal visions.

The Tarot card of The Moon is one of the most peculiar and dream-like images of the Major Arcana. It depicts a lobster or crayfish crawling from the water up onto the land. A long and winding path stretches ahead of it, flanked on either side by a dog and a wolf both howling at the resplendent orb, as well as a pair of ominous and mysterious towers in the mid-distance. The symbolism seems to hint at an evolutionary journey of sorts. Out of the primordial waters, we have life emerging in its most primitive form. Further along the path, we pass through a stage of more intelligent life characterized by the dog and wolf. The two towers are signs of human civilization, beyond which the path disappears into the great unknown. The mood of the card seems to hint that this journey is not without its dangers, and it is indeed very easy to get lost in the slippery waters of Pisces. This is, after all, a realm of nebulosity and illusion. The individuating focus of the Sun is buried from sight on the other side of the horizon, however its reflection in the Moon helps to shed light on the long road ahead. The evolutionary destiny of humanity is a *terra incognita,* beyond

The Moon

the borders of what we know. To get there requires that we pass through the Piscean realm of speculation and uncertainty. This journey through the darkness will not be an easy one, but with the reflection of the Solar Logos illuminating the night, the prophetic visions of Pisces will point the way to humanity's dreams.

Conclusion

As we come to the end of this study of the Tree of Life, the question arises: What does it actually mean, when we put it all together? What is the value of this diagram in practical terms? I think the key answer to this question is that the Tree of Life represents an ideal model of what the self-realized individual is made of, and how he or she comes together into a whole and into a fully functional creative being.

Speaking honestly, to live a human life is to be confused. This is true for all of us to a greater or lesser extent. To figure out who we are, what we want, and what we stand for is a lifelong process that never fully ends. If this were not an inherently challenging endeavor, then the journey would be over from the moment that it started. But the reality of our existence is that we have to *work* to make sense of our lives and of ourselves. By far, most of our confusion in life comes from the fact that we overcomplicate everything. In particular, we overcomplicate our own picture of who we are and what role we are supposed to play in the world around us. This is of course exacerbated by the competing demands placed upon us by society and by other people, all of whom project upon us their own expectations of who we are supposed to be and what we are supposed to represent.

To cut through this morass of confusion means to cut through the complexity, and to reduce things down to the simplest elements of what it means to be human. By taking things down to their essential simplicity, we experience them in their *purity*. The Tree of Life would seem to serve as a taxonomy of the simplest elements of existence, as well as the relationships which hold them together into a meaningful narrative. The value of the Tree is found then in its use as a framework for meditation and self-reflection. By separating the building blocks of reality into their discrete categories, we can ruminate upon each one of them individually, and dive deep into the pure essence of what it means to enact that particular mode of being-in-the-world. In this way, we can come closer to understanding what it means to act with pure consciousness, pure will, pure integrity, and so forth. The paths of the Tree, which represent the relationships between these simplest of elements, teach us to look at the entire structure holistically. None of the spheres exist in isolation. Each one finds its meaning in its relationships with the others. And so the twenty-two paths can be thought of as facets of the spheres, which collectively form a cohesive picture of what each part represents in the context of the whole.

We could say then that the value of Kabbalah is that it points us toward a vision of what it means to become a more complete human being. The arc of evolution, both physical and spiritual, strives toward the embodiment of greater and greater creative potential. To expand this creative capacity demands that we actualize and balance every facet of what it means to be fully human. In reality, each one of us reflects our own set of strengths and weaknesses. There are strong points and gaps in every personality, and so we move through life emphasizing different aspects of the human condition, while perhaps falling short in the expression of others. Some of us are introverts, and others are extroverts. Some are impeccably rational, while others process life emotionally. Some move with the impetuosity of fire, while others embody the cautious stability of earth. The ultimate goal, however, is to become a perfect synthesis and balance of all the energies that make up the human psyche.

The Tree of Life is just this representation of the perfectly balanced human being. As we reflect upon the spheres and the interconnections between them, we see how each one of these elements occupies a role in the overall system which is just as important as all the rest. And so our personal evolution becomes a matter of identifying those aspects in which we are less developed, and meditating upon them to bring them more fully into focus. The key point to understand in all of this is that ultimately, none of these aspects of the Tree are in opposition to one another. They are all complementary, fitting together like pieces of a puzzle. And so life becomes a question of understanding how to make these puzzle pieces work together in a well-tuned harmony.

In summary, then, the most meaningful understanding of the Kabbalah is perhaps the recognition that the clarity and simplicity of the Tree of Life gives us an intuition of what it means to be pure in our own self-expression. That is to say, *how we engage* with the present moment is just as important as *what we are doing* in the present moment. As each one of us has a unique role to play in the grand tapestry of human existence, it is incumbent upon each of us to understand the full depth and meaning of that role. The Tree of Life offers an outline of the core truths of what it means to play the human part. By comprehending each one of these truths in its full scope and totality, we acquire the tools and the understanding needed to become that which we are truly meant to be.

www.ingramcontent.com/pod-product-compliance
Lightning Source LLC
Chambersburg PA
CBHW030548080526
44585CB00012B/298